Broadway Translations

THE HISTORY OF THE
DAMNABLE LIFE and DESERVED DEATH
OF
DOCTOR JOHN FAUSTUS
1592

TOGETHER WITH

THE SECOND REPORT OF FAUSTUS
CONTAINING HIS APPEARANCES AND THE DEEDS OF WAGNER

1594

Both modernized and edited by

WILLIAM ROSE, M.A., Ph.D.
LECTURER IN THE UNIVERSITY OF LONDON, KING'S COLLEGE

With an Introduction

With 24 Illustrations chiefly from Woodcuts

LONDON
GEORGE ROUTLEDGE & SONS LTD.
NEW YORK: E. P. DUTTON & CO.

AN ALLEGED FAUST PORTRAIT
By Jan Joris van Vliet

After a Sketch by Rembrandt. *About* 1630

PRINTED IN GREAT BRITAIN BY
THE MAYFLOWER PRESS, WILLIAM BRENDON AND SONS LTD.

CONTENTS

THE HISTORIE OF DR. JOHN FAUSTUS

CONTENTS

CONTENTS

CONTENTS

CONTENTS

CONTENTS

THE SECOND REPORT OF DR. JOHN FAUSTUS

CONTENTS

CONTENTS

LIST OF ILLUSTRATIONS

FOREWORD

THE printed version of the earliest extant English Faust Book that has been modernized for the present edition is the reprint by H. Logeman in the *Recueil de Travaux de l'Université de Gand* [24ᵉ fascicule. Gand, 1900]. This is the only reprint of the unique copy of the English Faust Book of 1592, which is in the British Museum, and with which I was able to compare it.

The first edition of the English Wagner Book has likewise only been reprinted once, after one of the two copies in the Bodleian Library at Oxford, by Alfred E. Richards in *Literarhistorische Forschungen* [XXXV. Heft. Berlin, 1907], and this edition I have used for the present modernization.

Those who wish to read the Faust and Wagner Books in the old orthography, I would refer to the careful editions of these two scholars. I have only modernized the old spellings and occasionally, for the sake of clarity, the punctuation, but have made no syntactical alterations whatever. Even where, in the case of the Wagner Book, the syntax sometimes obscured the meaning, I have thought it best to let it stand.

The versions printed by Thoms in his *Early*

FOREWORD

English Prose Romances are later than those printed in this volume. His Faust Book is undated, but the British Museum Catalogue gives it the suppositional date 1700. His Wagner Book reproduces the text of 1680. His introduction is, of course, out of date and practically useless.

W. R.

INTRODUCTION

THE story of the man who sells his soul to the powers of evil in return for material gain, is one of the most ancient in the history of humanity. It is perhaps as old as humanity, for when the light of self-consciousness first began to dawn on man, he no doubt desired to know more than his limited intellect could tell him, or to possess something that the world could not or would not give him. When he looked around, and was frightened at his own littleness, he created gods for his protection, and these gods he endeavoured to propitiate, until they became his tyrants. They were the symbols of his hopes and fears, so that when he was propitiating his gods he was stereotyping the limitations of his own mind. And the most important of those limitations was that he must not look beyond his manufactured gods for the hidden causes of things. A profound instinct nevertheless urged him to probe beyond, and the resulting spiritual unrest, which has always manifested itself spasmodically in the human race, underwent various personifications at different times. The elements of the Faust story were already present in the Garden of Eden—the Tree of Knowledge, the personification of Evil in the Serpent, and the Woman who was tempted to overstep the bounds of what was

B

permitted by the orthodox authority, in order to grasp the Forbidden Fruit. It is significant for the peculiar construction of the human mind, that it was always the Spirit of Evil which led the way to spiritual emancipation. In order to give concrete expression to his almost unconscious thirst for greater knowledge, man had to pretend to himself that this craving was pernicious. His very attempts to free himself from superstition provide the strongest evidence of the tortuous way in which his mind had to work, for it could only rise to a higher conception of its own worth by playing a game of self-deception.

The Faust problem was not peculiar to the Christian era. The Jews had their Solomon and the Greeks their Prometheus, but it was only at the end of the Middle Ages, when the old world was in the melting-pot, that there arose the most famous of all these legends, the most curious element in which is perhaps the fact that there was at the source of it an actual person.

I

The Historical Personage

THE first record of an actual magician or adventurer
of the name of Faust occurs in a letter written in Latin
by the Abbot Trithemius of Würzburg, formerly of
the Benedictine monastery of Sponheim, near Kreuznach in the Palatinate, to the mathematician and
Court astrologer, Johann Virdung, on the 20th of
August, 1507. The learned abbot, whose name is
the Latinized form of Johannes Tritheim, writes to
his friend in Heidelberg to warn him against a certain
Faust from whom the astrologer is expecting a visit :—

" That man, about whom you have written to me,
Georgius Sabellicus, who has ventured to call himself
the prince of necromancers is a vagabond, an empty
babbler and a knave : worthy to be whipped, that he
might no longer profess publicly abominable matters
which are opposed to the holy Church. For what are
the titles which he assumes, other than the signs of
a most stupid and senseless mind, which proves that
he is a fool and no philosopher ? Thus he has adopted
the following title : *Magister Georgius Sabellicus,
Faustus junior*, fountain of necromancers, astrologer,
magus secundus, chiromancer, aëromancer, pyromancer,
second in hydromancy. Behold the foolish temerity
of the man ; what madness is necessary to call oneself

the fountain of necromancy. A man who is, in truth, entirely devoid of education, should rather call himself a fool than a *magister*. But his wickedness is not unknown to me. When some years ago I was returning from the March of Brandenburg, I met this man in the town of Gelnhausen, where I was told in the inn of many frivolous things promised by him with great audacity. When he heard of my presence, he fled forthwith from the inn and could not be persuaded by anyone to present himself to me.

He sent to me also by a citizen the advertisement of his foolishness, which I remember he sent to you. In that town I was told by priests, that he had said in the presence of many people that he had attained such great knowledge and memory of all wisdom, that if all the works of Plato and Aristotle, together with all their philosophy, had been absolutely wiped out of human memory, he would restore them, like a second Hebrew Ezra, by his genius, totally and more excellently than before.

When I was later on in Speyer, he came to Würzburg, and is said to have boasted with similar conceit in the presence of many people, that the miracles of our Redeemer Christ are no cause for astonishment ; he himself could do everything that Christ had done, as often as and whenever he wished. This year, during the last days of Lent, he came to Kreuznach, where he made vast promises in a similar swaggering manner, and said that in alchemy he was the most perfect of any that had ever lived, and knew and could perform whatever the people wished. During this time the office of schoolmaster in this town was vacant, and it was conferred upon him through the intercession of Franz von Sickingen, the steward of your prince, a man who is exceedingly ardent with regard to mystical matters. But soon afterwards he began to practise a most infamous kind of fornication, forsooth, with the boys, and he fled, when the matter came to light, from his imminent punishment.

This is what is evident to me, according to the most certain testimony, concerning that man whose visit you are awaiting with such eagerness."

The accusations of the abbot are to be taken with a pinch of salt, for he was himself suspected of dabbling in magic, and his indignation may have been coloured by more than a tinge of jealousy. He is known to have declaimed before the Emperor Maximilian against the followers of the black art, and there is a letter, written by him only four days before the above epistle to Virdung, in which he protests against the imputing to him of magic practices. He was even rumoured to have conjured up the spirits of the dead in the presence of the Emperor. At any rate, he does not seem to have been anxious for popular inclusion among the necromancers. Neither is it at all certain that there is any truth in the scandal about the school at Kreuznach, for that was the sort of vice which it was usual to attribute to dissolute magicians.

It cannot be explained why Faust should have called himself *junior*, for there is no trace of any earlier magician of the same name. Whether *Sabellicus* was his real name, and *Faustus junior* a kind of professional title, or whether George Faust attached the title

INTRODUCTION

Sabellicus to his name as an allusion to the magic art of the Sabines, is likewise a mystery. It will be noticed that he is called *George*, and the same Christian name occurs again, six years later, in the second existing reference to Faust.

Conrad Mutianus Rufus (Conrad Mut, Canon at Gotha, called Rufus on account of his red hair), a friend of Reuchlin and Melanchthon, and one of the most cultured of the Humanists, makes the following statement in a letter written from Erfurt to his friend Heinrich Urbanus on the 7th of October, 1513 :—

" There came a week ago to Erfurt a certain chiromancer named Georgius Faustus, *Helmitheus Hedebergensis*, a mere braggart and fool. The professions of this man and of all the fortune-tellers are vain. The rude people marvel at him, the priests should denounce him. I heard him swaggering at the inn. I did not reprove his boastfulness, for why should I bother about the foolishness of others ? "

These two George Fausts are obviously the same person. The term *Helmitheus Hedebergensis* may be meant for *Hemitheus Hedelbergensis*, half-god of Heidelberg, where the charlatan perhaps pretended to have studied.[1] There was a Bachelor named Johann Faust, of Simmern, at Heidelberg in the year 1509, but it is unlikely that he has any connection with our Faust.

There is a legend that Faust was given asylum at the monastery of Maulbronn by the Abbot Entenfuss

[1] H. Düntzer : *Die Sage von Dr. Joh. Faust* [Scheible's Kloster, 1847].

6

in the year 1516, and that he there pursued his alchemistic activities. The well-known " Faust tower " which is still shown there was, however, not built until nearly a hundred years later.

The next reference we find is an entry in the account book of the Bishop of Bamberg by the latter's chamberlain, under the date 12th of February, 1520 :—

" Item 10 gulden given and presented to Doctor Faustus *philosophus* in honour of his having cast for my gracious master a nativity or *indicium*, paid on Sunday after Scholastica by the order of Reverendissimus."

A less flattering entry is that in the minutes of the resolutions of the Town Council of Ingolstadt in 1528 :—

" To-day, Wednesday after St. Vitus, 1528. The fortune-teller shall be ordered to leave the town and spend his penny elsewhere." This is supplemented by another entry in the record of expulsions : " To-day, Wednesday after St. Vitus, 1528, one who calls himself Dr. Jörg Faustus of Heidelberg has been told to spend his penny elsewhere, and has promised not to resent or mock such summons of the authorities."

It will be noticed that the same Christian name again occurs, in conjunction with the reference to Heidelberg.

There is then a gap of some eleven years before we meet the name again in the *Index Sanitatis* of the

physician Philipp Begardi of Worms, published in
1539 :—

" There is also to be found a renowned and bold
man ; I did not wish to have mentioned his name, but
it will not be hidden or unknown. For some years
ago he wandered through almost every province,
principality and kingdom, made his name known to
everybody, and boasted loudly of his great art, not
only in medicine, but also in chiromancy, necromancy,
physiognomy, crystal-gazing and more of such arts.
And not only boasted, but also gave himself out to
be and wrote himself as a famous and experienced
master. He also himself acknowledged and did not
deny, that he was, and was called Faust, and signed
himself *Philosophus Philosophorum*, etc. There has,
however, been a great number of people, who have
complained to me, that they have been swindled
by him. His promises were as great as those
of Thessalus. Similarly his fame, like that of Theo-
phrastus also ; but the fulfilment, as I learn, was found
to be very small and fraudulent ; yet he was not slow
in taking money, and at his departure many people
were cheated. But what can one do about it, gone is
gone."

When Philipp von Hutten, the cousin of the more
famous Ulrich von Hutten, was about to start on his
first expedition to Venezuela in 1534, Faust pro-
phesied that the voyage would be unfortunate, and he
was right, for von Hutten, in a description of the voyage
written in 1540, writes : " I must acknowledge that
the philosopher Faustus divined it correctly, for we

have had a very bad year." A rival fortune-teller, Joachim Camerarius, who had declared that the voyage would be lucky, asks in a letter to a friend, written in 1536, what Faust can prophesy about the German Emperor's next battle with the King of France.

Johann Gast, a protestant clergyman at Basle, relates two anecdotes of Faust in the edition of his *Sermones Convivales* which appeared in 1548 :—

" *Concerning the Necromancer Faust.*

He once turned into a very wealthy monastery, in order to spend the night there. A brother sets before him ordinary, weak, not very tasty wine. Faust asks him for better wine from another barrel, which is usually given to distinguished guests. The brother says : ' I haven't the keys. The prior is asleep, and I may not rouse him.' Faust replies : ' The keys lie in that corner ; take them and open that barrel on the left and bring me a drink ! ' The brother refuses and declares that he has no permission from the prior to give the guests other wine. When Faust hears this, he says : ' In a short time thou wilt experience strange things, inhospitable brother ! ' Early next morning he went away full of bitterness, without taking leave, and sent a raging devil into the monastery, who made an uproar day and night, and set everything in motion in the church and in the rooms of the monks, so that they had no peace, whatever they did. At last they consulted as to whether they should abandon the monastery or totally destroy it. They therefore announced their misfortune to the Count Palatine, who took the monastery under his protection and sent away the monks, to whom he allows every year what they need, keeping the rest for himself. Some assert that even now, when monks enter the monastery, there arises such a tumult, that the inhabitants have no peace. The devil knows how to manage that.

Another Instance of Faust.

When I was dining with him in the great College at Basle, he gave the cook birds of various kinds, concerning which I did not know where he had bought them or who had given them to him, since at that time none was being sold in Basle, and they were birds such as I have never seen in our neighbourhood. He had with him a dog and a horse, which, as I believe, were devils, since they could do everything. Some people told me that the dog had sometimes assumed the form of a servant and brought him food. The wretched man came to a terrible end ; for the devil strangled him ; his corpse lay on the bier on its face all the time, although it was turned round five times."

The chronicler appears to have been a superstitious person, and he is the first to refer to Faust as being in league with the Devil, for Trithemius had looked upon him as a dissolute, wandering scholar, and Begardi thought him little more than a common charlatan. None of the last three authorities quoted above has mention of Faust's Christian name, but he appears as *Johannes* in a book compiled by Johannes Manlius (Johann Mennel) in 1563, *Locorum Communium Collectanea,* which consists mainly of reports of conversations with Melanchthon, to whom the following reminiscence is also to be attributed :—

"I knew a man named Faustus of Kundling, a little town near my home. When he studied at Cracow, he had learned Magic, which was formerly keenly studied there and where public lectures were delivered about this art. Later he wandered about in many places and spoke about secret things. When he wanted to create a sensation at Venice, he announced that he was going to fly into the heavens. The devil then lifted him up in the air, but let him fall to earth again, so that he nearly gave up the ghost. A few years ago, this Johannes Faustus sat very downcast on his last day in a village in the duchy of Württemberg. Mine host asked him why he was so downcast, this not being his custom or habit ; for he was usually a graceless rogue, who led a dissolute life, so that at one time and another his love affairs had nearly brought him to his death. He thereupon replied to the host in that village : ' Do not be frightened to-night ! ' At midnight the house was shaken. Since on the next morning Faustus had not risen and it was already noon, the host went into his room and found him lying beside the bed with his face twisted round, as the devil had killed him. During his life, he kept a dog, which was the devil. . . . This Faustus escaped from our town of Wittenberg, when the excellent prince, duke Johann, had given the order that he was to be arrested. In a similar way, he is said to have escaped likewise in Nuremberg. At the beginning of the meal, he felt warm ; he immediately rose from the table and paid his scot to the host. He was hardly outside the door when the minions came and asked for him. This magician Faustus, an infamous beast, a cesspool (*cloaca*) of many devils, boasted that all the victories which had been won by the imperial armies in Italy, had been obtained for them by him through his magic, which was a most shameless lie."

This story is repeated by Andreas Hondorff in his *Promptuarium Exemplorum*, which appeared five years later, in 1568 :—

" Such a necromancer was Johann Faustus, who practised many tricks through his black art. He had with him always a black dog, which was a devil. When he came to Wittenberg he would have been arrested by order of the Prince Elector, if he had not escaped. The same would have happened to him in Nuremberg also, where he likewise escaped. But this was his reward. When his time was up, he was in a tavern in a village of Württemberg. Upon the host asking him why he was so downcast, he replied, ' Do not be afraid to-night, if you hear a great banging and shaking of the house.' In the morning he was found lying dead in his room, with his neck twisted round."

There is a casual reference to Faust in the *Table-talk of Martin Luther*, edited by Johannes Aurifaber (Johann Goldschmidt) in 1566 :—

" But when in the evening, at table, mention was made of a necromancer named Faustus, Doctor

Martin says earnestly, 'the devil does not employ the services of magicians against me ; had he been able to do me hurt, he would have done it long ago. He has no doubt had me often by the head, but he nevertheless had to let me go again.' "

In a chronicle concluded in the same year by the Count Froben Christoph von Zimmern, the scene of Faust's death is given as Staufen in Breisgau :—

" But that the practice of such art (of soothsaying) is not only godless, but extremely perilous, that is undeniable, as is proved by experience, and we know how it went with the famous necromancer Faustus. He, after many wonderful things which he did during his life, about which one could write a special treatise, was at last, at an advanced age, slain by the evil spirit in the province of Staufen in Breisgau."

And there is further a reference to his revenge on the inhospitable monks :—

" About that time (i.e. after 1539), Faustus died at, or at least not far from Staufen, the little town in Breisgau. During his life, he was a strange necromancer, who in our times could be found in German provinces and had so many strange dealings, that he will not easily be forgotten for many years. He lived to be an old man, and, as is said, died wretchedly. Many people have thought that he was killed by the evil spirit, whom in his lifetime he only called his brother-in-law (*Schwager*). The books which he left behind have come into the possession of the lord of

Staufen, in whose province he died, and many people have afterwards tried to obtain them, and in my opinion desired in them a perilous and unlucky treasure. He charmed a spirit into the monastery of the monks of Lüxheim in Wasgau, which they could not get rid of for many years, and which troubled them strangely ; for the sole reason that they had once been unwilling to give him shelter for the night, that was why he had procured for them this turbulent visitor ; at the same time, it is said, that a similar spirit was attached to the former abbot of St. Diesenberg by an envious wandering scholar."

The last considerable reference, before the publication of the folk-book, is in the edition of *De Praestigiis Daemonum* by Johannes Wierus (Johann Weyer, or Wier), which appeared in 1568. A German edition of this book was published eighteen years later. Wierus was one of the most distinguished and enlightened physicians of his time, and he fought for years, at first with some success, against the fanatical persecution of witches which was providing human torches in every village in Germany. In this book on the illusions of the devils, he protests against the witch-burnings, and it is noticeable that he does not definitely refer to Faust's alleged compact with the Devil :—

" When formerly at Cracow in Poland necromancy was taught publicly, there came one of the name of Johannes Faustus, of Kundling, who in a short time understood this art so well, that a short time ago, before the year 1540, he practised it to the amazement of many and with many lies and frauds in Germany, publicly and without fear. What a strange hoaxer and adventurer he was, and what strange tricks he was able to perform, I will here only demonstrate to the reader by one instance, but with the instruction that he promise me beforehand that he will not imitate him. When on one occasion this necromancer Faustus on account of his wicked tricks was imprisoned at Battenburg, which lies on the River Maas and borders on the Duchy of Geldern, in the absence of the Count Hermann, the chaplain of that place, Dr. Johann Dorsten, a pious, simple man, showed him much kindness, because he had promised to teach him many good arts and make him a profoundly experienced man. Therefore, when he saw that Faust was very fond of drink, he sent him wine so long till the barrel was empty. But when the magician Faustus noticed that, and the chaplain also prepared to go to Graven to get a shave, he told him that if he would procure for him more wine, he would teach him an art, how to remove his beard without a razor or anything. When the chaplain forthwith agreed, he bade him take some arsenic and rub well his beard and chin with it, not telling him to prepare it beforehand and mix it with other things. When he did this, his chin began to burn, so that not only the hair fell out, but the skin and flesh came off as well.

I knew another man who had a black beard, and was yellowish of face on account of his melancholy complexion. When he visited the magician Faust, the latter said to him : ' Really, I thought you were my brother-in-law, my sister's husband ; and so I looked immediately at your feet, to see whether you had long, crooked claws !' Thus he compared the good man, because he was swarthy, to the devil, and called him also, as was always his custom, his brother-in-law. But he received his reward at last. For, as is said, he was found dead one morning beside his bed in a village in Württemberg, his face turned towards his back, and the previous night there was such a turmoil in the house, that the whole house shook."

And lastly, there is a reference to Faust's conjuring up the dead in Wolffgang Bütner's *Epitome Historiarum*, in 1576 :—

" I have heard that Faustus, at Wittenberg, showed to the students and to an exalted man N——, Hector, Ulysses, Hercules, Æneas, Samson, David and others, who came forth with fierce bearing and earnest countenance and disappeared again, and princely personages are also said to have been present at the time and to have looked on."

At this point it will be well to summarize what we have learnt about Faust from contemporary references. The difficulty with regard to his Christian name has already been mentioned. If his real name was *Georg*, it may have been forgotten and replaced by the more common one of *Johann*, or there may have been two magicians of the name of Faust, the older one named Georg and the later one Johann, who may have taken the name of Faust because it had already been rendered famous by his predecessor. The latter hypothesis is, however, extremely unlikely, and there seems very little reason to doubt that all the references are to the same individual. It has been suggested that the name Johann may have originated through confusion with Johann Fust, the printer, but the latter died in the year 1466, and it was only during the seventeenth century that the Faust legend was attributed to him. The earliest investigators thought that the whole story was a mere legend, and possibly invented by the monks as an expression of their hatred of the inventor of printing, though as a matter of fact, it was only through financial sharp practice that Fust obtained possession of the printing outfit of the real inventor, Gutenberg.

As early as 1683, however, a professor of theology at Wittenberg brought forward evidence of the actual existence of an individual of the name of Faust.[1]

According to Manlius-Melanchthon, Faust was born in Knittlingen and studied at the University of Cracow, though he appears later to have said he came from Heidelberg. About the year 1505, the Abbot Trithemius came in contact with him at Gelnhausen, though he did not speak to him, and does not even say that he actually saw him. He was later in Würzburg, and in 1507 he came to Kreuznach where he obtained a post as schoolmaster, though he was soon compelled to flee on account of alleged immorality. In the year 1513, he was in Erfurt, where he called himself the half-god of Heidelberg. He may have stayed at Maulbronn during the year 1516, but we hear nothing definite until he casts the horoscope of the Bishop of Bamberg in 1520. Eight years later, he was expelled

---

[1] J. G. Neumann : *Disquisitio historica de Fausto Praestigiatore.*

from Ingolstadt, and six years after we find Philipp von Hutten seeking his advice about a forthcoming expedition. Another five years elapse, and a physician of Worms refers to the complaints of people who had been swindled by him ; the remark " gone is gone " may allude to the disappearance or death of Faust, though it is more likely that it refers to the money of the victims. The Zimmern Chronicle mentions the village of Staufen, near Freiburg in Breisgau, as the scene of his death, and gives the date as some time after 1539. Wierus places the period of his activity before 1540, and when Gast writes in 1548, he refers to Faust as being already dead. He appears to have travelled extensively, for there are additional allusions to his presence in Wittenberg, Nuremberg, Battenburg on the Maas, and Basle, where Gast met him.

There seems no doubt that Doctor Faust surpassed all the wandering scholars of his time both in pretensions and notoriety. His attempts to fly and to conjure up spirits, to say nothing of the boast that he could restore lost manuscripts of classical authors, are all intelligent anticipations of what has been done or pretended in the present century. He was rather indiscreet in declaring that he had helped the Imperial armies to victory in Italy, but he may have been emboldened by patronage such as that of Philipp von Hutten and the Bishop of Bamberg, though the distinguished humanists and reformers would have nothing to do with the braggart. The students appear to have been greatly impressed by him and he certainly imposed on the uneducated people.

Soon after his death the historical facts become

blurred, and the mysterious circumstances surrounding his disappearance may have given an additional impulse to the subsequent legend, which appears, indeed, to have started even during his lifetime. The later contemporary references are already coloured with imaginative detail, and anecdotes relating to his various pranks, real or alleged, were circulating among all classes of the people. These soon became the nucleus of a large collection of stories, some of which had formerly been related of other magicians and were now fathered on Faust, until in the year 1587, scarcely fifty years after his death, the first printed account of the life of " Dr Johann Faust, the notorious Magician and Necromancer " was published, as a warning to all readers, at Frankfort-on-the-Main. It is astonishing that he should so soon have become a myth, but an explanation may perhaps be sought in the ferment and unrest of an age which stands between the medieval and the modern, when old conceptions were tumbling and new worlds, both material and intellectual, were being discovered. Literature was no longer a diversion for the upper classes, and the dreams and traditions of the people were finding their way into print. Till Owlglass, the Wandering Jew, Doctor Faust are all types in which have been concentrated the lore and myth of centuries. In these representative figures, the people have focussed their longings and their aversions, their hopes and fears, and none of the wizards of popular superstition was more familiar to them than the man who had put forth his pretensions in all the market-places of Germany.

The Zimmern Chronicle declares that when Faust

died, he left behind him various books which came into the possession of the lord of Staufen, and that many people had endeavoured to obtain these works. Whether there is any truth in this statement is a matter for considerable doubt, but the booksellers were not long in turning the belief to their own advantage and supplying the demand for books of an occult nature. There were at first manuscripts in circulation, which gave instructions how to practise the various magic arts attributed to Faust, the most famous of them being the *Höllenzwang*, or *Conquest of Hell.* They were usually disposed of secretly by disreputable people at exorbitant prices,[1] but later the publishers brought out volumes which they ascribed to the authorship of Faust, and some of these were even supplied with false dates, to give them an appearance of antiquity.

One such manuscript bears the following title :—

" Secret and hidden, highly-authenticated Magic Writings, for the advantage of all, which have been truly tested by me, Doctor Johann Faust, and found trustworthy in each and every case, to the purpose that I have set down herein honestly and without falseness or deceit the principles of all the arts of the world, how I have practised them all myself and come thereby to great fortune ; likewise I have presented openly everything which I have herein recounted to my successors, necromantic as well as cabalistic, that I may be well remembered ; all Spirits have been

---

[1] One enthusiast in Holland is said to have paid eight thousand gilders for four magic seals contained in a book of this kind.

subject to me through these my Writings, they have been compelled to fetch for me and do all my bidding. Nothing further have I written but these twelve parts. Let him who finds and obtains them use them with caution and take strict heed of all therein, that you may not endanger body and life, against which I warn you in all sincerity."

A *Höllenzwang* printed in the year 1607 explains in greater detail the benefits to be attained by its aid :—

" Dr. Johann Faust's Juggler's Bag, concerning all kinds of unheard-of, secret, merry feats, mysteries

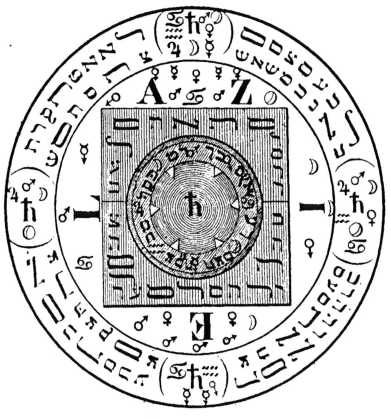

THE SEAL OF AZIEL

From Faust's *Triple Conquest of Hell.*

21

and inventions whereby a man may interpret dreams, tell fortunes, open locked doors, cure the gout, recognize adulterers and fornicators, inspire strange men, women and maids with love, increase his height by some ells, make himself invisible or invulnerable, change his shape, rouse the thunder and lightning, collect and disperse snakes, catch pigeons, fish or birds in his hands, overcome his enemies, and perform other innumerable, incredible and extravagant feats, both merry and advantageous, together with five other extravagant, excellent and authentic devices. Now for the first time from the Original written with his own hand by Dr. Faust, published for the particular pleasure of all artists by Johann de Luna, Christoph Wagner's former disciple and well-experienced in the Magic Arts."[1]

[1] K. Engel: *Zusammenstellung der Faust-Schriften vom 16. Jh. bis Mitte* 1884 [Oldenburg, 1885], pp. 150 and 158.

II

The German Faust Book

IT was not long before a publisher saw the business possibilities of the legend, for in the autumn of the year 1587 there appeared at Frankfort-on-the-Main the first printed account of the life and death of Faust :—

Historia Von D. Johann Fausten, dem weitbeschreyten Zauberer unnd Schwartzkünstler, Wie er sich gegen dem Teuffel auff eine benandte zeit verschrieben, Was er hierzwischen für seltzame Abentheuwer gesehen, selbs angerichtet und getrieben, bisz er endtlich seinen wol verdienten Lohn empfangen. Mehrertheils ausz seinen eygenen hinderlassenen Schrifften, allen hochtragenden, fürwitzigen und Gottlosen Menschen zum schrecklichen Beyspiel, abscheuwlichen Exempel, und treuwhertziger Warnung zusammen gezogen, und in den Druck verfertiget. Iacobi IIII. Seyt Gott underthänig, widerstehet dem Teuffel, so fleuhet er von euch. Cum Gratia et Privilegio. Gedruckt zu Franckfurt am Mayn, durch Johann Spies. M.D.LXXXVII. [History of D. Johann Faust, the notorious Magician and Necromancer, how he sold himself for a stipulated Time to the Devil, What strange Things he saw, performed and practised during this Time, until at last he received his well-merited Reward. For the most Part extracted

INTRODUCTION

*and herewith printed from his own posthumous Writings
as an awful and abominable Example and sincere Warning
to all presumptuous, inquisitive and godless Persons.
" Submit yourselves to God. Resist the Devil, and he
will flee from you " (James iv). Cum Gratia et Privilegio.
Printed at Frankfort-on-the-Main by Johann Spies.
M.D.LXXXVII.*]

The story is preceded by a dedication to two friends
of the publisher, and a *Preface to the Christian Reader*,
in the former of which there is reference to the wide-
spread popularity of the legend : " Since many years
ago there was great and universal talk in Germany
about the various adventures of Doct. Johannes
Faustus, the notorious magician and necromancer,
and everywhere there is a great demand for the history
of the said Faustus at entertainments and gatherings,
and since likewise there is now and then mention in
the works of some modern historians of this magician,
his devilish arts and fearful end, it has often been a
matter of astonishment to me that nobody has composed a regular account of this fearful story and
published it as a warning to the whole of Christendom.
I have also not hesitated to enquire from scholars and
wise people whether this history has perhaps already
been written down by anyone, but I have never been
able to discover anything certain, until recently it
was communicated and sent to me by a good friend
in Speyer, with the request that I should publish and
present it as a fearful example of devilish deceit,
murder of body and soul, as a warning to all Christians."
This dedication is dated Monday, the 4th of September,

24

1587, and signed by Johann Spies himself. The Preface to the Christian Reader, amid much quoting of the Bible, declares that, " The exorcisers of the devil seldom come to a good end, as is to be seen in the case of Dr. Johann Faustus, who was alive within the memory of man, signed a compact and league with the devil, experienced many strange adventures and practised abominable infamy and vice, with guzzling, swilling, fornication and all kinds of sensual pleasure, until at last the devil gave him his deserved reward and wrung his neck in a dreadful manner."

This little volume must have been enormously popular, for although it appeared so late in the season, there were before the end of the year at least four reprints, a new original edition, and a further edition containing eight new chapters. The *editio princeps* (of which there is a copy in the British Museum) contains 69 chapters.

It is not long since an older version of the *Historia* in manuscript, dating from the seventies or early eighties of the sixteenth century, was discovered.[1] It contains a different preface and two more chapters, one of which describes how Faust releases a nobleman and old schoolfellow named von Reuttpüffel from captivity in Turkey, and brings him home just after his wife has married again. The story is told with all

[1] By Gustav Milchsack in the library at Wolfenbüttel, and edited by him in *Historia D. Johannis Fausti des Zauberers* [Wolfenbüttel, 1892–7]. Milchsack promised at the time to follow up this publication with a second volume containing the results of his researches, but he has not yet done so, and according to German custom, other scholars have hitherto refrained from trespassing on his preserves, so the problems raised by the discovery of this manuscript have not yet been fully investigated.

the hearty bawdiness of the time, and the wife is made to feel thankful that her vigorous first husband has returned to her, after her single, disappointing experience with the second one. There are in addition a few prophecies made by Faust in his last year concerning the Papacy, including one concerning the Massacre of St. Bartholomew in 1572. It was written, of course, after the event. The preface states that the manuscript was translated from the Latin, but whether the first version of the Faust book was really written in any other language than German it is impossible to say.

It is already obvious from the Preface to the Faust book that the publication of the wicked life and dreadful doom of Faust was intended as a warning to all who could not find peace and content in the bosom of the Church, but would seek to explore beyond, with the treacherous aid of science, which at that time, of course, included magic. Curiosity in theological matters was regarded as an unhealthy symptom, and was only playing into the hands of the Devil, who, in the words of the Epistle of Peter, quoted in the Preface, as a roaring lion, walketh about, seeking whom he may devour. Faust represents the spirit of enquiry, which was regarded as fatal to the soul, but nobody seems to have wondered whether a soul that had to be so jealously guarded and could be so easily lost was worth having at all. The strong Lutheran tendency which was a characteristic of the activities of Spies as a publisher, is also a marked feature of the Faust book. Martin Luther himself shared the prevailing view of the time, that the world is divided into two camps, that of God and that of the Devil, and the latter is mentioned frequently in his writings. Faust can, with some reservation, be looked upon as the great counterpart of Luther ; they are the two poles of the sixteenth century. In the book, the contrast is all the more striking since it does not appear as an intentional element in the work. The views of Luther are not definitely defended, but are taken as a matter of course, and the contrast between the theologian and the sceptic develops naturally from the theme, though the Lutheran doctrine occasionally comes prominently to the fore. Both the Faust of the legend and Luther were Doctors of Theology and closely connected with Wittenberg, the cradle of the Reformation. Starting from the same point, they reached goals which were diametrically opposed. They both lectured on the culture of antiquity, and they had both been in Rome, but whereas Luther had set out with feelings of reverence, only to return in disappointment and indignation, Faust was merely amused and contemplated with cynical complacency the license of the Vatican, where the priests were no better than himself. Luther married in accordance with the tenets of the Church, but Faust rejected the sacrament of marriage for the pagan Helena. Luther based his faith on the Bible, Faust was not content to accept the Holy Writ, but sought to penetrate the forbidden mysteries beyond it. Faust entered into league with the Devil, while Luther hurled his inkstand at him.[1]

It is true that it was not in the spirit of Luther to conceive of the defection from orthodox theology as

[1] W. Scherer : *Das älteste Faustbuch* [Berlin, 1884].

defection from God, and the ridicule to which the Church of Rome and its priests are exposed in the Faust book, even the Devil himself appearing in the guise of a monk, would quite possibly even have appealed to his robust sense of humour. Nevertheless, there seems little reason to doubt that the book was written from the Lutheran standpoint. Since, however, in the field of German literary research, it seems impossible for any definite point of view, with whatever weight of proof it may be supported, to be maintained for very long, before a scholar brings forward its exact opposite, which he defends with equally weighty evidence, there has recently been an attempt to prove that the tendency of the Faust book was not Lutheran but Catholic.[1] The author of this theory does not deny that the intention of some passages is obviously hostile to Catholicism, but he declares that they are later interpolations, and endeavours to prove that the book is a parody on Luther, who is represented as a modern Bacchus and companion of the Devil. The first direct anti-clerical reference is the taunt at the celibacy of the clergy in Faust's conversation with Mephostophiles concerning the former's desire to take a wife. The Devil endeavours to dissuade him by declaring that marriage is a divine institution, but Faust retorts that the monks and nuns do not marry. This passage is lacking in the Wolfenbüttel MS. In the chapter which deals with the journey through Europe, Faust remarks at Cologne that the Devil is in the Church of St. Ursula with the 11,000 virgins. The MS. has *Tempel* instead of *Teufel*.

[1] Eugen Wolff: *Faust und Luther* [Halle, 1912].

When Faust arrives in Rome, he spends three days and nights invisible in the pope's palace, finding that " these pigs at Rome are fattened and all ready to roast and cook," and after his experience in the harem at Constantinople, he mounts up in the air in the vestments of a pope. These last two adventures are also to be found in the MS., but Dr. Wolff declares them to be interpolations. His evidence, however, is not convincing, and there is little reason to assume that the spirit of any literary version of the Faust book which may have been extant before 1587 was different from the tendency of the edition published by Spies.

The development from historical fact to legend was influenced considerably by contact with other myths of the same type. There were numerous alleged covenanters with the Devil in the Middle Ages, of whom the most akin to Faust was Theophilus of Adana. But Theophilus was saved eventually from eternal damnation by the intervention of the Virgin Mary, and if the Faust book had really been of Catholic origin, there is little doubt that the Madonna and the Saints would have saved him. The fires of Hell are essential to the spirit of the Faust book; the pact is irrevocable. Many features formerly attributed to other wizards were transferred to Faust, including the Devil in the form of a black dog which always accompanied Cornelius Agrippa of Nettesheim, the enchanted garden conjured up by Albertus Magnus for the Emperor in the midst of winter, and the exorcising of the spirit of Alexander the Great and other Greek heroes by the Abbot Trithemius. The incident

INTRODUCTION

of Helena may be due to the connection with Simon Magus, who was accompanied on his journeys by a courtesan named Helen. The fame of all these magicians sank into obscurity, and the one figure that carried on into future centuries the memory of their deeds was Faust.

When the oral legend was cast into literary form, the anonymous author appears to have consulted many works of reference. The long chapter which describes the journey of Faust and Mephostophiles, as well as the description of Paradise, is based on the *Book of Chronicles* of Hartmann Schedel, which appeared in 1493. The peculiar zig-zag nature of the journey is due to the fact that Schedel gives the towns in chronological order, according to the supposed year in which they were founded, and the author of the Faust book has copied them mechanically. Similarly he has taken from the German-Latin dictionary of the Swiss humanist Dasypodius, in alphabetical order, the list of fish, game and wine with which Faust entertains his guests at the court of the Count (really Prince) of Anhalt. For example, the fish are mentioned in the following order : *Aal, Barben, Bersing, Bickling, Bolchen, Aschen, Forell, Hecht, Karpffen, Krebs, Moschel, Neunaugen, Platteissen, Salmen* and *Schleyen*, and the wines are *Burgunder, Brabänder, Coblentzer, Crabatischer, Elsässer, Engelländer, Frantzösische, Rheinische, Spanische*, etc. The conversations concerning the physical sciences and celestial phenomena can be traced to *Elucidarius*, a collection of scientific dialogues.

Augustin Lercheimer's (pseudonym for Professor

Hermann Witekind of Heidelberg) *Christliche Bedenken und Erinnerung von Zauberei*, which first appeared in 1585, was formerly thought to have been a direct source of the Faust book, but it is possible that Lercheimer himself borrowed from an earlier manuscript of the Faust book. He anticipates modern science when he protests against the witch-burnings, and declares that witches should be sent to the physician rather than to the judge. In the third edition of his book, which was published in 1597, Lercheimer denounces the Faust book as a libel on the University and Church of Wittenberg :—

" It is all malicious lies. . . . He had neither house nor yard at Wittenberg or elsewhere, was never at home, lived like a vagabond, was a parasite, guzzled, swilled and lived by his conjuring. How could he have a house and yard by the outer gate of the town in the Scheergasse, since there never was a suburb and therefore no outer gate ? Neither was there ever a Scheergasse there. That in such a University, a man whom Melanchthon used to call a cesspool of many devils should have been made Master, to say nothing of Doctor of Theology, which would be an eternal disgrace to the degree and honourable title, who believes that ? . . . About all the other vanity, lies and *Teufelsdreck* in the book, I will say nothing. . . . It is, to be sure, nothing new and no cause for surprise that such calumnies are issued by the enemies of our religion, but it is unwarrantable and lamentable that our printers also should publish such books without shame, whereby honest people are slandered and inquisitive youths led to attempt similar magic feats ; to say nothing of the abuse of the beautiful and noble art of printing, which has been conferred on us by God."

The fact that Lercheimer, who was an ardent adherent of Luther, should have condemned the book in such terms, cannot be regarded as evidence of its anti-Lutheran tendency.

Another important manuscript was discovered recently in Nuremberg.[1] A certain Christoph Rosshirt, a teacher of Nuremberg, who had studied in Wittenberg, copied into an album about the year 1575, amidst other matter, anecdotes relating to various magicians, including Doctor Faust. It will be noticed that Faust's Christian name is given here as *George*. The Faust stories are four in number :—

1. When Dr. Georgius Faustus is lecturing to the students at the University of Ingolstadt on philosophy and necromancy, he invites some friends to dinner, and tells them that the food and drink they are enjoying come from the wedding-feast of the King of England. He instructs them to hold on to the edge of the towel when water is brought for them to wash their hands, and he will take them to the dance at the King's wedding. When they are discovered in the ball-room, they are taken for spies and arrested. They are condemned to be hanged, but Faust rescues them in the same way that he had brought them there. They wash their hands in England and dry them in Germany.

[1] By Wilhelm Meyer, and edited by him in *Nürnberger Faustgeschichten* [Munich, 1895].

2. Faust asks a Jewish merchant at the Frankfort Fair to change him some French money into good talers. The merchant promises to call on Faust at his inn and bring him the money, but when he arrives, Faust is lying on a couch, apparently asleep. The Jew puts his bag of talers on the table and shakes Faust by the arm, but cannot rouse him; he becomes annoyed and shakes him violently by the leg, which comes off in his hand. He rushes in terror from the house, leaving behind him cloak and money-bag which are shared by Faust and his servant.

3. Faust sells a swineherd in Bamberg some fat pigs, but warns him against driving them into flowing water. On the next day the swineherd neglects the warning and the pigs are turned into bundles of straw. By this time Faust is well on the way to Nuremberg.

4. On the evening before he is due to fulfil his pact with the Devil, Faust arrives at a village inn and asks for a room for the night. In the tap-room there is a crowd of drunken, noisy peasants, who refuse to be quiet when Faust asks them. The magician bewitches them so that they remain sitting with their mouths wide open, and he is able to have his last meal in peace. He pays his bill, tips all the servants, and goes to bed, but is persuaded by the host to disenchant the drunken clowns. On the next morning, Faust is found dead in bed.

As some of these stories had already been in circulation about other magicians, it is obvious that Faust was already becoming in popular imagination the prototype, and it is possible to see the myth in progress of development. The magician who sold his soul to the Devil was not a new factor in the superstitious fantasy of the people, but it was convenient to father all the floating rumours on some outstanding personality of whom everybody had heard and who had, in the memory of many, boasted in public of his wicked art. It is of interest to note that whereas Bütner declares that it was at Wittenberg, the leading Lutheran University, that Faust conjured up the Greek heroes, this Nuremberg manuscript transfers his teaching activities in philosophy and necromancy to the centre of Catholic doctrine, Ingolstadt. Later on the scene is shifted to Erfurt, the seat of humanism.

The enlarged edition which appeared in 1587, with a different sequence of chapters and eight new ones added, has drawn for its new matter mainly on the *De Praestigiis Daemonum* of Wierus and the *Christliche Bedenken und Erinnerung von Zauberei* of Augustin Lercheimer, where the anecdotes are related for the most part about other magicians. The title-page of this edition states that it was printed by Spies, but his printer's ornament is lacking, so the statement is most probably false.

The stories are as follows :—

1. Faust meets a peasant who has lost his horse, and tells him that he has just seen a man riding away on it. The peasant hurries after the supposed thief and there is a gory fight, until he notices that the other man's horse is a stallion, whereas his own was a gelding.

2. Faust meets a priest in Cologne hastening to

church with his breviary in his hand, and turns the sacred book into a pack of cards.

3. Faust enters an inn, where he is refused entertainment, as there is no food in the house. He taps the window with his finger, and says " Bring what you have " ; then putting his hand outside the window, he draws in a large dish full of boiled pike and a large can of good Rhine wine.

4. A castle in which Faust is living is besieged by the Spanish troops of the Emperor Charles. He shoots fragments from a tree under which a Spanish colonel is sitting, although the latter is not visible from the castle, and catches the Spanish cannon-balls in his hands.

5. Faust swallows a servant in an inn, because he fills the glasses too full, and washes the morsel down with a bucket of water. The servant is afterwards discovered in the yard all wet and dripping.

6. Faust cuts off a man's head in an inn, but is prevented from setting it on again by the mysterious influence of one of the spectators ; so he causes a lily to grow on the table, from which he slices off the head, and immediately one of the spectators falls decapitated from his seat. Faust then sets the first man's head on his shoulders again.

7. Faust invites some gentlemen to dinner, but when they arrive they find the table empty. Their host bids his spirit fetch food from a neighbouring wedding-party, and after the feast the guests ask him to show them one of his tricks. He causes a vine to grow on the table, with grapes for each of his guests, and tells

35

each one to pick his own fruit with one hand and put his knife to the stalk with the other, but to be very careful not to cut. He then leaves the room, and when he returns they are all grasping their own noses with one hand and holding their knives in dangerous proximity with the other.

8. Faust teaches a chaplain how to remove his beard with arsenic.

The edition of 1589 is important, because it contains the six extra " Erfurt Chapters," which were most probably based on local tradition in that town. Faust is seen here as a lecturer at the University. The following is a summary of these extra chapters :—

1. Some students invite Faust to accompany them to the Leipzig Fair, and after they have inspected the town and the University they come to a wine-

cellar, where some draymen are endeavouring without success to roll out a huge barrel. Faust mocks their efforts, and they return his jeers with interest, but the owner of the barrel offers to make a present of the contents to whoever can lift it out. Faust goes into the cellar, sits astride the barrel as though it were a horse and rides out. The host has to keep his promise, and Faust shares the contents with his companions.

2. Faust was for some years at Erfurt and lectured at the University. On one occasion, when he is lecturing on Homer, the students request him to conjure up the ancient heroes of Greece. He promises to do so at his next lecture, which is consequently very fully attended. The heroes duly appear in their armour— Menelaus, Achilles, Hector, Priam, Alexander, Ulysses,

Ajax, Agamemnon and others, followed by the one-eyed giant Polyphemus, with the extremities of a man he is eating still projecting from between his teeth. The spectators are terrified, but Faust laughs and orders the spirits to go away again, which they all do with the exception of Polyphemus, who looks as though he would like to devour one or two of the students. However, he also is persuaded to retire, but the students do not ask Faust to repeat the experiment.

3. Faust offers to bring to light the lost comedies of Terence and Plautus, though only for a sufficient length of time to enable them to be copied. The theologians and members of the University council, however, think that there are enough books in existence from which the students can learn Latin, and in any case there is the possibility of the Devil inserting in the newly discovered works all kinds of poison and bad examples, and the disadvantage might outbalance the gain. So Faust is not given the opportunity this time of proving his skill.

4. While Faust is in Prague, a friend of his, who is giving a party in Erfurt, desires his presence, and presently there is a knock at the door and Faust is seen to have just alighted from his horse. He says he cannot stay long as he must be back in Prague on the morrow. He gets intoxicated, and asks the guests whether they would not like to try some foreign wines. He thereupon bores four holes in the table and puts plugs into them. Glasses are fetched, Faust draws the plugs and serves each man with the wine he desires. It appears that his horse, who is devouring all the oats in the stable and looking for more, is really Mephostophiles. Early in the morning Faust rides away, and the guests who accompany him to the door see his horse rise with him into the air.

5. Faust invites some friends to his lodging, and when they arrive there is neither food nor drink, fire nor smoke. Their host raps on the table with his knife, and a servant comes in. Faust asks, "How swift are you?" and the reply is, "Like an arrow."

" No," says Faust, " you cannot serve me, go back whence you came." He raps again, and another servant enters, who tells Faust that he is as swift as the wind. He also is sent away. A third servant is as swift as thought and is accepted by Faust, who orders him to bring food and drink for the feast. The goblets are put on the table empty, but Faust asks each of his guests what kind of wine or beer he would like, holds the goblet out of the window and draws it in again full of the desired liquor.

6. A famous Franciscan monk, named Dr. Kling, who was well acquainted with Dr. Martin Luther, endeavours to convert Faustus. But Faust declares it would be dishonourable to go back on his pact with the Devil, which he has signed with his own blood. " The Devil has honourably kept his part of the bargain, therefore I will keep mine." The monk reports this conversation to the Rector and Council of the University, and Faust is compelled to quit Erfurt.

These stories are also to be found in a seventeenth-century manuscript chronicle of Thuringia and the town of Erfurt, based on an Erfurt Chronicle of the previous century which is now lost. The author of this earlier chronicle appears to have heard the anecdotes, in the year 1556, from a neighbour of the Franciscan monk who tried to convert Faust. The story of how Faust rode the barrel of wine out of the cellar is recorded in two paintings on the wall of Auerbach's wine-cellar in Leipzig, which bear the date 1525, but are in reality no earlier than the seventeenth century. The wine-cellar itself was not built till 1530.

INTRODUCTION

There were further editions of the Faust book in 1590 and 1592, as well as a rhymed version, which appeared at Tübingen in the winter of 1587–8. It is probably the authors of this book who are referred to in the complaint of the ducal commissioners to the senate of the University of Tübingen, which is recorded in the minutes of the senate on the 15th of April, 1588. The publisher and authors are ordered to be incarcerated for a couple of days, and sternly reprimanded.

In the year 1599 there was published at Hamburg a considerably enlarged edition, of which the end of each chapter was adorned with an edifying commentary, called an *Erinnerung*, or Remonstrance, and it is this version which became the basis of the subsequent editions. The story becomes more anti-Catholic than in the earlier editions, and the anti-papal moral is driven home in each *Erinnerung*. The editor, Georg Rudolf Widman, has successfully eliminated any element of titanism or poetry which may have been present in the original book, and Faust becomes merely a young man led astray by the Church of Rome. Widman has even been delicate enough to condense the Helena episode to a mere reference in a footnote.

Widman's version was again subjected to re-arrangement in the year 1674, by the Nuremberg physician Johann Nicolaus Pfitzer, who modified the former polemic against the Catholic Church, and in 1725 Pfitzer's version was published in abbreviated form by an anonymous editor who called himself a *Christlich-Meynender*, or Man of Christian Sentiments. This volume is exceedingly slim, but it was sold everywhere and became the popular chap-book. It is important in that it contains the germ of the Gretchen episode in Goethe's drama. Faust tries to seduce a servant-girl, but she is proof against temptation and he offers to marry her; Lucifer, however, dissuades him and gives him Helena instead.

III

Faust in England

THE earliest mention of Faust in England is in a translation by R. H. of a book by Ludwig Lavater, *Of Ghostes and Spirites*, published in 1572 :—

" There are also conjurers founde even at this day, who bragge of themselves that they can so by inchauntments saddle an horse, that in a fewe houres they will dispatch a very long journey. God at the last will chasten these men with deserved punishment. What straunge things are reported of one Faustus a German, which he did in these our dayes by inchauntments ? "

The History of the Damnable Life and Deserved Death of Doctor John Faustus, which was published in London in 1592, was, as the title-page announces, newly printed and in places amended, so there must have been an earlier edition of which all trace is lost. This was in all likelihood translated from the *editio princeps* of 1587, but as we are uncertain of its date, it is not impossible that one of the slightly later German editions was used. There occurs in the Stationers' Registers under the date 28th of February, 1589, the entry of " A ballad of the life and deathe of Doctor FFAUSTUS the great Cunngerer. Allowed under the hand of the Bishop of London."

This ballad has been preserved only in later versions of the seventeenth century,[1] and it is not possible to say definitely whether or no it was founded on the English translation of the German Faust book, though that is the most likely theory. There is little doubt that the latter appeared before the ballad. In any case, *The Tragical History of Doctor Faustus*, by Christopher Marlowe, which was in all probability on the stage as early as 1589, was based directly, as is shown by internal evidence, on the English Faust book, and it is unlikely that Marlowe was acquainted with the German version.[2] So even if the ballad was founded on Marlowe's tragedy, which is very improbable, and not on the English Faust book, the latter must have been published an astonishingly short time after the appearance of the original German *Historia*. The translator is called P. F. *Gent.* (i.e. Gentleman, and not, as some editors have thought, his surname), but in later editions these initials appear as P. R. or P. K. His identity cannot be established, and it is not even possible to estimate definitely his knowledge of German. To quote Logeman ; " That P. F. . . . must have known some German is of course evident from the whole of the translation and more especially from some passages where a smaller light would have blundered. But that his own cannot have shone very brightly is apparent from the number of lesser and greater blunders in which we have caught our translator, and also from the fact that some passages which

[1] See Appendix B.

[2] *Marlowe's Faustus, etc.*, edited by A. W. Ward [4th ed., Oxford, 1901], and *Faustus-Notes*, by H. Logeman [Gand, 1898].

present considerable difficulties will be found to have been omitted." We cannot, however, judge a sixteenth-century translator by present-day standards, for he was at liberty to adapt or modify as he listed. For example, where the German original states that Faust blew in the pope's face, the translator renders *blew* by *smote*, thus altering the whole sense, and it is doubtful whether the false translation is due to P. F.'s sense of humour or his ignorance of German. The description of Florence is even more confused than in the original, and he adds strange lore of his own, such as the mythical story of the Brazen Virgin on the bridge at Breslau, who was used for the disposal of unruly children. It is possible that P. F. had really visited eastern Germany and the Polish or Galician regions, such as Prague and Cracow, but it is just as likely that he obtained his extra knowledge from a travelled friend. He frequently tones down the German author's denunciation of Faust's wicked ways, and emphasizes the fantasies and cogitations rather than the presumption and arrogance of the sorcerer. The English Faust book is therefore the first step in the deepening of the Faust character, and this conception is developed by Marlowe.[1]

There is in the original legend of Faust little of that titanic discontent with the spiritual limits of humanity, which is now regarded as the fundamental characteristic of the Faustian nature. It is not the desire to solve the riddle of the universe that drives him to the pact with the Devil, but the less worthy

[1] R. Rohde: *Das Englische Faustbuch und Marlowes Tragödie* [Halle, 1910].

44

desire for power and pleasure. It is true that " he took to himself eagles' wings and wanted to fathom all the causes in heaven and earth," but the Promethean defiance which some scholars have sought to establish as his guiding motive, was a preconception implanted in their own minds by a study of the Faust of Goethe. The Faust of the *Historia* obliges the Devil to answer all his questions and shows afterwards a lively interest in the organization of heaven and hell, but the first-fruits of the pact are food, wine and women. Even Marlowe's Faustus promises himself merely treasure, delicacies and power from intercourse with the spirits ; philosophy, medicine, law and theology are all inadequate for the man who longs to " raise the wind, or rend the clouds," but when his league with hell has endowed him with supernatural powers, the only use he finds for them is to gratify his sensual desires or indulge in practical jokes. It cannot be said that Marlowe has realized in his tragedy the potentiality of the legend, though he seems to have had an inkling of it. The Helen episode gives rise to the finest poetical passage in the play :—

" Was this the face that launch'd a thousand ships,
   And burnt the topless towers of Ilium ? "—

and the final scene, with Faust's death presaged by the striking of the clock, is impressive, but the author has done little to raise the conception to a higher plane.

After the production of Marlowe's play the name of Faustus appears to have become a household word, and there are various allusions to the character in contemporary writings, including a reference in Shakespeare's *Merry Wives*. William Prynne relates

INTRODUCTION

in his *Histrio-Mastix, The Players' Scourge*, 1663, a curious incident which occurred during a performance. He is quoting the tragic end of many who have been slain in playhouses in London, " Nor yet to recite the sudden fearful burning even to the ground, both of the Globe and Fortune Playhouses, no man perceiving how these fires came : together with the visible apparition of the Devil on the Stage at the Belsavage Playhouse, in Queen Elizabeth's days (to the great amazement both of the Actors and Spectators) whiles they were there profanely playing the History of Faustus, . . . there being some distracted with that fearful sight."

There was no further development of the theme in this country, for it degenerated into a subject for farce and pantomime. There were further editions of the English Faust book, and in the year 1664 there was published in London *The History of Doctor John Faustus ; Compiled in Verse, very pleasant and Delightfull*, with a doggerel dedication to the reader :—

> " Reader, I would not have you think,
> That I intend to waste my ink,
> While Faustus Story I reherse,
> And here do write his life in verse.
> For seeing Fryer Bacons Story,
> (In whom Oxford still may glory)
> For want of better pen comes forth,
> Compos'd in Rymes of no great worth :
> I call'd my Muse to task, and pend
> Faustus life, and death, and end.
> And when it cometh forth in print,
> If you like it not, the Devil's in't."

A farce by the actor W. Mountford, *Life and Death of Doctor Faustus, with the Humours of Harlequin and*

Scaramuch, was acted at the Queen's Theatre in Dorset Gardens between 1684 and 1688, and revived later at the theatre in Lincoln's Inn Fields. It was borrowed for the most part, with the exception, of course, of the harlequinade, from Marlowe.

The poet Alexander Pope declares that Faust was the subject of a set of farces, which lasted in vogue two or three seasons, and in which both Drury Lane and Covent Garden strove to outdo each other for some years. John Thurmond, a dancing master, composed a *Harlequin Dr. Faustus*, which was performed at Drury Lane, and published in the year 1724, and there is a record of a *Harlequin Dr. Faustus, Pantomime ; altered from the Necromancer*, by a Mr. Woodward, which was acted at Covent Garden as late as 1766. These are but casual references to what must have been numerous Faust farces, and there were in addition performances of Faust puppet-plays in the Punch and Judy Theatre of Martin Powell opposite St. Paul's Church in Covent Garden. Neither the pantomimes nor the puppet-plays appear to derive from Marlowe, but since the appearance of the latter's tragedy, the Faust story appears definitely to have abandoned the epic form for the dramatic, and it is in its original home, Germany, that further development took place. Although in England the theme degenerated until it was employed for the most insipid type of theatrical entertainment, it was the English dramatist who first gave it the form in which, two centuries later, it was to inspire the greatest of all the poets who have sought to express the strivings of humanity in the figure of Faust.

47

IV

The Faust Drama in Germany

THROUGHOUT the stagnant literary period of the seventeenth century and the first half of the eighteenth, it was not the various editions of the Faust book that kept the legend green in Germany, but the popular drama which developed from Marlowe's *Faustus*. Towards the end of the sixteenth century, companies of English actors began to tour the Continent, and in their repertories were the plays of the Elizabethans, much mangled and adapted to the taste of their uncultivated audiences. The popularity of these *English Comedians*, as they were called, was greatest in Germany, and we find traces of them throughout the first half of the seventeenth century. Acting as a profession began in Germany with these English companies. At first they played only in English, but later they produced German translations of their repertory, even German original plays, and recruited their ranks from among German actors. Soon German troupes were formed on the same lines, who still, however, called themselves "English Comedians," since the advertisement was of value. The English actors laid great weight on visual effect, for the language difficulty had at first to be surmounted. The actors themselves were for the most part minstrels and dancers, and the most important character was the clown who appeared in every production, however tragic it might be. Even when the play was performed in English, the clown spoke German, and he was known under various names, such as *Pickelhäring*, while later on he was called *Hans Wurst*. The plays were not written down and there was plenty of scope allowed for gagging, so that eventually they were distorted out of all recognition and were practically the work of the actors themselves. Among the plays which were produced and gradually adapted in this manner was Marlowe's tragedy, and in its more spectacular form it provided the public with the two somewhat contradictory essentials, plenty of coarse humour and plenty of blood.

The earliest record of a performance of Marlowe's play by the English strolling players is one at Gräz in 1608. In 1626, a *Tragödia von Dr. Faust* was produced at Dresden on the 7th of July, and this was no doubt also Marlowe's play. We know what the main outline of the popular drama must have been from a comparison of the various puppet-plays which were performed in comparatively recent times in Germany and Austria, for when the Faust drama ceased to be performed by living actors, it was taken over by the proprietors of marionette theatres, and in this form it survived till well into the nineteenth century. The main points which the popular drama possessed in common with Marlowe's tragedy were the expository opening monologue, the appearance of the good and evil angels, and the presaging of Faust's impending end by the striking of the clock. The humorous and melodramatic scenes had no doubt been supplemented and exaggerated by other hands even on the English stage. There is no ground for assuming that there was already a Faust play of German origin on the German stage before the arrival of the English Comedians.

The following is an amusing specimen of the type of programme which was issued by the strolling players. It refers to a performance by the famous Neuber troupe in Hamburg, on the 7th of July, 1738[1] :—

" The wicked Life and fearful End of the World-famous Arch-sorcerer D. Johann Faust.

The following Scenes will be presented, among others : A great outer Court in the underworld Palace of Pluto, by the Rivers Lethe and Acheron. On the River comes Charon in a Boat, and to him Pluto on a fiery Dragon, followed by the whole of his underworld Retinue and Spirits.

Dr. Faust's Study and Library. An agreeable Spirit of the upper World will sing the following touching Aria, accompanied by tender Music :

[A song of three verses.]

A Raven flies out of the Air and fetches the Manuscript of Dr. Faust. Hans Wurst breaks in accidentally on his Master, Dr. Faust's Magic. He must stand still and cannot move from the spot until he has taken off his Shoes. The Shoes then dance together in a merry Manner.

An insolent Court-menial, who mocks Dr. Faust, is endowed with a pair of Horns.

[1] K. Engel: *Zusammenstellung der Faust-Schriften* [Oldenburg, 1885], pp. 188 ff.

A Peasant buys a Horse from Dr. Faust, and as soon as he rides it, the Horse turns into a Bundle of Hay. The Peasant wants to call Dr. Faust to Account, Faust pretends to be asleep, the Peasant tugs him and pulls off his Leg.

Hans Wurst wants to have a lot of Money, and to please him, Mephostophiles causes him to rain Money.

The lovely Helena sings, to the Accompaniment of pleasant Music, an Aria which is unpleasant to Dr. Faust, for it presages his Doom.

Dr. Faust takes Leave from his Famulus Christoph Wagner. Hans Wurst also departs, and the Spirits fetch Dr. Faust to the Accompaniment of Fire-works, which play in an ingenious Manner.

The underworld Palace of Pluto is seen once more. The Furies have Possession of Dr. Faust and dance a Ballet round him, because they have brought him safely into their Domain.

The Rest will be more pleasant in the Seeing then here in the Reading.

Commencement at half past four, in the so-called Opera House in the Goosemarket at Hamburg."

Another programme from Frankfort of the year 1742 announces that after the play there will be a dance, after the dance a ballet, and if time permits, after the ballet there will be a merry comedy.

It will thus be seen to what depths the story of Faust had fallen, before the time came to raise it to the plane of the world's greatest tragedies. It was Lessing who first saw the potentialities of the theme, and he pointed them out in the famous seventeenth

INTRODUCTION

Literaturbrief of the 16th of February, 1759, which commenced a new era for German literature, henceforth to turn away from French models and seek inspiration from Shakespeare. The stilted superficiality of French literature was to yield to the more congenial vigour of the English. It is true that Lessing did not recognize the worth of Marlowe, who stood in the shadow of his greater contemporary, but he declares that the old German plays had possessed much of the English quality. " To mention only the best known of them : *Doctor Faust* has a number of scenes, which could only have been imagined by a Shakespearean genius. And how deeply was, and in part still is, Germany in love with her Doctor Faust ! One of my friends possesses an old draft of this tragedy, and he has communicated a scene to me in which there is undoubtedly much that is great." He then prints a scene, which was really composed by himself, and among his papers after his death were found sketches relating to his plan for a Faust drama. It is certain that Lessing intended to reject the obsolete orthodox view that Faust must necessarily pay for his sins by an eternity of damnation. The Catholic theologians had permitted sorcerers to be saved by repentance, but the spirit of the Reformation demanded that Faust forfeit his soul, and from this inevitable doom there was no appeal. The age of Enlightenment, on the other hand, looked upon the intellect as supreme, and it was obviously absurd that Faust's attempt to solve an intellectual problem should lead to the loss of his soul. It is to Lessing that is due the fundamental change in the conception of the Faust problem, whereby Faust is not damned, but saved. The longing to penetrate the mysteries of the universe is no longer regarded as an instinct implanted in humanity by the Devil.

So far as we can judge from the fragments, Lessing's Faust was to be driven to the pact solely by his thirst for knowledge. Goethe was to create the eternal type, the man who seeks to encompass the universe, who demands complete and ultimate satisfaction for the limitless craving of the human soul. The first impulse to create a Faust drama of his own came to Goethe from a marionette version of the popular drama, a performance of which he saw in Leipzig in his student days, for he never saw it performed by living actors, and neither the Folk book nor Marlowe's tragedy came into his hands until much later. It was a task which occupied him all his life. His original draft, the *Urfaust*, has only been discovered in manuscript in recent times, but in the year 1790 he published *Faust. A Fragment*. The first part of the completed tragedy appeared in 1808, and the second part in 1833, a year after Goethe's death.

The fundamental difference between Goethe's conception of the problem and all that had gone before is typified in the fact that it is not a *pact* into which Faust enters with Mephisto, but a *wager*. There are indeed two wagers. In the Prologue in Heaven, Mephisto discusses Faust with the Lord and says,[1]

" What will you bet ?   There's still a chance to gain him,
    If unto me full leave you give,
    Gently upon *my* road to train him ! "

[1] Bayard Taylor's translation.

INTRODUCTION

The Lord enters into the spirit of the thing and replies,

> " As long as he on earth shall live,
> So long I make no prohibition,
> While Man's desires and aspirations stir,
> He cannot choose but err.
>
> A good man, through obscurest aspiration,
> Has still an instinct of the one true way."

The opening monologue, which shows Faust in his study fighting with the realization that " here, poor fool ! with all my lore I stand, no wiser than before," is an echo of the initial monologue of Marlowe's tragedy, which came to Goethe through the medium of the popular drama and the puppet-show. Hitherto the pact had been for a definite period of twenty-four years, during which Faust was to enjoy all that the Devil could give him and then to fulfil without hope of mercy his part of the bargain. Goethe's Faust, however, demands more than the fulfilment of transitory desires. He wants to grasp the moment of supreme satisfaction, and if Mephisto cannot give him that, Faust's soul remains his own :—

> " When on an idler's bed I stretch myself in quiet,
> There let, at once, my record end !
> Canst thou with lying flattery rule me,
> Until, self-pleased, myself I see,—
> Canst thou with rich enjoyment fool me,
> Let that day be the last for me !
> The bet I offer ! . . .
>
> When thus I hail the Moment flying :
> ' Ah, still delay—thou art so fair ! '
> Then bind me in thy bonds undying,
> My final ruin then declare ! "

54

That is the important point. Mephisto plunges Faust in the pleasures of revelry, love, power and classic beauty, but in spite of his burning craving for supreme happiness, he is incapable of enjoying the blissful moment. There never is a fleeting moment to which he can say " Ah, still delay—thou art so fair ! " There is no absolute truth or absolute beauty, and therefore no absolute happiness. The blissful moment does not exist, and the only satisfaction which man is free to enjoy is in striving after an imaginary absolute. Faust never becomes absorbed in a moment of ecstasy and therefore the Devil loses the wager. By using his power unselfishly to further the lot of others, he is the instrument of his own salvation ; he redeems himself by an ever higher and purer form of activity, as Goethe himself said, and dies with the conviction that

> " He only earns his freedom and existence,
> Who daily conquers them anew."

When Mephisto summons his devils to carry the soul to hell, a host of angels flies from heaven to repel them, and as they bear Faust's immortal soul into the upper air, they proclaim

> " Whoe'er aspires unweariedly
> Is not beyond redeeming."

The Devil had not given Faust the blissful moment, but had only enabled him to find a compromise between dream and reality by creative work. Faust's craving remained unfulfilled, and his reconcilement to the conditions of life was only temporary. But as that is the only possibility, as man's highest aspirations never can be completely satisfied, the wager was from the first destined to be unfulfilled.

In Goethe's *Faust* the theme received the highest treatment of which it was capable. At the time when he first came in contact with the story, Faust dramas were being announced by authors from all corners of Germany, and perhaps it would not be too much to say that every German poet since Goethe has cherished the hope of some day creating his own Faust. Of the tragedies, farces, operas, pantomimes, ballets, novels, short stories, poems, folk-songs and even parodies on the subject, it may be said that their name is legion, and it appears to have been cast into every possible art-form. It will, perhaps, suffice to mention here a dance-poem which was written by the poet Heinrich Heine in 1851 for performance at Drury Lane. Lumley, the director of the theatre, had already made preparations for the production, when it was laid aside as unsuitable. One of the latest treatments of the theme is *Faust and the City*, by Lunacharski, the Minister of Education in Soviet Russia.

V

The Wagner Book

THE first edition of the German Wagner book was published anonymously, without mention even of its place of origin, in 1593, under a title of which the following is a translation :—

Second part of D. Johann Faust's History, in which is described the Pact of Christopher Wagner, Faust's former Disciple, contracted with the Devil, called Auerhan, who appeared to him in the form of an Ape, also his adventurous Ribaldries and Pranks, which he performed with the Aid of the Devil, and fearful End which at last overtook him.

Together with an excellent Description of the New Isles, what People live therein, what Fruits grow there, what Religion and Idol-worship they have there, and how they are captured by the Spaniards, all drawn from his posthumous Writings and, for it is very amusing to read, put into Print. By Fridericus Schotus Tolet : Now at P. 1593.

Unlike the publisher of the Faust book, the author of the Wagner book appears to have taken all precautions to hide his identity, for Fridericus Schotus is a pseudonym, and Tolet is Toledo, where there were supposed to be celebrated schools of magic. At the end of his book the author declares that he has translated from a Spanish original, printed seventy years ago, which he received from a Brother Martin of the Order of St. Benedict. That is obviously false, since the Faust legend did not exist in 1523, and certainly could not have been in print in Spain. The author also declares that he has refrained from saying anything that might be considered detrimental to the Church of Rome, but this promise he has not kept very successfully. In an edition which appeared in the following year, the town of origin is given as " Gerapoli," which is fictitious and may contain an anagram of " Prague," since the first edition states that it was published at " P."

The Wagner story is essentially a paraphrase of the Faust legend, and the author keeps to the outline of his hero's character which is given in the Faust book. The sole difference is in some of the external incidents.

The English Wagner book was licensed about six months after the German Wagner book, according to an entry in the Stationers' Registers under the 16th of November, 1593, and the date on the title-page is 1594. It is *not* a translation of the German Wagner book, but an extremely faint imitation, into which the author has introduced many new details. He appears only to have taken the basic idea, though there are occasional quotations from the German book, and it is practically an independent work. The 1680 edition was, in fact, translated into German and published in Scheible's *Kloster*.

WILLIAM ROSE.

1925.

THE
HISTORIE

of the damnable

life, and deserued death of
Doctor Iohn Faustus,

Newly imprinted, and in conueni-
ent places imperfect matter amended:
according to the true Copie printed
at Franckfort, *and translated into*
Englisb by P.F. Gent.

Scene and allowed.

Imprinted at London *by* Thomas Orwin, *and are to be*
solde by Edward White, *dwelling at the little North*
doore of Paules, *at the signe of the Gun.* 1592.

HERE FOLLOWETH THE CONTENTS OF THIS BOOK

THE CONTENTS OF THIS BOOK

64

A Discourse of the most famous Doctor
John Faustus of Wittenberg in Germanie, Coniurer,
and Necromancer: wherein is declared many strange
things that he himselfe hath seene, and done in the
earth and in the Ayre, with his bringing vp,
his trauailes, studies, and last end

CHAPTER I

Of his Parentage and Birth

JOHN FAUSTUS, born in the town of Rhode,
lying in the province of Weimer in Germanie,
his father a poor husbandman, and not able well to
bring him up : but having an uncle at Wittenberg,
a rich man, and without issue, took this J. Faustus
from his father, and made him his heir, in so much
that his father was no more troubled with him, for he
remained with his uncle at Wittenberg, where he was
kept at the University in the same city to study
Divinity. But Faustus being of a naughty mind and
otherwise addicted, applied not his studies, but took
himself to other exercises : the which his uncle often-
times hearing, rebuked him for it, as Eli oft-times
rebuked his children for sinning against the Lord :
even so this good man laboured to have Faustus apply
his study of Divinity, that he might come to the

knowledge of God and his laws. But it is manifest that many virtuous parents have wicked children, as Cain, Ruben, Absolom, and such-like have been to their parents : so this Faustus having godly parents, and seeing him to be of a toward wit, were very desirous to bring him up in those virtuous studies, namely, of Divinity : but he gave himself secretly to study Necromancy and Conjuration, in so much that few or none could perceive his profession.

But to the purpose : Faustus continued at study in the University, and was by the Rectors and sixteen Masters afterwards examined how he had profited in his studies ; and being found by them, that none for his time were able to argue with him in Divinity, or for the excellency of his wisdom to compare with him, with one consent they made him Doctor of Divinity. But Doctor Faustus within short time after he had obtained his degree, fell into such fantasies and deep cogitations, that he was marked of many, and of the most part of the Students was called the Speculator ; and sometime he would throw the Scriptures from him as though he had no care of his former profession : so that he began a very ungodly life, as hereafter more at large may appear ; for the old proverb saith, Who can hold that will away ? so, who can hold Faustus from the Devil, that seeks after him with all his endeavour ? For he accompanied himself with divers that were seen in those Devilish Arts, and that had the Chaldean, Persian, Hebrew, Arabian, and Greek tongues, using Figures, Characters, Conjurations, Incantations, with many other ceremonies belonging to these infernal Arts, as Necromancy, Charms, Soothsaying, Witchcraft, Enchantment, being delighted with their books, words, and names so well, that he studied day and night therein : in so much that he could not abide to be called Doctor of Divinity, but waxed a worldly man, and named himself an Astrologian, and a Mathematician : and for a shadow sometimes a Physician, and did great cures, namely, with herbs, roots, waters, drinks, receipts, and clysters. And without doubt he was passing wise, and excellent perfect in the holy scriptures : but he that knoweth his master's will and doth it not, is worthy to be beaten with many stripes. It is written, no man can serve two masters : and, thou shalt not tempt the Lord thy God : but Faustus threw all this in the wind, and made his soul of no estimation, regarding more his worldly pleasure than the joys to come : therefore at the day of judgment there is no hope of his redemption.

CHAPTER II

How Doctor Faustus began to practise in his Devilish Art, and how he conjured the Devil, making him to appear and meet him on the morrow at his own house

YOU have heard before, that all Faustus' mind was set to study the arts of Necromancy and Conjuration, the which exercise he followed day and night : and taking to him the wings of an Eagle, thought to fly over the whole world, and to know the secrets of heaven and earth ; for his Speculation was so wonderful, being expert in using his Vocabula, Figures, Characters, Conjurations, and other Ceremonial actions, that in all the haste he put in practice to bring the Devil before him. And taking his way to a thick Wood near to Wittenberg, called in the German tongue Spisser Waldt : that is in English the Spissers Wood (as Faustus would often-times boast of it among his crew being in his jollity), he came into the same wood towards evening into a cross way, where he made with a wand a Circle in the dust, and within that many more Circles and Characters : and thus he passed away the time, until it was nine or ten of the clock in the night, then began Doctor Faustus to call for Mephostophiles the Spirit, and to charge him in the name of Beelzebub to appear there personally without any long stay : then presently the Devil began so great a rumour in the Wood, as if heaven and earth would have come together with wind, the trees bowing their tops to the ground, then fell the Devil to blare as if the whole Wood had been full of Lions, and suddenly about the Circle ran the Devil as if a thousand Wagons had been running together on paved stones. After this at the four corners of the Wood it thundered horribly, with such lightnings as if the whole world, to his seeming, had been on fire. Faustus all this while half amazed at the Devil's so long tarrying, and doubting whether he were best to abide any more such horrible Conjurings, thought to leave his Circle and depart ; whereupon the Devil made him such music of all sorts, as if the Nymphs themselves had been in

68

place : whereat Faustus was revived and stood stoutly in his circle aspecting his purpose, and began again to conjure the Spirit Mephostophiles in the name of the Prince of Devils to appear in his likeness : whereat suddenly over his head hanged hovering in the air a mighty Dragon : then calls Faustus again after his Devilish manner, at which there was a monstrous cry in the Wood, as if Hell had been open, and all the tormented souls crying to God for mercy ; presently not three fathoms above his head fell a flame in manner of a lightning, and changed itself into a Globe : yet Faustus feared it not, but did persuade himself that the Devil should give him his request before he would leave : Often-times after to his companions he would boast, that he had the stoutest head (under the cope of heaven) at commandment : whereat they answered, they knew none stouter than the Pope or Emperor : but Doctor Faustus said, the head that is my servant is above all on earth, and repeated certain words out of Saint Paul to the Ephesians to make his argument good : The Prince of this world is upon earth and under heaven. Well, let us come again to his Conjuration where we left him at his fiery Globe : Faustus vexed at the Spirit's so long tarrying, used his Charms with full purpose not to depart before he had his intent, and crying on Mephostophiles the Spirit ; suddenly the Globe opened and sprang up in height of a man : so burning a time, in the end it converted to the shape of a fiery man. This pleasant beast ran about the Circle a great while, and lastly appeared in manner of a gray Friar, asking Faustus what was his request. Faustus commanded that the

next morning at twelve of the clock he should appear
to him at his house ; but the Devil would in no wise
grant. Faustus began again to conjure him in the
name of Beelzebub, that he should fulfil his request :
whereupon the Spirit agreed, and so they departed
each one his way.

CHAPTER III

*The conference of Doctor Faustus with the Spirit
Mephostophiles the morning following at his
own house*

DOCTOR FAUSTUS having commanded the Spirit to
be with him, at his hour appointed he came and
appeared in his chamber, demanding of Faustus
what his desire was : then began Doctor Faustus
anew with him to conjure him that he should be
obedient unto him, and to answer him certain Articles,
and to fulfil them in all points.

1. That the Spirit should serve him and be obedient
unto him in all things that he asked of him from that
hour until the hour of his death.

2. Farther, anything that he desired of him he should
bring it to him.

3. Also, that in all Faustus his demands or Inter-
rogations, the Spirit should tell him nothing but that
which is true.

Hereupon the Spirit answered and laid his case
forth, that he had no such power of himself, until

he had first given his Prince (that was ruler over him) to understand thereof, and to know if he could obtain so much of his Lord : therefore speak farther that I may do thy whole desire to my Prince : for it is not in my power to fulfil without his leave. Shew me the cause why (said Faustus). The Spirit answered : Faustus, thou shalt understand, that with us it is even as well a kingdom, as with you on earth : yea, we have our rulers and servants, as I my self am one, and we name our whole number the Legion : for although that Lucifer is thrust and fallen out of heaven through his pride and high mind, yet he hath notwithstanding a Legion of Devils at his commandment, that we call the Oriental Princes ; for his power is great and infinite. Also there is an host in <u>Meridie</u>, in Septentrio, in Occidente : and for that Lucifer hath his kingdom under heaven, we must change and give ourselves unto men to serve them at their pleasure. It is also certain, we have never as yet opened unto any man the truth of our dwelling, neither of our ruling, neither what our power is, neither have we given any man any gift, or learned him anything, except he promise to be ours.

Doctor Faustus upon this arose where he sat,[1] and said, I will have my request, and yet I will not be damned. The Spirit answered, Then shalt thou want thy desire, and yet art thou mine notwithstanding : if any man would detain thee it is in vain, for thine infidelity hath confounded thee.

Hereupon spake Faustus : Get thee hence from me,

---

[1] A mistranslation of the German text, " entsetzt sich darob," i.e. " was terrified at this."

71

and take Saint Valentine's farewell and Crisam[1] with thee, yet I conjure thee that thou be here at evening, and bethink thyself on that I have asked thee, and ask thy Prince's counsel therein. Mephostophiles the Spirit, thus answered, vanished away, leaving Faustus in his study, where he sat pondering with himself how he might obtain his request of the Devil without loss of his soul : yet fully he was resolved in himself, rather than to want his pleasure, to do whatsoever the Spirit and his Lord should condition upon.

CHAPTER IV

The second time of the Spirit's appearing to Faustus in his house, and of their parley

FAUSTUS continuing in his Devilish cogitations, never moving out of the place where the Spirit left him (such was his fervent love to the Devil) the night approaching, this swift flying Spirit appeared to Faustus, offering himself with all submission to his service, with full authority from his Prince to do whatsoever he would request, if so be Faustus would promise to be his : this answer I bring thee, and an answer must thou make by me again, yet will I hear what is thy desire, because thou hast sworn me to be here at this time. Doctor Faustus gave him this answer, though faintly (for his soul's sake), That his request

---

[1] Saint Valentine's sickness is epilepsy.
Crisam is Gk. *chrisma*, a composition of oil and balm.

was none other but to become a Devil, or at the least a limb of him, and that the Spirit should agree unto these Articles as followeth.

1. That he might be a Spirit in shape and quality.

2. That Mephostophiles should be his servant, and at his commandment.

3. That Mephostophiles should bring him anything, and do for him whatsoever.

4. That at all times he should be in his house, invisible to all men, except only to himself, and at his commandment to shew himself.

5. Lastly, that Mephostophiles should at all times appear at his command, in what form or shape soever he would.

Upon these points the Spirit answered Doctor Faustus, that all this should be granted him and fulfilled, and more if he would agree unto him upon certain Articles as followeth.

First, that Doctor Faustus should give himself to his Lord Lucifer, body and soul.

Secondly, for confirmation of the same, he should make him a writing, written with his own blood.

Thirdly, that he would be an enemy to all Christian people.

Fourthly, that he would deny his Christian belief.

Fifthly, that he let not any man change his opinion, if so be any man should go about to dissuade, or withdraw him from it.

Further, the Spirit promised Faustus to give him certain years to live in health and pleasure, and when such years were expired, that then Faustus should be fetched away, and if he should hold these Articles and conditions, that then he should have all whatsoever his heart would wish or desire ; and that Faustus should quickly perceive himself to be a Spirit in all manner of actions whatsoever. Hereupon Doctor Faustus his mind was so inflamed, that he forgot his soul, and promised Mephostophiles to hold all things as he had mentioned them : he thought the Devil was not so black as they used to paint him, nor Hell so hot as the people say, *etc*.

CHAPTER V

The third parley between Doctor Faustus and Mephostophiles about a conclusion

AFTER Doctor Faustus had made his promise to the Devil, in the morning betimes he called the Spirit before him and commanded him that he should always come to him like a Friar, after the order of Saint Francis, with a bell in his hand like Saint Anthony, and to ring it once or twice before he appeared, that he might know of his certain coming : Then Faustus demanded the Spirit, what was his name ? The Spirit answered, my name is as thou sayest, Mephostophiles, and I am a prince, but servant to Lucifer : and all the circuit from Septentrio to the Meridian, I rule under him. Even at these words was this wicked wretch Faustus inflamed, to hear himself to have gotten so great a Potentate to be his servant, forgot the Lord his maker, and Christ his redeemer,

74

became an enemy unto all mankind, yea, worse than the Giants whom the Poets feign to climb the hills to make war with the Gods : not unlike that enemy of God and his Christ, that for his pride was cast into Hell : so likewise Faustus forgot that the high climbers catch the greatest falls, and that the sweetest meat requires the sourest sauce.

After a while, Faustus promised Mephostophiles to write and make his Obligation, with full assurance of the Articles in the Chapter before rehearsed. A pitiful case, (Christian Reader), for certainly this Letter or Obligation was found in his house after his most lamentable end, with all the rest of his damnable practices used in his whole life. Therefore I wish all Christians to take an example by this wicked Faustus, and to be comforted in Christ, contenting themselves with that vocation whereunto it hath pleased God to call them, and not to esteem the vain delights of this life, as did this unhappy Faustus, in giving his Soul to the Devil : and to confirm it the more assuredly, he took a small penknife, and pricked a vein in his left hand, and for certainty thereupon, were seen on his hand these words written, as if they had been written with blood, ô HOMO FUGE : whereat the Spirit vanished, but Faustus continued in his damnable mind, and made his writing as followeth.

CHAPTER VI

How Doctor Faustus set his blood in a saucer on warm ashes, and writ as followeth

I, JOHANNES FAUSTUS, Doctor, do openly acknowledge with mine own hand, to the greater force and strengthening of this Letter, that siththence I began to study and speculate the course and order of the Elements, I have not found through the gift that is given me from above, any such learning and wisdom, that can bring me to my desires : and for that I find, that men are unable to instruct me any farther in the matter, now have I Doctor John Faustus, unto the hellish prince of Orient and his messenger Mephostophiles, given both body and soul, upon such condition, that they shall learn me, and fulfil my desire in all things, as they have promised and vowed unto me, with due obedience unto me, according unto the Articles mentioned between us.

Further, I covenant and grant with them by these presents, that at the end of twenty-four years next ensuing the date of this present Letter, they being expired, and I in the meantime, during the said years be served of them at my will, they accomplishing my desires to the full in all points as we are agreed, that then I give them full power to do with me at their pleasure, to rule, to send, fetch, or carry me or mine, be it either body, soul, flesh, blood, or goods, into their habitation, be it wheresoever : and hereupon, I defy God and his Christ, all the host of heaven, and all living creatures that bear the shape of God, yea all that lives ; and again I say it, and it shall be so. And to the more strengthening of this writing, I have written it with mine own hand and blood, being in perfect memory, and hereupon I subscribe to it with my name and title, calling all the infernal, middle, and supreme powers to witness of this my Letter and subscription.

John Faustus, approved in the Elements,
and the spiritual Doctor.

CHAPTER VII

How Mephostophiles came for his writing, and in what manner he appeared, and his sights he shewed him : and how he caused him to keep a copy of his own writing

DOCTOR FAUSTUS sitting pensive, having but one only boy with him, suddenly there appeared his Spirit Mephostophiles, in likeness of a fiery man, from whom issued most horrible fiery flames, in so much that the boy was afraid, but being hardened by his master, he bade him stand still and he should have no harm : the Spirit began to blare as in a singing manner. This pretty sport pleased Doctor Faustus well, but he would not call his Spirit into his Counting house, until he had seen more : anon was heard a rushing of armed men, and trampling of horses : this ceasing, came a kennel of hounds, and they chased a great

77

Hart in the hall, and there the Hart was slain. Faustus took heart, came forth, and looked upon the Hart, but presently before him there was a Lion and a Dragon together fighting, so fiercely, that Faustus thought they would have brought down the house, but the Dragon overcame the Lion, and so they vanished.

After this, came in a Peacock, with a Peahen, the cock brustling of his tail, and turning to the female, beat her, and so vanished. Afterward followed a furious Bull, that with a full fierceness ran upon Faustus, but coming near him, vanished away. Afterward followed a great old Ape, this Ape offered Faustus the hand, but he refused : so the Ape ran out of the hall again. Hereupon fell a mist in the hall, that Faustus saw no light, but it lasted not, and so soon as it was gone, there lay before Faustus two great sacks, one full of gold, the other full of silver.

Lastly, was heard by Faustus all manner Instruments of music, as Organs, Clarigolds,[1] Lutes, Viols, Citterns,[2] Waits,[3] Hornpipes, Flutes, Anomes,[4] Harps, and all manner of other Instruments, the which so ravished his mind, that he thought he had been in another world, forgot both body and soul, in so much that he was minded never to change his opinion concerning that which he had done. Hereat, came Mephostophiles into the Hall to Faustus, in apparel like unto a Friar, to whom Faustus spake, thou hast done me a wonderful pleasure in shewing me this pastime,

[1] A stringed musical instrument, or clarichord.
[2] A kind of guitar.   [3] A wind instrument.
[4] This instrument is unknown.

if thou continue as thou hast begun, thou shalt win me heart and soul, yea and have it. Mephostophiles answered, this is nothing, I will please thee better : yet that thou mayest know my power and all, ask what thou wilt request of me, that shalt thou have, conditionally hold thy promise, and give me thy handwriting : at which words, the wretch thrust forth his hand, saying, hold thee, there hast thou my promise : Mephostophiles took the writing, and willing Faustus to take a copy of it, with that the perverse Faustus being resolute in his damnation, wrote a copy thereof, and gave the Devil the one, and kept in store the other. Thus the Spirit and Faustus were agreed, and dwelt together : no doubt there was a virtuous housekeeping.

CHAPTER VIII

The manner how Faustus proceeded with his damnable life, and of the diligent service Mephostophiles used towards him

DOCTOR FAUSTUS having given his soul to the Devil, renouncing all the powers of heaven, confirming this lamentable action with his own blood, and having already delivered his writing now into the Devil's hand, the which so puffed up his heart, that he had forgot the mind of a man, and thought rather himself to be a spirit. This Faustus dwelt in his uncle's house at Wittenberg, who died, and bequeathed it in his Testament to his Cousin Faustus. Faustus kept a boy with him that was his scholar, an unhappy wag, called Christopher Wagner, to whom this sport and life that he saw his master follow seemed pleasant. Faustus loved the boy well, hoping to make him as good or better seen in his Devilish exercise than himself ; and he was fellow with Mephostophiles : otherwise Faustus had no more company in his house ; but himself, his boy and his Spirit, that ever was diligent at Faustus' command, going about the house, clothed like a Friar, with a little bell in his hand, seen of none but Faustus. For his victual and other necessaries, Mephostophiles brought him at his pleasure from the Duke of Saxon, the Duke of Bavaria, and the Bishop of Saltzburg : for they had many times their best wine stolen out of their cellars by Mephostophile : Likewise their provision for their own table, such meat as Faustus wished for, his Spirit brought him in : besides that, Faustus himself was become so cunning, that when he opened his window, what fowl soever he wished for, it came presently flying into his house, were it never so dainty. Moreover, Faustus and his boy went in sumptuous apparel, the which Mephostophiles stole from the Mercers at Norenberg, Auspurg, Franckeford, and Liptzig : for it was hard for them to find a lock to keep out such a thief. All their maintenance was but stolen and borrowed ware : and thus they lived an odious life in the sight of God, though as yet the world were unacquainted with their wickedness. It must be so, for their fruits be none other : as Christ saith through John, where he calls the Devil a thief, and a murderer : and that found Faustus, for he stole him away both body and soul.

CHAPTER IX

*How Doctor Faustus would have married, and how
the Devil had almost killed him for it*

DOCTOR FAUSTUS continued thus in his Epicurish
life day and night, and believed not that there was
a God, hell, or Devil : he thought that body and soul
died together, and had quite forgotten Divinity or
the immortality of his soul, but stood in his damnable
heresy day and night. And bethinking himself of
a wife, called Mephostophiles to counsel ; which
would in no wise agree : demanding of him if he
would break the covenant made with him, or if he
had forgot it. Hast not thou (quoth Mephostophiles)
sworn thyself an enemy to God and all creatures ?
To this I answer thee, thou canst not marry ; thou
canst not serve two masters, God, and my Prince :
for wedlock is a chief institution ordained of God,
and that hast thou promised to defy, as we do all, and
that hast thou also done : and moreover thou hast
confirmed it with thy blood : persuade thyself, that
what thou dost in contempt of wedlock, it is all to
thine own delight. Therefore Faustus, look well
about thee, and bethink thyself better, and I wish
thee to change thy mind : for if thou keep not what
thou hast promised in thy writing, we will tear thee
in pieces like the dust under thy feet. Therefore
sweet Faustus, think with what unquiet life, anger,
strife, and debate thou shalt live in when thou takest
a wife : therefore change thy mind.

THE FAMOUS HISTORY

Doctor Faustus was with these speeches in despair : and as all that have forsaken the Lord, can build upon no good foundation : so this wretched Faustus having forsook the rock, fell in despair with himself, fearing if he should motion Matrimony any more, that the Devil would tear him in pieces. For this time (quoth he to Mephostophiles) I am not minded to marry. Then you do well, answered his Spirit. But shortly and that within two hours after, Faustus called his Spirit, which came in his old manner like a Friar. Then Faustus said unto him, I am not able to resist nor bridle my fantasy, I must and will have a wife, and I pray thee give thy consent to it. Suddenly upon these words came such a whirlwind about the place, that Faustus thought the whole house would come down, all the doors in the house flew off the hooks : after all this, his house was full of smoke, and the floor covered over with ashes : which when Doctor Faustus perceived, he would have gone up the stairs : and flying up, he was taken and thrown into the hall, that he was not able to stir hand nor foot : then round about him ran a monstrous circle of fire, never standing still, that Faustus fried as he lay, and thought there to have been burned. Then cried he out to his Spirit Mephostophiles for help, promising him he would live in all things as he had vowed in his handwriting. Hereupon appeared unto him an ugly Devil, so fearful and monstrous to behold, that Faustus durst not look on him. The Devil said, what wouldst thou have Faustus ? how likest thou thy wedding ? what mind art thou in now ? Faustus answered, he had forgot his promise, desiring him of

THE JOURNEY TO THE WITCHES' SABBATH

After P. Cornelius

83

pardon, and he would talk no more of such things.
The Devil answered, thou were best so to do, and so
vanished.

After appeared unto him his Friar Mephostophiles
with a bell in his hand, and spake to Faustus : It is
no jesting with us, hold thou that which thou
hast vowed, and we will perform as we have promised : and more than that, thou shalt have thy heart's
desire of what women soever thou wilt, be she alive or
dead, and so long as thou wilt, thou shalt keep her
by thee.

These words pleased Faustus wonderful well, and
repented himself that he was so foolish to wish himself
married, that might have any woman in the whole
City brought to him at his command ; the which he
practised and persevered in a long time.

CHAPTER X

*Questions put forth by Doctor Faustus unto his
Spirit Mephostophiles*

DOCTOR FAUSTUS living in all manner of pleasure that
his heart could desire, continuing in his amorous
drifts, his delicate fare, and costly apparel, called on
a time his Mephostophiles to him : which being come,
brought with him a book in his hand of all manner
of Devilish and enchanted arts, the which he gave
Faustus, saying : hold my Faustus, work now thy
heart's desire : The copy of this enchanting book

was afterward found by his servant Christopher Wagner. Well (quoth Faustus to his Spirit) I have called thee to know what thou canst do if I have need of thy help. Then answered Mephostophiles and said, my Lord Faustus, I am a flying spirit : yea, so swift as thought can think, to do whatsoever. Here Faustus said : but how came thy Lord and master Lucifer to have so great a fall from heaven ? Mephostophiles answered : My Lord Lucifer was a fair Angel, created of God as immortal, and being placed in the Seraphims, which are above the Cherubims, he would have presumed unto the Throne of God, with intent to have thrust God out of his seat. Upon this presumption the Lord cast him down headlong, and where before he was an Angel of light, now dwells he in darkness, not able to come near his first place, without God send for him to appear before him as Raphael : but unto the lower degree of Angels that have their conversation with men he was come, but not unto the second degree of Heavens that is kept by the Archangels, namely, Michael and Gabriel, for these are called Angels of God's wonders : yet are these far inferior places to that from whence my Lord and Master Lucifer fell. And thus far Faustus, because thou art one of the beloved children of my Lord Lucifer, following and feeding thy mind in manner as he did his, I have shortly resolved thy request, and more I will do for thee at thy pleasure. I thank thee Mephostophiles (quoth Faustus) come let us now go rest, for it is night : upon this they left their communication.

CHAPTER XI

How Doctor Faustus dreamed that he had seen hell in his sleep, and how he questioned with his Spirit of matters as concerning hell, with the Spirit's answer

THE night following, after Faustus his communication had with Mephostophiles, as concerning the fall of Lucifer, Doctor Faustus dreamed that he had seen a part of hell : but in what manner it was, or in what place he knew not : whereupon he was greatly troubled in mind, and called unto him Mephostophiles his Spirit, saying to him, my Mephostophiles, I pray thee resolve me in this doubt : what is hell, what substance is it of, in what place stands it, and when was it made ? Mephostophiles answered : my Faustus, thou shalt know, that before the fall of my Lord Lucifer there was no hell, but even then was hell ordained : it is of no substance, but a confused thing : for I tell thee, that before all Elements were made, and the earth seen, the Spirit of God moved on the waters, and darkness was over all : but when God said, let it be light, it was so at his word, and the light was on God's right hand, and God praised the light. Judge thou further : God stood in the middle, the darkness was on his left hand, in the which my Lord was bound in chains until the day of judgment : in this confused hell is nought to find but a filthy, Sulphurish, fiery, stinking mist or fog. Further, we Devils know not what substance it is of, but a confused thing. For as a bubble of water flieth before the wind, so doth hell before the breath of God. Further, we Devils know not how God hath laid the foundation of our hell, nor whereof it is : but to be short with thee Faustus, we know that hell hath neither bottom nor end.

CHAPTER XII

The second question put forth by Doctor Faustus to his Spirit, what Kingdoms there were in hell, how many, and what were their rulers' names

FAUSTUS spake again to Mephostophiles, saying : thou speakest of wonderful things, I pray thee now tell me what Kingdoms is there in your hell, how many are there, what are they called, and who rules them : the Spirit answered him : my Faustus, know that hell is as thou wouldst think with thyself another world, in the which we have our being, under the earth, and above the earth, even to the Heavens ; within the circumference whereof are contained ten Kingdoms, namely :

1. Lacus mortis.   6. Gehenna.
2. Stagnum ignis.   7. Herebus.
3. Terra tenebrosa.   8. Barathrum.
4. Tartarus.   9. Styx.
5. Terra oblivionis. 10. Acheron.

The which Kingdoms are governed by five kings, that is, Lucifer in the Orient, Beelzebub in Septentrio,

Belial in Meridie, Astaroth in Occidente, and Phlegeton in the middest of them all : whose rule and dominions have none end until the day of Doom. And thus far Faustus, hast thou heard of our rule and Kingdoms.

CHAPTER XIII

Another question put forth by Doctor Faustus to his Spirit concerning his Lord Lucifer, with the sorrow that Faustus fell afterwards into

DOCTOR FAUSTUS began again to reason with Mephostophiles, requiring him to tell him in what form and shape, and in what estimation his Lord Lucifer was when he was in favour with God. Whereupon his Spirit required of him three days' respite, which Faustus granted. The three days being expired, Mephostophiles gave him this answer : Faustus, my Lord Lucifer (so called now, for that he was banished out of the clear light of heaven) was at the first an Angel of God, he sat on the Cherubims, and saw all the wonderful works of God, yea he was so of God ordained, for shape, pomp, authority, worthiness, and dwelling, that he far exceeded all other the creatures of God, yea our gold and precious stones : and so illuminated, that he far surpassed the brightness of the Sun and all other Stars : wherefore God placed him on the Cherubims, where he had a kingly office, and was always before God's seat, to the end he might be the more perfect in all his beings : but when he

88

began to be high-minded, proud, and so presumptuous that he would usurp the seat of his Majesty, then was he banished out from amongst the heavenly powers, separated from their abiding into the manner of a fiery stone, that no water is able to quench, but continually burneth until the end of the world.

Doctor Faustus, when he had heard the words of his Spirit, began to consider with himself, having diverse and sundry opinions in his head : and very pensively (saying nothing unto his Spirit) he went into his chamber, and laid him on his bed, recording the words of Mephostophiles ; which so pierced his heart, that he fell into sighing and great lamentation, crying out : alas, ah, woe is me ! what have I done ? Even so shall it come to pass with me : am not I also a creature of God's making, bearing his own Image and similitude, into whom he hath breathed the Spirit of life and immortality, unto whom he hath made all things living subject : but woe is me, mine haughty mind, proud aspiring stomach, and filthy flesh, hath brought my soul into perpetual damnation ; yea, pride hath abused my understanding, in so much that I have forgot my maker, the Spirit of God is departed from me. I have promised the Devil my Soul : and therefore it is but a folly for me to hope for grace, but it must be even with me as with Lucifer, thrown into perpetual burning fire : ah, woe is me that ever I was born. In this perplexity lay this miserable Doctor Faustus, having quite forgot his faith in Christ, never falling to repentance truly, thereby to attain the grace and holy Spirit of God again, the which would have been able to have resisted the strong assaults of Satan : for although he had made him a promise, yet he might have remembered through true repentance sinners come again into the favour of God ; which faith the faithful firmly hold, knowing they that kill the body, are not able to hurt the soul : but he was in all his opinions doubtful, without faith or hope, and so he continued.

CHAPTER XIV

Another disputation betwixt Doctor Faustus and his Spirit, of the power of the Devil, and of his envy to mankind

AFTER Doctor Faustus had a while pondered and sorrowed with himself of his wretched estate, he called again Mephostophiles unto him, commanding him to tell him the judgment, rule, power, attempts, tyranny and temptation of the Devil, and why he was moved to such kind of living : whereupon the Spirit answered, this question that thou demandest of me, will turn thee to no small discontentment : therefore thou shouldst not have desired me of such matters, for it toucheth the secrets of our Kingdom, although I cannot deny to resolve thy request. Therefore know thou Faustus, that so soon as my Lord Lucifer fell from heaven, he became a mortal enemy both to God and man, and hath used (as now he doth) all manner of tyranny to the destruction of man, as is manifest by divers examples, one falling suddenly dead, another hangs himself, another drowns himself, others stab themselves, others unfaithfully despair, and so come to utter confusion : the first man Adam that was made perfect to the similitude of God, was by my Lord his policy, the whole decay of man : yea, Faustus, in him was the beginning and first tyranny of my Lord Lucifer used to man : the like did he with Cain, the same with the children of Israel, when they worshipped strange Gods, and fell to whoredom with strange women : the like with Saul : so did he by the seven husbands of her that after was the wife of Tobias : likewise Dagon our fellow brought to destruction thirty thousand men, whereupon the Ark of God was stolen : and Belial made David to number his men, whereupon were slain sixty thousand, also he deceived King Solomon that worshipped the Gods of the heathen : and there are such Spirits innumerable that can come by men and tempt them, drive them to sin, weaken their belief : for we rule the hearts of Kings and Princes, stirring them up to war and bloodshed ; and to this intent do we spread ourselves throughout all the world, as the utter enemies of God, and his Son Christ, yea and all those that worship them : and that thou knowest by thyself Faustus, how we have dealt with thee. To this answered Faustus, why then thou didst also beguile me. Yea (quoth Mephostophiles) why should not we help thee forwards : for so soon as we saw thy heart, how thou didst despise thy degree taken in Divinity, and didst study to search and know the secrets of our Kingdom ; even then did we enter into thee, giving thee divers foul and filthy cogitations, pricking thee forward in thine intent, and persuading thee that thou couldst never attain to thy desire, until thou hast the help of some Devil : and when thou wast delighted with this, then took we root in thee ; and so firmly, that thou gavest thyself unto us, both body and soul the which thou (Faustus) canst not deny. Hereat answered Faustus, Thou sayest true Mephostophiles, I cannot deny it : Ah, woe is me miserable Faustus ; how have I been deceived ? had not I desired to know so much, I had not been in this case : for having studied the lives of the holy Saints and Prophets, and thereby thought myself to understand sufficient in heavenly matters, I thought myself not worthy to be called Doctor Faustus, if I should not also know the secrets of hell, and be associated with the furious Fiend thereof ; now therefore must I be rewarded accordingly. Which speeches being uttered, Faustus went very sorrowfully away from Mephostophiles.

CHAPTER XV

How Doctor Faustus desired again of his Spirit to know the secrets and pains of hell ; and whether those damned Devils and their company might ever come into the favour of God again or not?

DOCTOR FAUSTUS was ever pondering with himself how he might get loose from so damnable an end as he had given himself unto, both of body and soul : but his repentance was like to that of Cain and Judas, he thought his sins greater than God could forgive, hereupon rested his mind : he looked up to heaven, but saw nothing therein ; for his heart was so possessed with the Devil, that he could think of nought else but of hell, and the pains thereof. Wherefore in all the haste he calleth unto him his Spirit Mephostophiles, desiring him to tell him some more of the secrets of hell, what pains the damned were in, and how they were tormented, and whether the damned souls might get again the favour of God, and so be released out of their torments or not : whereupon the Spirit answered, my Faustus, thou mayest well leave to question any more of such matters, for they will but disquiet thy mind, I pray thee what meanest thou ? Thinkest thou through these thy fantasies to escape us ? No, for if thou shouldst climb up to heaven, there to hide thyself, yet would I thrust thee down again ; for thou art mine, and thou belongest unto our society : therefore sweet Faustus, thou wilt repent this thy foolish demand, except thou be content that I shall tell thee nothing. Quoth Faustus ragingly, I will know, or I will not live, wherefore dispatch and tell me : to whom Mephostophiles answered, Faustus, it is no trouble unto me at all to tell thee, and therefore sith thou forcest me thereto, I will tell thee things to the terror of thy soul, if thou wilt abide the hearing. Thou wilt have me tell thee of the secrets of hell, and of the pains thereof : know Faustus, that hell hath many figures, semblances, and names, but it cannot be named nor figured in such sort unto the living that are damned, as it is unto those that are dead, and do both see and feel the torments thereof : for hell is said to be deadly, out of the which came never any to life again but one, but he is as nothing for thee to reckon upon, hell is bloodthirsty, and is never satisfied ; hell is a valley, into the which the damned souls fall : for so soon as the soul is out of man's body, it would gladly go to the place from whence it came, and climbeth up above the highest hills, even to the heavens; where being by the Angels of the first Mobile denied entertainment (in consideration of their evil life spent on the earth) they fall into the deepest pit or valley which hath no bottom, into a perpetual fire, which shall never be quenched : for like as the Flint thrown into the water, loseth not his virtue, neither is his fire extinguished ; even so the hellish fire is unquench-able : and even as the Flint stone in the fire being burned is red hot, and yet consumeth not : so likewise the damned souls in our hellish fire are ever burning, but their pains never diminishing. Therefore is hell called the everlasting pain, in which is neither hope nor mercy : So is it called utter darkness, in which we see neither the light of Sun, Moon, nor Star : and were our darkness like the darkness of the night, yet were there hope of mercy, but ours is perpetual darkness, clean exempt from the face of God. Hell hath also a place within it called Chasma, out of the which issueth all manner of thunders, lightnings, with such horrible shriekings and wailings, that oft-times the very Devils themselves stand in fear thereof : for one while it sendeth forth winds with exceeding snow, hail, and rain congealing the water into ice ; with the which the damned are frozen, gnash their teeth, howl and cry, and yet cannot die. Otherwhiles, it sendeth forth most horrible hot mists or fogs, with flashing flames of fire and brimstone, wherein the sorrowful souls of the damned lie broiling in their reiterated torments : yea Faustus, hell is called a prison wherein the damned lie continually bound ; it is also called Pernicies, and Exitium, death, destruction, hurtfulness, mischief, a mischance, a pitiful and an evil thing, world without end. We have also with us in hell a ladder, reaching of an exceeding height, as though it would touch the heavens, on which the damned ascend to seek the blessing of God ; but through their infidelity, when they are at the very highest degree, they fall down again into their former miseries, complaining of the heat of that unquenchable fire : yea sweet Faustus, so must thou understand of hell, the while thou art so desirous to know the secrets of our Kingdom. And mark Faustus, hell is the nurse of death, the heat of all fire, the shadow of heaven and earth, the oblivion of all goodness, the pains unspeakable, the griefs unremovable, the dwelling of Devils, Dragons, Serpents, Adders, Toads, Crocodiles, and all manner of venomous creatures, the puddle of sin, the stinking fog ascending from the Stygian lake, Brimstone, Pitch, and all manner of unclean metals, the perpetual and unquenchable fire, the end of whose miseries was never purposed by God : yea, yea Faustus, thou sayest, I shall, I must, nay I will tell thee the secrets of our Kingdom, for thou buyest it dearly, and thou must and shalt be partaker of our torments, that (as the Lord God said) never shall cease : for hell, the woman's belly, and the earth are never satisfied ; there shalt thou abide horrible torments, trembling, gnashing of teeth, howling, crying, burning, freezing, melting, swimming in a labyrinth of miseries, scalding, burning, smoking in thine eyes, stinking in thy nose, hoarseness of thy speech, deafness of thine ears, trembling of thy hands, biting thine own tongue with pain, thy heart crushed as in a press, thy bones broken, the Devils tossing fire-brands upon thee, yea thy whole carcass tossed upon muckforks from one Devil to another, yea Faustus, then wilt thou wish for death, and he will fly from thee, thine unspeakable torments shall be every day augmented more and more, for the greater the sin, the greater is the punishment : how likest thou this, my Faustus, a resolution answerable to thy request?

Lastly, thou wilt have me tell thee that which belongeth only to God, which is, if it be possible for the damned to come again into the favour of God, or not : why Faustus, thou knowest that this is against thy promise, for what shouldst thou desire to know that, having already given thy soul to the Devil to have the pleasure of this world, and to know the secrets of hell ? therefore art thou damned, and how canst thou then come again to the favour of God ? Wherefore I directly answer, no ; for whomsoever God hath forsaken and thrown into hell, must there abide his wrath and indignation in that unquenchable fire, where is no hope nor mercy to be looked for, but abiding in perpetual pains world without end : for even as much it availeth thee Faustus, to hope for the favour of God again, as Lucifer himself, who indeed although he and we all have a hope, yet is it to small avail, and taketh none effect, for out of that place God will neither hear crying nor sighing ; if he do, thou shalt have as little remorse, as Dives, Cain, or Judas had : what helpeth the Emperor, King, Prince, Duke, Earl, Baron, Lord, Knight, Squire or Gentleman, to cry for mercy being there ? Nothing : for if on the earth they would not be Tyrants, and self-willed, rich with covetousness ; proud with pomp, gluttons, drunkards, whoremongers, backbiters, robbers, murderers, blasphemers, and such-like, then were there some hope to be looked for : therefore my Faustus, as thou comest to hell with these qualities, thou must say with Cain, My sins are greater than can be forgiven, go hang thyself with Judas : and lastly, be content to suffer torments with Dives. Therefore know Faustus, that the damned have neither end nor time appointed in the which they may hope to be released, for if there were any such hope, that they but by throwing one drop of water out of the Sea in a day, until it were all dry : or if there were an heap of sand as high as from the earth to the heavens, that a bird carrying away but one corn in a day, at the end of this so long labour ; that yet they might hope at the last, God would have mercy on them, they would be comforted : but now there is no hope that God once thinks upon them, or that their howlings shall never be heard ; yea, so impossible, as it is for thee to hide thyself from God, or impossible for thee to remove the mountains, or to empty the sea, or to tell the number of the drops of rain that have fallen from Heaven until this day, or to tell what there is most of in the world, yea and for a Camel to go through the eye of a needle : even so impossible it is for thee Faustus, and the rest of the damned, to come again into the favour of God. And thus Faustus hast thou heard my last sentence, and I pray thee how dost thou like it? But know this, that I counsel thee to let me be unmolested hereafter with such disputations, or else I will vex thee every limb, to thy small contentment. Doctor Faustus departed from his Spirit very pensive and sorrowful, laid him on his bed, altogether doubtful of the grace and favour of God, wherefore he fell into fantastical cogitations : fain he would have had his soul at liberty again, but the Devil had so blinded him, and taken such deep root in his heart, that he could never think to crave God's mercy, or if by chance he had any good motion, straightways the Devil would thrust him a fair Lady into his chamber, which fell to kissing and dalliance with him, through which means, he threw his godly motions in the wind, going forward still in his wicked practices, to the utter ruin both of his body and soul.

CHAPTER XVI

Another question put forth by Doctor Faustus to his Spirit Mephostophiles of his own estate

DOCTOR FAUSTUS, being yet desirous to hear more strange things, called his Spirit unto him, saying : My Mephostophiles, I have yet another suit unto thee, which I pray thee deny not to resolve me of. Faustus (quoth the Spirit) I am loth to reason with thee any further, for thou art never satisfied in thy mind, but always bringest me a new. Yet I pray thee this once (quoth Faustus) do me so much favour, as to tell me the truth in this matter, and hereafter I will be no more so earnest with thee. The Spirit was altogether against it, but yet once more he would abide him : well (said the Spirit to Faustus), what demandest thou of me ? Faustus said, I would gladly know of thee, if thou wert a man in manner and form as I am ; what wouldest thou do to please both God and man ? Whereat the Spirit smiled saying : my Faustus, if I were a man as thou art, and that God had adorned me with those gifts of nature as thou once haddest ; even so long as the breath of God were by, and within me, would I humble myself unto his Majesty, endeavouring in all that I could to keep his Commandments, praise him, glorify him, that I might continue in his favour, so were I sure to enjoy the eternal joy and felicity of his Kingdom. Faustus said, but that have not I done. No, thou sayest true (quoth Mephostophiles) thou hast not done it, but thou hast denied thy Lord and maker, which gave thee the breath of life, speech, hearing, sight, and all other thy reasonable senses that thou mightest understand his will and pleasure, to live to the glory and honour of his name, and to the advancement of thy body and soul, him I say being thy maker hast thou denied and defied, yea wickedly thou hast applied that excellent gift of thine understanding, and given thy soul to the Devil : therefore give none the blame but thine own self-will, thy proud and aspiring mind, which hath brought thee into the wrath of God and utter damnation. This is most true (quoth Faustus), but tell me Mephostophiles, wouldst thou be in my case as I am now? Yea, saith the Spirit (and with that fetched a great sigh) for yet would I so humble myself, that I would win the favour of God. Then (said Doctor Faustus) it were time enough for me if I amended. True (said Mephostophiles), if it were not for thy great sins, which are so odious and detestable in the sight of God, that it is too late for thee, for the wrath of God resteth upon thee. Leave off (quoth Faustus) and tell me my question to my greater comfort.

CHAPTER XVII

Here followeth the second part of Doctor Faustus his life, and practices, until his end

DOCTOR FAUSTUS having received denial of his Spirit, to be resolved any more in such-like questions propounded; forgot all good works, and fell to be a Calendar maker by help of his Spirit; and also in short time to be a good Astronomer or Astrologian: he had learned so perfectly of his Spirit the course of the Sun, Moon, and Stars, that he had the most famous name of all the Mathematicks[1] that lived in his time; as may well appear by his works dedicated unto sundry Dukes and Lords: for he did nothing without the advice of his Spirit, which learned him to presage of matters to come, which have come to

[1] i.e. Mathematicians.

pass since his death. The like praise won he with his Calendars, and Almanacs making, for when he presaged upon any change, Operation, or alteration of the weather, or Elements ; as wind, rain, fogs, snow, hail, moist, dry, warm, cold, thunder, lightning : it fell so duly out, as if an Angel of heaven had forewarned it. He did not like the unskilful Astronomers of our time, that set in Winter cold, moist, airy, frosty ; and in the Dog-days, hot, dry, thunder, fire, and such-like : but he set in all his works, day and hour, when, where, and how it should happen. If anything wonderful were at hand, as death, famine, plague, or wars, he would set the time and place in true and just order, when it should come to pass.

CHAPTER XVIII

A question put forth by Doctor Faustus to his Spirit
concerning Astronomy

DOCTOR FAUSTUS falling to practice, and making his Prognostications, he was doubtful in many points : wherefore he called unto him Mephostophiles his Spirit, saying : I find the ground of this science very difficult to attain unto : for that when I confer Astronomia and Astrologia, as the Mathematicians and ancient writers have left in memory, I find them to vary and very much to disagree : wherefore I pray thee to teach me the truth in this matter. To whom his Spirit answered, Faustus, thou shalt know that the practitioners or speculators, or at least the first inventors of these Arts, have done nothing of themselves certain, whereupon thou mayest attain to the true prognosticating or presaging of things concerning the heavens, or of the influence of the Planets : for if by chance some one Mathematician or Astronomer hath left behind him anything worthy of memory : they have so blinded it with Enigmatical words, blind Characters, and such obscure figures ; that it is impossible for an earthly man to attain unto the knowledge thereof, without the aid of some Spirit, or else the special gift of God ; for such are the hidden works of God from men : yet do we Spirits that fly and fleet in all Elements, know such, and there is nothing to be done, or by the Heavens pretended, but we know it, except only the day of Doom. Wherefore (Faustus) learn of me, I will teach thee the course and recourse of ♄. ♃. ♂. ☉. ♀. ☿ and ☽.[1] the cause of winter and summer, the exaltation and declination of the Sun, the eclipse of the Moon, the distance and height of the Poles, and every fixed Star, the nature and operation of the elements, fire, air, water, and earth, and all that is contained in them, yea herein there is nothing hidden from me, but only the fifth essence, which once thou hadst Faustus at liberty, but now Faustus thou hast lost it past recovery ; wherefore leaving that which will not be again had, learn now of me to make thunder, lightning, hail, snow, and rain : the clouds to rend, the earth and craggy rocks to shake and split in sunder, the Seas to swell, and roar, and over-run their

[1] The symbols of Saturn, Jupiter, Mars, the Sun, Venus, Mercury, and the Moon.

marks. Knowest not thou that the deeper the Sun shines, the hotter he pierces ? so, the more thy Art is famous whilst thou art here, the greater shall be thy name when thou art gone. Knowest not thou that the earth is frozen cold and dry ; the water running, cold and moist ; the air flying, hot and moist ; the fire consuming, hot and dry ? Yea Faustus, so must thy heart be enflamed like the fire to mount on high : learn, Faustus, to fly like myself, as swift as thought from one kingdom to another, to sit at princes' tables, to eat their daintiest fare, to have thy pleasure of their fair Ladies, wives and concubines, to use their jewels, and costly robes as things belonging to thee, and not unto them : learn of me, Faustus, to run through walls, doors, and gates of stone and iron, to creep into the earth like a worm, to swim in the water like a fish, to fly in the air like a bird, and to live and nourish thyself in the fire like a Salamander ; so shalt thou be famous, renowned, far-spoken of, and extolled for thy skill : going on knives, not hurting thy feet ; carrying fire in thy bosom, and not burning thy shirt ; seeing through the heavens as through a Crystal, wherein is placed the Planets, with all the rest of the presaging Comets, the whole circuit of the world from the East to the West, North and South : there shalt thou know, Faustus, wherefore the fiery sphere above ♄ and the signs of the Zodiac doth not burn and consume the whole face of the earth, being hindered by placing the two moist elements between them, the airy clouds and the wavering waves of water : yea, Faustus, I will learn thee the secrets of nature, what the causes that the Sun in summer being at the highest, giveth all his heat downwards on the earth ; and being in winter at the lowest, giveth all his heat upward into the heavens : that the snow should be of so great virtue, as the honey ; and the Lady Saturnia ♓[1] in Occulto more hotter than the Sun in Manifesto. Come on my Faustus, I will make thee as perfect in these things as myself, I will learn thee to go invisible, to find out the mines of gold and silver, the fodines[2] of precious stones, as the Carbuncle, the Diamond, Sapphire, Emerald, Ruby, Topaz, Jacinth, Garnet, Jasper, Amethyst, use all these at thy pleasure, take thy heart's desire : thy time Faustus weareth away, then why wilt thou not take thy pleasure of the world ? Come up, we will go visit Kings at their own courts, and at their most sumptuous banquets be their guests, if willingly they invite us not, then perforce we will serve our own turn with their best meat and daintiest wine : Agreed, quoth Faustus ; but let me pause a while upon this thou hast even now declared unto me.

CHAPTER XIX

How Doctor Faustus fell into despair with himself : for having put forth a question unto his Spirit, they fell at variance, whereupon the whole route of Devils appeared unto him, threatening him sharply

DOCTOR FAUSTUS revolving with himself the speeches of his Spirit, he became so woeful and sorrowful in

[1] The symbol of Pisces in the Zodiac.   [2] Mines.

his cogitations, that he thought himself already frying in the hottest flames of hell, and lying in his muse, suddenly there appeared unto him his Spirit, demanding what thing so grieved and troubled his conscience, whereat Doctor Faustus gave no answer : yet the Spirit very earnestly lay upon him to know the cause ; and if it were possible, he would find remedy for his grief, and ease him of his sorrows. To whom Faustus answered, I have taken thee unto me as a servant to do me service, and thy service will be very dear unto me ; yet I cannot have any diligence of thee farther than thou list thyself, neither dost thou in anything as it becometh thee. The Spirit replied, my Faustus, thou knowest that I was never against thy commandments as yet, but ready to serve and resolve thy questions, although I am not bound unto thee in such respects as concern the hurt of our Kingdom, yet was I always willing to answer thee, and so I am still : therefore my Faustus say on boldly, what is thy will and pleasure ? At which words, the Spirit stole away the heart of Faustus, who spake in this sort, Mephostophiles, tell me how and after what sort God made the world, and all the creatures in them, and why man was made after the Image of God ?

The Spirit hearing this, answered, Faustus thou knowest that all this is in vain for thee to ask, I know that thou art sorry for that thou hast done, but it availeth thee not, for I will tear thee in thousands of pieces, if thou change not thine opinions, and hereat he vanished away. Whereat Faustus all sorrowful for that he had put forth such a question, fell to weeping and to howling bitterly, not for his sins towards

God, but for that the Devil was departed from him so suddenly, and in such a rage. And being in this perplexity, he was suddenly taken in such an extreme cold, as if he should have frozen in the place where he sat, in which, the greatest Devil in hell appeared unto him, with certain of his hideous and infernal company in the most ugliest shapes that it was possible to think upon, and traversing the chamber round about where Faustus sat, Faustus thought to himself, now are they come for me though my time be not come, and that because I have asked such questions of my servant Mephostophiles : at whose cogitations, the chiefest Devil which was his Lord, unto whom he gave his soul, that was Lucifer, spake in this sort : Faustus, I have seen thy thoughts, which are not as thou hast vowed unto me, by virtue of this letter, and shewed him the Obligation that he had written with his own blood, wherefore I am come to visit thee and to shew thee some of our hellish pastimes, in hope that will draw and confirm thy mind a little more stedfast unto us. Content quoth Faustus, go to, let me see what pastime you can make. At which words, the great Devil in his likeness sat him down by Faustus, commanding the rest of the Devils to appear in their form, as if they were in hell : first entered Belial in form of a Bear, with curled black hair to the ground, his ears standing upright : within the ear was as red as blood, out of which issued flames of fire, his teeth were a foot at least long, as white as snow, with a tail three ells long (at the least) having two wings, one behind each arm, and thus one after another they appeared to Faustus in form as they were in hell. Lucifer himself sat in manner of a man, all hairy, but of a brown colour like a Squirrel, curled, and his tail turning upwards on his back as the Squirrels use, I think he could crack nuts too like a Squirrel. After him came Beelzebub in curled hair of horse-flesh colour, his head like the head of a Bull, with a mighty pair of horns, and two long ears down to the ground, and two wings on his back, with pricking stings like thorns : out of his wings issued flames of fire, his tail was like a Cow. Then came Astaroth in form of a worm, going upright on his tail ; he had no feet, but a tail like a slow-worm : under his chaps grew two short hands, and his back was coal black, his belly thick in the middle, and yellow like gold, having many bristles on his back like a Hedgehog. After him came Chamagosta, being white and gray mixed, exceeding curled and hairy : he had a head like the head of an Ass, the tail like a Cat, and Claws like an Ox, lacking nothing of an ell broad. Then came Anobis ; this Devil had a head like a Dog, white and black hair in shape of a Hog, saving that he had but two feet, one under his throat, the other at his tail : he was four ells long, with hanging ears like a Bloodhound. After him came Dythycan, he was a short thief in form of a Pheasant, with shining feathers, and four feet : his neck was green, his body red, and his feet black. The last was called Brachus, with four short feet like an Hedgehog, yellow and green : the upper side of his body was brown, and the belly like blue flames of fire ; the tail red, like the tail of a Monkey. The rest of the Devils were in form of insensible beasts, as Swine, Harts, Bears, Wolves, Apes, Buffs, Goats, Antelopes, Elephants, Dragons,

Horses, Asses, Lions, Cats, Snakes, Toads, and all manner of ugly odious Serpents and Worms : yet came in such sort, that every one at his entry into the Hall, made their reverence unto Lucifer, and so took their places, standing in order as they came, until they had filled the whole Hall : wherewith suddenly fell a most horrible thunder-clap, that the house shook as though it would have fallen to the ground, upon which every monster had a muck-fork in his hand, holding them towards Faustus as though they would have run a tilt at him : which when Faustus perceived, he thought upon the words of Mephostophiles, when he told him how the souls in hell were tormented, being cast from Devil to Devil upon muck-forks, he thought verily to have been tormented there of them in like sort. But Lucifer perceiving his thought, spake to him, my Faustus, how likest thou this crew of mine ? Quoth Faustus, why came you not in another manner of shape ? Lucifer replied, we cannot change our hellish form, we have shewed ourselves here, as we are there ; yet can we blind men's eyes in such sort, that when we will we repair unto them, as if we were men or Angels of light, although our dwelling be in darkness. Then said Faustus, I like not so many of you together, whereupon Lucifer commanded them to depart, except seven of the principal, forthwith they presently vanished, which Faustus perceiving, he was somewhat better comforted, and spake to Lucifer, where is my servant Mephostophiles, let me see if he can do the like, whereupon came a fierce Dragon, flying and spitting fire round about the house, and coming towards Lucifer, made reverence, and then changed himself to the form of a Friar, saying, Faustus, what wilt thou ? Saith Faustus, I will that thou teach me to transform myself in like sort as thou and the rest have done : then Lucifer put forth his Paw, and gave Faustus a book, saying hold, do what thou wilt, which he looking upon, straightways changed himself into a Hog, then into a Worm, then into a Dragon, and finding this for his purpose, it liked him well. Quoth he to Lucifer, and how cometh it that all these filthy forms are in the world ? Lucifer answered, they are ordained of God as plagues unto men, and so shalt thou be plagued (quoth he) where-upon, came Scorpions, Wasps, Emmets, Bees, and Gnats, which fell to stinging and biting him, and all the whole house was filled with a most horrible stinking fog, in so much, that Faustus saw nothing, but still was tormented ; wherefore he cried for help saying, Mephostophiles my faithful servant, where art thou, help, help, I pray thee : hereat his Spirit answered nothing, but Lucifer himself said, ho ho ho Faustus, how likest thou the creation of the world, and incontinent it was clear again, and the Devils and all the filthy Cattle were vanished, only Faustus was left alone ; seeing nothing, but hearing the sweetest music that ever he heard before, at which he was so ravished with delight, that he forgot the fears he was in before : and it repented him that he had seen no more of their pastime.

CHAPTER XX

How Doctor Faustus desired to see hell, and of the manner how he was used therein

Doctor Faustus bethinking how his time went away, and how he had spent eight years thereof, he meant to spend the rest to his better contentment, intending quite to forget any such motions as might offend the Devil any more : wherefore on a time he called his Spirit Mephostophiles, and said unto him, bring thou hither unto me thy Lord Lucifer, or Belial : he brought him (notwithstanding) one that was called Beelzebub, the which asked Faustus his pleasure. Quoth Faustus, I would know of thee if I may see hell and take a view thereof ? That thou shalt (said the Devil) and at midnight I will fetch thee. Well, night being come, Doctor Faustus awaited very diligently for the coming of the Devil to fetch him, and thinking that he tarried all too long, he went to the window, where he pulled open a casement, and looking into the Element, he saw a cloud in the North more black, dark, and obscure, than all the rest of the Sky, from whence the wind blew most horrible right into Faustus his chamber, filled the whole house with smoke, that Faustus was almost smothered : hereat fell an exceeding thunder-clap, and withal came a great rugged black Bear, all curled, and upon his back a chair of beaten gold, and spake to Faustus, saying, sit up and away with me : and Doctor Faustus that had so long abode the smoke, wished rather to be in hell than there, got on the

Devil, and so they went together. But mark how the Devil blinded him, and made him believe that he carried him into hell, for he carried him into the air, where Faustus fell into a sound sleep, as if he had sat in a warm water or bath : at last they came to a place which burneth continually with flashing flames of fire and brimstone, whereout issued an exceeding mighty clap of thunder, with so horrible a noise, that Faustus awaked, but the Devil went forth on his way and carried Faustus thereinto, yet notwithstanding,

howsoever it burnt, Doctor Faustus felt no more heat, than as it were the glimpse of the Sun in May : there heard he all manner of music to welcome him, but saw none playing on them ; it pleased him well, but he durst not ask, for he was forbidden it before. To meet the Devil and the guest that came with him, came three other ugly Devils, the which ran back again before the Bear to make them way, against whom there came running an exceeding great Hart, which would have thrust Faustus out of his chair, but being defended by the other three Devils, the Hart was put to the repulse : thence going on their way Faustus looked, and behold there was nothing but Snakes, and all manner of venomous beasts about him, which were exceeding great, unto the which Snakes came many Storks, and swallowed up all the whole multitude of Snakes, that they left not one : which when Faustus saw, he marvelled greatly : but proceeding further on their hellish voyage, there came forth of a hollow cliff an exceeding great flying Bull, the which with such a force hit Faustus his chair with his head and horns, that he turned Faustus and his Bear over and over, so that the Bear vanished away, whereat Faustus began to cry : oh, woe is me that ever I came here : for he thought there to have been beguiled of the Devil, and to make his end before his time appointed or conditioned of the Devil : but shortly came unto him a monstrous Ape, bidding Faustus be of good cheer, and said, get upon me ; all the fire in hell seemed to Faustus to have been put out, whereupon followed a monstrous thick fog, that he saw nothing, but shortly it seemed to him to wax clear, where he saw two great Dragons fastened to a waggon, into the which the Ape ascended and set Faustus therein ; forth flew the Dragons into an exceeding dark cloud, where Faustus saw neither Dragon nor Chariot wherein he sat, and such were the cries of tormented souls, with mighty thunder-claps and flashing lightnings about his ears, that poor Faustus shook for fear. Upon this came they to a water, stinking and filthy, thick like mud, into the which ran the Dragons, sinking under with waggon and all ; but Faustus felt no water but as it were a small mist, saving that the waves beat so sore upon him, that he

saw nothing under and over him but only water, in the
which he lost his Dragons, Ape, and waggon ; and
sinking yet deeper and deeper, he came at last as it
were upon an high Rock, where the waters parted and
left him thereon : but when the water was gone, it
seemed to him he should there have ended his life, for
he saw no way but death : the Rock was as high from
the bottom as Heaven is from the earth : there sat
he, seeing nor hearing any man, and looked ever upon
the Rock ; at length he saw a little hole, out of the
which issued fire ; thought he, how shall I now do ? I
am forsaken of the Devils, and they that brought me
hither, here must I either fall to the bottom, or burn
in the fire, or sit still in despair : with that in his madness he gave a leap into the fiery hole, saying : hold
you infernal Hags, take here this sacrifice as my last
end ; the which I justly have deserved : upon this
he was entered, and finding himself as yet unburned
or touched of the fire, he was the better appayed,[1] but
there was so great a noise as he never heard the like
before, it passed all the thunder that ever he had
heard ; and coming down further to the bottom of
the Rock, he saw a fire, wherein were many worthy
and noble personages, as Emperors, Kings, Dukes,
and Lords, and many thousands more of tormented
souls, at the edge of which fire ran a most pleasant,
clear, and cool water to behold, into the which many
tormented souls sprang out of the fire to cool themselves ; but being so freezing cold, they were constrained to return again into the fire, and thus wearied
themselves and spent their endless torments out of

[1] i.e. pleased.

one labyrinth into another, one while in heat, another while in cold : but Faustus standing thus all this while gazing on them were thus tormented, he saw one leaping out of the fire and screeching horribly, whom he thought to have known, wherefore he would fain have spoken unto him, but remembering that he was forbidden, he refrained speaking. Then this Devil that brought him in, came to him again in likeness of a Bear, with the chair on his back, and bade him sit up, for it was time to depart : so Faustus got up, and the Devil carried him out into the air, where he had so sweet music that he fell asleep by the way. His boy Christopher being all this while at home, and missing his master so long, thought his master would have tarried and dwelt with the Devil for ever : but whilst his boy was in these cogitations, his master came home, for the Devil brought him home fast asleep as he sat in his chair, and so he threw him on his bed, where (being thus left of the Devil) he lay until day. When he awaked, he was amazed, like a man that had been in a dark dungeon ; musing with himself if it were true or false that he had seen hell, or whether he was blinded or not : but he rather persuaded himself that he had been there than otherwise, because he had seen such wonderful things : wherefore he most carefully took pen and ink, and wrote those things in order as he had seen : the which writing was afterwards found by his boy in his study ; which afterwards was published to the whole city of Wittenberg in open print, for example to all Christians.

CHAPTER XXI

How Doctor Faustus was carried through the air up to the heavens to see the world, and how the Sky and Planets ruled: after the which he wrote one letter to his friend of the same to Liptzig, how he went about the world in eight days

THIS letter was found by a freeman and Citizen of Wittenberg, written with his own hand, and sent to his friend at Liptzig a Physician, named John Victor, the contents of which were as followeth.

Amongst other things (my loving friend and brother) I remember yet the former friendship had together, when we were schoolfellows and students in the University at Wittenberg, whereas you first studied Physic, Astronomy, Astrology, Geometry, and Cosmography ; I to the contrary (you know) studied Divinity : notwithstanding now in any of your own studies I am seen (I am persuaded) further then your self : for sithence I began I have never erred, for (might I speak it without affecting my own praise) my Calendars and other practices have not only the commendations of the common sort, but also of the chiefest Lords and Nobles of this our Dutch Nation : because (which is chiefly to be noted) I write and presaged of matters to come, which all accord and fall out so right, as if they had been already seen before. And for that (my beloved Victori) you write to know my voyage which I made into the Heavens, the which (as you certify me you have had some suspicion of, although you partly persuaded yourself, that it is a thing impossible) no matter for that, it is as it is, and let it be as it will, once it was done, in such manner as now according unto your request I give you here to understand.

I being once laid on my bed, and could not sleep for thinking on my Calendar and practice, I marvelled with myself how it were possible that the Firmament should be known and so largely written of men, or whether they write true or false, by their own opinions, or supposition, or by due observations and true course of the heavens. Behold, being in these my muses, suddenly I heard a great noise, in so much that I thought my house would have been blown down, so that all my doors and chests flew open, whereat I was not a little astonied, for withal I heard a groaning voice which said, get up, the desire of thy heart, mind, and thought shalt thou see : at the which I answered, what my heart desireth, that would I fain see, and to make proof, if I shall see I will away with thee. Why then (quoth he) look out at thy window, there cometh a messenger for thee, that did I, and behold, there stood a Waggon, with two Dragons before it to draw the same, and all the Waggon was of a light burning fire, and for that the Moon shone, I was the willinger at that time to depart : but the voice spake again, sit up and let us away : I will, said I, go with thee, but upon this condition, that I may ask after all things that I see, hear, or think on : the voice answered, I am content for this time. Hereupon I got me into the Waggon, so that the Dragons carried me upright into the air. The Waggon had also four wheels the which rattled so, and made such a noise as if we had been all this while running on the stones : and round about us flew out flames of fire, and the higher that I came, the more the earth seemed to be darkened, so that methought I came out of a dungeon, and looking down from Heaven, behold, Mephostophiles my Spirit and servant was behind me, and when he perceived that I saw him, he came and sat by me, to whom I said, I pray thee Mephostophiles whither shall I go now ? Let not that trouble thy mind, said he, and yet they carried us higher up. And now will I tell thee good friend and schoolfellow, what things I have seen and proved ; for on the Tuesday went I out, and on Tuesday seven-nights following I came home again, that is, eight days, in which time I slept not, no not one wink came in mine eyes, and we went invisible of any man : and as the day began to appear, after our first night's journey, I said to my Spirit Mephostophiles, I pray thee how far have we now ridden, I am sure thou knowest : for methinks that we are ridden exceeding far, the World seemeth so little : Mephostophiles answered me, my Faustus believe me, that from the place from whence thou camest, unto this place where we are now, is already forty-seven leagues right in height, and as the day increased, I looked down upon the World, there saw I many kingdoms and provinces, likewise the whole world, Asia, Europa, and Africa, I had a sight of : and being so high, quoth I to my Spirit, tell me now how these Kingdoms lie, and what they are called, the which he denied not, saying, see this on our left hand is Hungaria, this is also Prussia on our left hand, and Poland, Muscovia, Tartascelesia,[1] Bohemia, Saxony :

[1] Probably a corruption of Tartary and Silesia.

117

and here on our right hand, Spain, Portugal, France, England, and Scotland : then right out before us lie the Kingdoms of Persia, India, Arabia, the King of Alchar, and the great Cham : now are we come to Wittenberg, and are right over the town of Weim in Austria, and ere long will we be at Constantinople, Tripolie, and Jerusalem, and after will we pierce the frozen Zone, and shortly touch the Horizon, and the Zenith of Wittenberg. There looked I on the Ocean Sea, and beheld a great many of ships and Galleys ready to the battle, one against another : and thus I spent my journey, now cast I my eyes here, now there, toward South, North, East, and West, I have been in one place where it rained and hailed, and in another where the Sun shone excellent fair, and so I think that I saw the most things in and about the world, with great admiration that in one place it rained, and in another hail and snow, on this side the Sun shone bright, some hills covered with snow never consuming, others were so hot that grass and trees were burned and consumed therewith. Then looked I up to the heavens, and behold, they went so swift, that I thought they would have sprung in thousands. Likewise it was so clear and so hot, that I could not long gaze into it, it so dimmed my sight : and had not my Spirit Mephostophiles covered me as it were with a shadowing cloud, I had been burnt with the extreme heat thereof, for the Sky the which we behold here when we look up from the earth, is so fast and thick as a wall, clear and shining bright as a Crystal, in the which is placed the Sun, which casteth forth his rays or beams over the universal world, to the uttermost confines of the earth. But we think that the Sun is very little : no, it is altogether as big as the world. Indeed the body substantial is but little in compass, but the rays or stream that it casteth forth, by reason of the thing wherein it is placed, maketh him to extend and shew himself over the whole world : and we think that the Sun runneth his course, and that the heavens stand still : no, it is the heavens that move his course, and the Sun abideth perpetually in his place, he is permanent, and fixed in his place, and although we see him beginning to ascend in the Orient or East, at the highest in the Meridian or South, setting in the Occident or West, yet is he at the lowest in Septentrio or North, and yet he moveth not. It is the axle of the heavens that moveth the whole firmament, being a Chaos or confused thing, and for that proof, I will shew thee this example, like as thou seest a bubble made of water and soap blown forth of a quill, is in form of a confused mass or Chaos, and being in this form, is moved at pleasure of the wind, which runneth round about that Chaos, and moveth him also round : even so is the whole firmament or Chaos, wherein are placed the sun, and the rest of the Planets turned and carried at the pleasure of the Spirit of God, which is wind. Yea Christian Reader, to the glory of God, and for the profit of thy soul, I will open unto thee the divine opinion touching the ruling of this confused Chaos, far more than any rude German Author, being possessed with the Devil, was able to utter ; and to prove some of my sentence before to be true, look into Genesis unto the works of God, at the creation of the world, there shalt thou find, that the Spirit of

God moved upon the waters before heaven and earth were made. Mark how he made it, and how by his word every element took his place : these were not his works, but his words ; for all the words he used before, he concluded afterwards in one work, which was in making man : mark reader with patience for thy soul's health, see into all that was done by the word and work of God, light and darkness was, the firmament stood, and their great ⊙ and little light ☽ in it : the moist waters were in one place, the earth was dry, and every element brought forth according to the word of God : now followeth his works he made man like his own image, how ? out of the earth ? The earth will shape no image without water, there was one of the elements. But all this while where was wind ? all elements were at the word of God, man was made, and in a form by the work of God, yet moved not that work, before God breathed the Spirit of life into his nostrils, and made him a living soul, here was the first wind and Spirit of God out of his own mouth, which we have likewise from the same seed which was only planted by God in Adam, which wind, breath, or spirit, when he had received, he was living and moving on earth, for it was ordained of God for his habitation, but the heavens are the habitation of the Lord : and like as I shewed before of the bubble or confused Chaos made of water and soap, through the wind and breath of man is turned round, and carried with every wind ; even so the firmament wherein the Sun and the rest of the Planets are fixed, moved, turned, and carried with the wind, breath, or Spirit of God, for the heavens and firmament are movable as the Chaos, but the Sun is fixed in the firmament. And farther my good schoolfellow, I was thus nigh the heavens, where methought every Planet was but as half the earth, and under the firmament ruled the Spirits in the air, and as I came down I looked upon the world and the heavens, and methought that the earth was enclosed in comparison within the firmament, as the yolk of an egg within the white, and methought that the whole length of the earth was not a span long, and the water was as if it had been twice as broad and long as the earth, even thus at the eight days end came I home again, and fell asleep, and so I continued sleeping three days and three nights together : and the first hour that I waked, I fell fresh again to my Calendar, and have made them in right ample manner as you know, and to satisfy your request, for that you writ unto me, I have in consideration of our old friendship had at the University of Wittenberg, declared unto you my heavenly voyage, wishing no worse unto you, than unto myself, that is, that your mind were as mine in all respects. Dixi.

Doctor Faustus the Astrologian.

CHAPTER XXII

How Doctor Faustus made his journey through the principal and most famous lands in the world

DOCTOR FAUSTUS having overrun fifteen years of his appointed time, he took upon him a journey, with full pretence to see the whole world : and calling his spirit Mephostophiles unto him, he said : thou knowest that thou art bound unto me upon conditions, to perform and fulfil my desire in all things, wherefore my pretence is to visit the whole face of the earth visible and invisible when it pleaseth me : wherefore, I enjoin and command thee to the same. Whereupon Mephostophiles answered, I am ready my Lord at thy command and forthwith the Spirit changed himself unto the likeness of a flying horse, saying, Faustus sit up, I am ready. Doctor Faustus loftily sat upon him, and forward they went : Faustus came through many a land and Province ; as Pannonia, Austria, Germania, Bohemia, Slesia, Saxony, Missene, During, Francklandt, Shawblandt, Beyerlandt, Stiria, Carinthia, Poland, Litaw, Liefland, Prussia, Denmarke, Muscovia, Tartaria, Turkie, Persia, Cathai, Alexandria, Barbaria, Ginnie, Peru, the straits of Magelanes, India, all about the frozen Zone, and Terra Incognita, Nova Hispaniola, the Isles of Terzera, Mederi, S. Michael's, the Canaries, and the Tenorrifocie, into Spaine, the Mayne Land, Portugall, Italie, Campania, the Kingdom of Naples, the Isles of Sicilia, Malta, Majoria, Minoria, to the Knights of the Rhodes, Candie, or Creete, Ciprus, Corinth, Switzerland, France, Freesland, Westphalia, Zeland, Holland, Brabant, and all the seventeen Provinces in Netherland, England, Scotland, Ireland, all America, and Island, the out Isles of Scotland, the Orchades, Norway, the Bishopric of Breame, and so home again : all these Kingdoms, Provinces, and Countries he passed in twenty-five days, in which time he saw very little that

THE RIDE PAST THE GALLOWS

After P. Cornelius

delighted his mind : wherefore he took a little rest at home, and burning in desire to see more at large, and to behold the secrets of each Kingdom, he set forward again on his journey upon his swift horse Mephostophiles, and came to Treir, for that he chiefly desired to see this town, and the monuments thereof ; but there he saw not many wonders, except one fair Palace that belonged unto the Bishop, and also a mighty large Castle that was built of brick, with three walls and three great trenches, so strong, that it was impossible for any prince's power to win it ; then he saw a Church, wherein was buried Simeon, and the Bishop Popo : their Tombs are of most sumptuous large Marble stone, closed and joined together with great bars of iron : from whence he departed to Paris, where he liked well the Academy ; and what place or Kingdom soever fell in his mind, the same he visited. He came from Paris to Mentz, where the river of Mayne falls into the Rhine ; notwithstanding he tarried not long there, but went to Campania in the Kingdom of Neapolis, in which he saw an innumerable sort of Cloisters, Nunneries, and Churches, great and high houses of stone, the streets fair and large, and straight forth from one end of the town to the other as a line, and all the pavement of the City was of brick, and the more it rained in the town, the fairer the streets were ; there saw he the Tomb of Virgil ; and the highway that he cut through that mighty hill of stone in one night, the whole length of an English mile : then he saw the number of Galleys, and Argosies that lay there at the City head, the Windmill that stood in the water, the Castle in the water, and the houses above the water where under the Galleys might ride most safely from rain or wind; then he saw the Castle on the hill over the town, and many monuments within: also the hill called Vesuvius, whereon groweth all the Greekish wine, and most pleasant sweet Olives. From thence he came to Venice, whereat he wondered not a little to see a City so famously built standing in the Sea: where, through every street the water ran in such largeness, that great Ships and Barks might pass from one street to another, having yet a way on both sides the water, whereon men and horse might pass; he marvelled also how it was possible for so much victual to be found in the town and so good cheap, considering that for a whole league off nothing grew near the same. He wondered not a little at the fairness of Saint Mark's place, and the sumptuous Church standing therein called Saint Mark's; how all the pavement was set with coloured stones, and all the rood or loft of the Church double gilded over. Leaving this, he came to Padoa, beholding the manner of their Academy, which is called the mother or nurse of Christendom, there he heard the Doctors, and saw the most monuments in the town, entered his name into the University of the German nation, and wrote himself Doctor Faustus the insatiable Speculator: then saw he the worthiest monument in the world for a Church, named S. Anthony's Cloister, which for the pinnacles thereof and the contriving of the Church, hath not the like in Christendom. This town is fenced about with three mighty walls of stone and earth, betwixt the which runneth goodly ditches of water: twice every twenty-

125

four hours passeth boats betwixt Padoa and Venice with passengers, as they do here betwixt London and Gravesend, and even so far they differ in distance : Faustus beheld likewise the Council house and the Castle with no small wonder. Well, forward he went to Rome, which lay, and doth yet lie, on the river Tybris, the which divideth the City in two parts : over the river are four great stone bridges, and upon the one bridge called Ponte S. Angelo is the Castle of S. Angelo, wherein are so many great cast pieces as there are days in a year, and such Pieces that will shoot seven bullets off with one fire, to this Castle cometh a privy vault from the Church and Palace of Saint Peter, through the which the Pope (if any danger be) passeth from his Palace to the Castle for safeguard ; the City hath eleven gates, and a hill called Vaticinium,[1] whereon S. Peter's Church is built : in that Church the holy Fathers will hear no confession, without the penitent bring money in his hand. Adjoining to this Church, is the Campo Santo, the which Carolus Magnus built, where every day thirteen Pilgrims have their dinners served of the best : that is to say, Christ and his Twelve Apostles. Hard by this he visited the Church yard of S. Peter's, where he saw the Pyramid that Julius Cæsar brought out of Africa : it stood in Faustus his time leaning against the Church wall of Saint Peter's, but now Papa Sixtus hath erected it in the middle of S. Peter's Church yard ; it is twenty-four fathoms long and at the lower end six fathoms four square, and so forth smaller upwards, on the top is a Crucifix of beaten gold, the stone

[1] A mistake for *Vaticanum.*

standeth on four Lions of brass. Then he visited the seven Churches of Rome, that were S. Peter's, S. Paul's, S. Sebastian's, S. John Lateran, S. Laurence, S. Mary Magdalen, and S. Marie Majora : then went he without the town, where he saw the conduits of water that run level through hill and dale, bringing water into the town fifteen Italian miles off : other monuments he saw, too many to recite, but amongst the rest he was desirous to see the Pope's Palace, and his manner of service at his table, wherefore he and his Spirit made themselves invisible, and came into the Pope's Court, and privy chamber where he was, there saw he many servants attendant on his holiness, with many a flattering Sycophant carrying of his meat, and there he marked the Pope and the manner of his service, which he seeing to be so unmeasurable and sumptuous ; fie (quoth Faustus), why had not the Devil made a Pope of me ? Faustus saw notwithstanding in that place those that were like to himself, proud, stout, wilful, gluttons, drunkards, whoremongers, breakers of wedlock, and followers of all manner of ungodly exercises : wherefore he said to his Spirit, I thought that I had been alone a hog, or pork of the devil's, but he must bear with me yet a little longer, for these hogs of Rome are already fattened, and fitted to make his roast-meat, the Devil might do well now to spit them all and have them to the fire, and let him summon the Nuns to turn the spits : for as none must confess the Nun but the Friar, so none should turn the roasting Friar but the Nun. Thus continued Faustus three days in the Pope's Palace, and yet had no lust to his meat, but stood still in the Pope's chamber,

and saw everything whatsoever it was : on a time the
Pope would have a feast prepared for the Cardinal
of Pavia, and for his first welcome the Cardinal was
bidden to dinner : and as he sat at meat, the Pope
would ever be blessing and crossing over his mouth ;
Faustus could suffer it no longer, but up with his fist
and smote the Pope on the face, and withal he laughed
that the whole house might hear him, yet none of them
saw him nor knew where he was : the Pope persuaded
his company that it was a damned soul, commanding
a Mass presently to be said for his delivery out of
Purgatory, which was done : the Pope sat still at
meat, but when the latter mess came in to the Pope's
board, Doctor Faustus laid hands thereon saying ;
this is mine : and so he took both dish and meat and
fled unto the Capitol or Campadolia, calling his Spirit
unto him and said : come let us be merry, for thou
must fetch me some wine, and the cup that the Pope
drinks of, and hereupon Monte Caval will we make
good cheer in spite of the Pope and all his fat abbey
lubbers. His Spirit hearing this, departed towards
the Pope's chamber, where he found them yet sitting
and quaffing : wherefore he took from before the
Pope the fairest piece of plate or drinking goblet, and
a flagon of wine, and brought it to Faustus ; but when
the Pope and the rest of his crew perceived they
were robbed, and knew not after what sort, they persuaded themselves that it was the damned soul that
before had vexed the Pope so, and that smote him on
the face, wherefore he sent commandment through
all the whole City of Rome, that they should say Mass
in every Church, and ring all the bells for to lay the

THE SEVEN CHIEF CHURCHES OF ROME

Second Half of the 16th Century

walking Spirit, and to curse him with Bell, Book, and Candle, that so invisibly had misused the Pope's holiness, with the Cardinal of Pavia, and the rest of their company : but Faustus notwithstanding made good cheer with that which he had beguiled the Pope of, and in the midst of the order of Saint Barnard's bare-footed Friars, as they were going on Procession through the market place, called Campa de fiore, he let fall his plate dishes and cup, and withal for a farewell he made such a thunder-clap and a storm of rain, as though Heaven and earth should have met together, and so he left Rome, and came to Millain in Italie, near the Alps or borders of Switzerland, where he praised much to his Spirit the pleasantness of the place, the City being founded in so brave a plain, by the which ran most pleasant rivers on every side of the same, having besides within the compass or circuit of seven miles, seven small Seas : he saw also therein many fair Palaces and goodly buildings, the Duke's Palace, and the mighty strong Castle, which is in manner half the bigness of the town. Moreover, it liked him well to see the Hospital of Saint Mary's, with divers other things. He did nothing there worthy of memory, but he departed back again towards Bolognia, and from thence to Florence, where he was well pleased to see the pleasant walk of Merchants, the goodly vaults of the City, for that almost the whole City is vaulted, and the houses themselves are built outwardly, in such sort that the people may go under them as under a vault : then he perused the sumptuous Church in the Duke's Castle called Nostra Donna, our Lady's Church, in which he saw many monuments,

as a Marble door most huge to look upon : the gate
of the Castle was Bell metal, wherein are graven the
holy Patriarchs, with Christ and his twelve Apostles,
and divers other histories out of the old and new
Testament. Then went he to Sena, where he highly
praised the church and Hospital of Santa Maria
Formosa, with the goodly buildings, and especially
the fairness and greatness of the City, and beautiful
women. Then came he to Lyons in France, where he
marked the situation of the City, which lay between
two hills, environed with two waters : one worthy
monument in the City pleased him well, that was the
great Church with the Image therein ; he commended
the City highly for the great resort that it had unto
it of strangers. From thence he went to Cullin, which
lieth upon the River of Rhine, wherein he saw one
of the ancientest monuments of the world, the which
was the Tomb of the three Kings that came by the
Angel of God, and their knowledge they had in the
star, to worship Christ : which when Faustus saw, he
spake in this manner. Ah, alas good men how have
you erred and lost your way, you should have gone to
Palestina and Bethelem in Judea, how came you
hither ? or belike after your death you were thrown
into Mare Mediterraneum about Tripolis in Syria ;
and so you fleeted out of the Straits of Giblaterra
into the Ocean Sea, and so into the bay of Portugal ;
and not finding any rest you were driven along the
coast of Galicia, Biskay, and France, and into the
narrow Seas, then from thence into Mare Germanicum,
and so I think taken up about the town of Dort in
Holland, you were brought to Cullin to be buried :

131

or else I think you came more easily with a whirlwind over the Alps, and being thrown into the River of Rhine, it conveyed you to this place, where you are kept as a monument? There saw he the Church of S. Ursula, where remains a monument of the thousand Virgins: it pleased him also to see the beauty of the women. Not far from Cullin lieth the town of Ach. where he saw the gorgeous Temple that the Emperor Carolus Quartus[1] built of Marble stone for a remembrance of him, to the end that all his successors should there be crowned. From Cullin and Ach, he went to Geuf, a City in Savoy, lying near Switzerland: it is a town of great traffic, the Lord thereof is a Bishop, whose Wine-cellar Faustus, and his Spirit visited for the love of his good wine. From thence he went to Strasburg, where he beheld the fairest steeple that ever he had seen in his life before, for on each side thereof he might see through it, even from the covering of the Minster to the top of the Pinnacle, and it is named one of the wonders of the world: wherefore he demanded why it was called Strasburg: his Spirit answered, because it hath so many high ways coming to it on every side, for Stras in Dutch is a high way, and hereof came the name, yea (said Mephostophiles) the Church which thou so wonderest at, hath more revenues belonging to it, then the twelve Dukes of Slesia are worth, for there pertain unto this Church fifty-five Towns, and four hundred and sixty-three Villages besides many houses in the Town. From hence went Faustus to Basile in Switzerland, whereat the River of Rhine runneth through the town, parting

[1] This should be Carolus Magnus.

the same as the River of Thames doth London : in this town of Basile he saw many rich Monuments, the town walled with brick, and round about without it goeth a great trench : no Church pleased him but the Jesuits' Church, which was so sumptuously builded, and beset full of Alabaster pillars. Faustus demanded of his Spirit, how it took the name of Basyl : his Spirit made answer and said, that before this City was founded, there used a Basiliscus, a kind of Serpent, this Serpent killed as many men, women, and children, as it took a sight of : but there was a Knight that made himself a cover of Crystal to come over his head, and so down to the ground, and being first covered with a black cloth, over that he put the Crystal, and so boldly went to see the Basiliscus, and finding the place where he haunted, he expected his coming, even before the mouth of her cave : where standing a while, the Basylike came forth, who, when she saw her own venomous shadow in the Crystal, she split in a thousand pieces ; wherefore the Knight was richly rewarded of the Emperor : after the which the Knight founded this Town upon the place where he had slain the Serpent, and gave it the name of Basyl, in remembrance of his deed.

From Basyl Faustus went to Costuitz[1] in Sweitz, at the head of the Rhine, where is a most sumptuous Bridge, that goeth over the Rhine, even from the gates of the Town unto the other side of the stream : at the head of the River of Rhine, is a small Sea, called of the Switzers the black[2] Sea, twenty thousand paces

[1] i.e. Constance, which, however, is not in Switzerland.
[2] A mistranslation of the German *Bodensee*.

long, and fifty hundred paces broad. The town Costuitz took the name of this; the Emperor gave it to a Clown for expounding of his riddle, wherefore the Clowne named the Town Costuitz, that is in English, cost nothing. From Costuitz he came to Ulme, where he saw the sumptuous Town-house built by two and fifty of the ancient Senators of the City, it took the name of Ulma, for that the whole lands thereabout are full of Elms: but Faustus minding to depart from thence, his Spirit said unto him: Faustus think on the town as thou wilt, it hath three Dukedoms belonging to it, the which they have bought with ready money. From Ulme, he came to Wartzburg the chiefest town in Frankelandt, wherein the Bishop all together keepeth his Court, through the which Town passeth the River of Mayne that runs into the Rhine: thereabout groweth strong and pleasant wine, the which Faustus well proved. The Castle standeth on a hill on the North side of the Town, at the foot whereof runneth the River: this Town is full of beggarly Friars, Nuns, Priests, and Jesuits: for there are five sorts of begging Friars, besides three Cloisters of Nuns. At the foot of the Castle stands a Church, in the which there is an Altar, where are engraven all the four Elements, and all the orders and degrees in Heaven, that any man of understanding whosoever that hath a sight thereof, will say that it is the artificiallest thing that ever he beheld. From thence he went to Norenberg, whither as he went by the way, his Spirit informed him that the Town was named of Claudius Tiberius the Son of Nero the Tyrant. In the Town are two famous Cathedral Churches, the one called Saint Sabolt, the other Saint Laurence ; in which Church hangeth all the reliques of Carolus Magnus, that is his cloak, his hose and doublet, his sword and Crown, his Sceptre, and his Apple. It hath a very gorgeous gilden Conduit in the market of Saint Laurence, in which Conduit, is the spear that thrust our Saviour into the side, and a piece of the holy Cross ; the wall is called the fair wall of Norenberg, and hath five hundred and twenty-eight streets, one hundred and sixty wells, four great, and two small clocks, six great gates, and two small doors, eleven stone bridges, twelve small hills, ten appointed market places, thirteen common hothouses,[1] ten Churches, within the Town are thirty wheels of water-mills ; it hath one hundred and thirty-two tall ships,[2] two mighty Town walls of hewn stone and earth, with very deep trenches. The walls have one hundred and eighty Towers about them, and four fair plat-forms, ten Apothecaries, ten Doctors of the common law, fourteen Doctors of Physic. From Norenberg, he went to Auspurg, where at the break of the day, he demanded of his Spirit whereupon the Town took his name : this Town (saith he) hath had many names, when it was first built, it was called Vindelica : secondly, it was called Zizaria, the iron bridge : lastly by the Emperor Octavius Augustus, it was called Augusta, and by corruption of language the Germans have named it Auspurg. Now for because that Faustus had been there before, he departed without visiting

---

[1] i.e. hot baths.
[2] Probably a mistranslation of a German word ending in -schaft.

their monuments to Ravenspurg, where his Spirit certified him that the City had had seven names, the first Tyberia, the second Quadratis, the third Hyaspalis, the fourth Reginopolis, the fifth Imbripolis, the sixth Ratisbona, lastly Ravenspurg. The situation of the City pleased Faustus well, also the strong and sumptuous buildings : by the walls thereof runneth the River of Danubia, in Dutch called Donow, into the which not far from the compass of the City, falleth nearhand threescore other small Rivers and fresh waters. Faustus also liked the sumptuous stone bridge over the same water, with the Church standing thereon, the which was founded 1115, the name whereof is called S. Remedian : in this town Faustus went into the cellar of an Innholder, and let out all the Wine and Beer that was in his Cellar. After the which feat he returned unto Mentz[1] in Bavaria, a right princely Town, the Town appeared as if it were new, with great streets therein, both of breadth and length : from Mentz to Saltzburg, where the Bishop is always resident : here saw he all the commodities that were possible to be seen, for at the hill he saw the form of Abel[2] made in Crystal, an huge thing to look upon, that every year groweth bigger and bigger, by reason of the freezing cold. From hence, he went to Vienna, in Austria : this Town is of so great antiquity, that it is not possible to find the like : in this Town (said the Spirit) is more Wine than water, for all under the Town are wells, the which are filled every year with Wine, and all the water that they have, runneth by

---

[1] A mistake for Menchen (Munich).
[2] Perhaps " a bell."

the Town, that is the River Danubia. From hence, he went unto Prage, the chief City in Bohemia, this is divided into three parts, that is, old Prage, new Prage, and little Prage. Little Prage is the place where the Emperor's Court is placed upon an exceeding high mountain : there is a Castle, wherein are two fair Churches, in the one he found a monument, which might well have been a mirror to himself, and that was the Sepulchre of a notable Conjurer, which by his Magic had so enchanted his Sepulchre, that whosoever set foot thereon, should be sure never to die in their beds. From the Castle he came down, and went over the Bridge. This Bridge hath twenty and four Arches. In the middle of this Bridge stands a very fair monument, being a Cross builded of stone, and most artificially carved. From thence, he came into the old Prage, the which is separated from the new Prage, with an exceeding deep ditch, and round about enclosed with a wall of Brick. Unto this is adjoining the Jews' Town, wherein are thirteen thousand men, women, and children, all Jews. There he viewed the College and the Garden, where all manner of savage Beasts are kept ; and from thence, he fetched a compass round about the three Towns, whereat he wondered greatly, to see so mighty a City to stand all within the walls. From Prage, he flew into the air and bethought himself what he might do, or which way to take, so he looked round about, and behold, he had espied a passing fair City which lay not far from Prage, about some four and twenty miles, and that was Breslaw in Sclesia ; into which when he was entered, it seemed to him that he had been in Paradise, so neat and clean was the streets, and so sumptuous was their buildings. In this City he saw not many wonders, except the Brazen Virgin that standeth on a Bridge over the water, and under the which standeth a mill like a powder mill, which Virgin is made to do execution upon those disobedient town-born children that be so wild, that their parents cannot bridle them ; which when any such are found with some heinous offence, turning to the shame of their parents and kindred, they are brought to kiss this Virgin, which openeth her arms, the person then to be executed, kisseth her, then doth she close her arms together with such violence, that she crusheth out the breath of the person, breaketh his bulk, and so dieth : but being dead, she openeth her arms again, and letteth the party fall into the Mill, where he is stamped in small morsels, which the water carrieth away, so that not any part of him is found again. From Breslaw he went toward Cracovia, in the Kingdom of Polonia, where he beheld the Academy, the which pleased him wonderful well. In this City the King most commonly holdeth his Court at a Castle, in which Castle are many famous monuments. There is a most sumptuous Church in the same, in which standeth a silver altar gilded, and set with rich stones, and over it is a conveyance full of all manner silver ornaments belonging to the Mass. In the Church hangeth the jaw bones of an huge Dragon that kept the Rock before the Castle was edified thereon. It is full of all manner munition, and hath always victual for three years to serve two thousand men. Through the Town runneth a river called the Vistula or Wissel, where over is a fair wooden bridge.

This water divideth the Town and Casmere, in this Casmere dwelleth the Jews being a small walled Town by themselves, to the number of twenty-five thousand men, women, and children. Within one mile of the Town there is a salt mine, where they find stones of pure salt of a thousand pound, or nine hundred pound, or more in weight, and that in great quantity. This salt is as black as the Newcastle coals when it comes out of the mines, but being beaten to powder, it is as white as snow. The like they have four mile from thence, at a Town called Buchnia. From thence, Faustus went to Sandetz, the Captain thereof was called Don Spiket Iordan, in this Town are many monuments, as the tomb or sepulchre of Christ, in as ample manner as that is at Jerusalem, at the proper costs of a Gentleman that went thrice to Jerusalem from that place, and returned again. Not far from that Town is a new Town, wherein is a Nunnery of the order of Saint Dioclesian, into which order may none come, except they be Gentlewomen, and well formed and fair to look upon, the which pleased Faustus well : but having a desire to travel farther, and to see more wonders, mounting up towards the East over many lands and Provinces, as into Hungaria, Transilvania, Shede, Ingratz, Sardinia, and so into Constantinople, where the Turkish Emperor kept his Court. This City was surnamed by Constantine the founder thereof, being builded of very fair stone. In the same the great Turk hath three fair Palaces, the walls are strong, the pinnacles are very huge, and the streets large : but this liked not Faustus, that one man might have so many wives as he would. The Sea

runneth hard by the City, the wall hath eleven Gates :
Faustus abode there a certain time to see the manner
of the Turkish Emperor's service at his table, where he
saw his royal service to be such, that he thought if
all the Christian Princes should banquet together, and
everyone adorn the feast to the uttermost, they were
not able to compare with the Turk for his table, and
the rest of his Country service, wherefore it so spited
Faustus, that he vowed to be revenged of him, for
his pomp he thought was more fit for himself : wherefore as the Turk sat and ate, Faustus shewed him a
little apish play : for round about the privy Chamber,
he sent forth flashing flames of fire, in so much, that
the whole company forsook their meat and fled, except
only the great Turk himself, him Faustus had charmed
in such sort, that he could neither rise nor fall, neither
could any man pull him up. With this was the Hall
so light, as if the Sun had shined in the house, then
came Faustus in form of a Pope to the great Turk,
saying, all hail, Emperor, now art thou honoured that
I so worthily appear unto thee as thy Mahumet was
wont to do, hereupon he vanished, and forthwith it
so thundered, that the whole Palace shook : the Turk
greatly marvelled what this should be that so vexed
him, and was persuaded by his chiefest counsellors,
that it was Mahumet his Prophet, the which had so
appeared unto them, whereupon the Turk commanded
them to fall down on their knees, and to give him
thanks for doing them so great honour, as to shew
himself unto them ; but the next day Faustus went
into the Castle where he kept his Wives and Concubines, in the which Castle might no man upon pain

of death come, except those that were appointed by the great Turk to do them service, and they were all gelded. Which when Faustus perceived, he said to his Spirit Mephostophiles, how likest thou this sport, are not these fair Ladies greatly to be pitied, that thus consume their youth at the pleasure of one only man ? Why (quoth the Spirit) mayest not thou instead of the Emperor, embrace his fairest Ladies, do what thy heart desireth herein, and I will aid thee, and what thou wishest, thou shalt have it performed : wherefore Faustus (being before this counsel apt enough to put such matters in practice) caused a great fog to be round about the Castle, both within and without, and he himself appeared amongst the Ladies in all things as they use to paint their Mahumet, at which sight, the Ladies fell on their knees, and worshipped him, then Faustus took the fairest by the hand, and led her into a chamber, where after his manner he fell to dalliance, and thus he continued a whole day and night : and when he had delighted himself sufficiently with her, he put her away, and made his Spirit bring him another, so likewise he kept with her twenty-four hours' play, causing his Spirit to fetch him most dainty fare, and so he passed away six days, having each day his pleasure of a sundry Lady, and that of the fairest, all which time, the fog was so thick, and so stinking, that they within the house thought they had been in hell, for the time, and they without wondered thereat, in such sort, that they went to their prayers calling on their God Mahumet, and worshipping of his Image. Wherefore the sixth day Faustus exalted himself in the air, like to a Pope, in the sight of the great Turk and his people, and he had no sooner departed the Castle, but the fog vanished away, whence presently the Turk sent for his Wives and Concubines, demanding of them if they knew the cause why the Castle was beset with a mist so long? they said, that it was the God Mahumet himself that caused it, and how he was in the Castle personally full six days, and for more certainty, he hath lain with six of us these six nights one after another. Wherefore the Turk hearing this fell on his knees, and gave Mahumet thanks, desiring him to forgive him for being offended with his visiting his Castle and wives those six days: but the Turk commanded that those whom Mahumet had lain by, should be most carefully looked unto, persuading himself (and so did the whole people that knew of it) that out of their Mahumet should be raised a mighty generation, but first he demanded of the six Ladies if Mahumet had had actual copulation with them, according as earthly men have, yea my Lord, quoth one, as if you had been there yourself, you could not have mended it, for he lay with us stark naked, kissed and colled[1] us, and so delighted me, that for my part, I would he came two or three times a week to serve me in such sort again. From hence, Faustus went to Alkar, the which before time was called Chairam, or Memphis, in this City the Egyptian Soldan holdeth his Court. From hence the river Nilus hath his first head and spring, it is the greatest fresh-water river that is in the whole world, and always when the Sun is in Cancer, it overfloweth the whole land of Egypt: then he returned again

[1] Embraced.

142

towards the North-east, and to the Town of Ofen and Sabatz in Hungaria. This Ofen is the chiefest City in Hungaria, and standeth in a fertile soil, wherein groweth most excellent wine, and not far from the Town there is a well, called Zipzar, the water whereof changeth iron into Copper : here are mines of gold and silver, and all manner of metal, we Germans call this town Ofen[1], but in the Hungarian speech it is Start. In the town standeth a very fair Castle, and very well fortified. From hence he went to Austria, and through Slesia into Saxony, unto the Towns of Magdeburg and Liptzig, and Lubeck. Magdeburg is a Bishopric : in this City is one of the pitchers wherein Christ changed the water into wine at Cana in Galile. At Liptzig nothing pleased Faustus so well as the great vessel in the Castle made of wood, the which is bound about with twenty-four iron hoops, and every hoop weigheth two hundred pound weight, they must go upon a ladder of thirty steps high before they can look into it : he saw also the new church-yard, where it is walled, and standeth upon a fair plain, the yard is two hundred paces long, and round about in the inside of the wall, are goodly places separated one from each other to see sepulchres in, which in the middle of the yard standeth very sumptuous : therein standeth a pulpit of white work and gold. From hence he came to Lubeck and Hamburg, where he made no abode, but away again to Erfort in Duringen, where he visited the Freskold, and from Erfort he went home to

---

[1] This is Buda. The statement that the Hungarians call the town " Start " springs from a misunderstanding of his source by the author of the *German Faust Book*.

Wittenberg, when he had seen and visited many a strange place, being from home one year and a half, in which time he wrought more wonders than are here declared.

CHAPTER XXIII

How Faustus had a sight of Paradise

AFTER this, Doctor Faustus set forth again, visited these countries of Spain, Portugal, France, England, Scotland, Denmark, Sweden, Poland, Muscovy, India, Cataia, Africa, Persia, and lastly into Barbaria amongst the Blackamoors, and in all his wandering he was desirous to visit the ancient monuments and mighty hills, amongst the rest beholding the high hill called the Treno Riefe, was desirous to rest upon it : from thence he went into the Isle of Brittany, wherein he was greatly delighted to see the fair water and warm Baths, the divers sorts of metal, with many precious stones, and divers other commodities the which Faustus brought thence with him, he was also at the Orchades behind Scotland, where he saw the tree that bringeth forth fruit, that when it is ripe, openeth and falleth into the water, whereof engendereth a certain kind of Fowl or Bird : these Islands are in number twenty-three but ten of them are not habitable, the other thirteen are inhabited : from hence, he went to the hill of Caucasus, which is the highest in all that Tropic, it lieth near the borders of Scythia, hereon Faustus stood and beheld many lands and Kingdoms. Faustus being on such an high hill, thought to look over all the world and beyond, for he meant to see Paradise, but he durst not commune with his Spirit thereof : and being on the hill of Caucasus, he saw the whole land of India and Scythia, and towards the East as he looked he saw a mighty clear strike of fire coming from heaven upon the earth, even as it had been one of the beams of the Sun, he saw in the valley four mighty waters springing, one had his course towards India, the second towards Egypt, the third and fourth towards Armenia. When he saw these, he would needs know of his Spirit what waters they were, and from whence they came. His Spirit gave him gently an answer, saying ; it is Paradise that lieth so far in the East, the garden that God himself hath planted with all manner of pleasure, and the fiery stream that thou seest, is the walls or defence of the garden, but that clear light that thou seest so far off, is the Angel that hath the custody thereof, with a fiery sword : and although that thou thinkest thyself to be hard by, thou hast yet farther thither from hence, than thou hast ever been : the water that thou seest divided in four parts, is the water that issueth out of the Well in the middle of Paradise. The first is called Ganges or Phison, the second, Gihon or Nilus, the third Tigris, and the fourth Euphrates, also thou seest that he standeth under Libra and Aries right up towards the Zenith, and upon this fiery wall standeth the Angel Michael with his flaming sword to keep the tree of life the which he hath in charge ; but the Spirit said unto Faustus, neither thou, nor I, nor any after us, yea all men whosoever are denied to visit it, or to come any nearer than we be.

CHAPTER XXIV

Of a certain Comet that appeared in Germanie, and how Doctor Faustus was desired by certain friends of his to know the meaning thereof

IN Germanie over the Town of S. Eizleben was seen a mighty great Comet, whereat the people wondered ; but Doctor Faustus being there, was asked of certain of his friends his judgment or opinion in the matter. Whereupon he answered, it falleth out often by the course and change of the Sun and Moon, that the Sun is under the earth, and the Moon above ; but when the Moon draweth near the change, then is the Sun so strong that he taketh away all the light of the Moon, in such sort that he is as red as blood : and to the contrary, after they have been together, the Moon taketh her light again from him, and so increasing in light to the full, she will be as red as the Sun was before, and changeth herself into divers and sundry colours, of the which springeth a prodigious monster, or as you call it, a Comet, which is a figure or token appointed of God as a forewarning of his displeasure : as at one time he sendeth hunger, plague, sword, or such-like : being all tokens of his judgment : the which Comet cometh through the conjunction of the Sun and Moon begetting a monster, whose father is the Sun, and whose mother is the Moon, ☉ and ☽.

CHAPTER XXV

A question put forth to Doctor Faustus, concerning the Stars

THERE was a learned man of the Town of Halberstat, named N. V. W. invited Doctor Faustus to his table, but falling into communication before supper was ready, they looked out of the window, and seeing many stars in the firmament, this man being a Doctor of Physic and a good Astrologian, said : Doctor Faustus, I have invited you as my guest, hoping that you will take it in good part with me, and withal I request you to impart unto me some of your experience in the Stars and Planets. And seeing a Star fall, he said : I pray you, Faustus, what is the condition, quality, or greatness of the Stars in the firmament ? Faustus answered him : My friend and Brother, you see that the Stars that fall from heaven when they come on the earth they be very small to our thinking as candles, but being fixed in the firmament there are many as great as this City, some as great as a Province or Dukedom, other as great as the whole earth, other some far greater than the earth : for the length and breadth of the heavens is greater than the earth twelve times, and from the height of the heavens there is scarce any earth to be seen, yea the Planets in the heavens are some so great as this land, some so great as the whole Empire of Rome, some as Turkie, yea one so great as the whole world.

CHAPTER XXVI

*How Faustus was asked a question concerning the
Spirits that vex men*

THAT is most true (saith he to Faustus) concerning
the Stars and Planets : but I pray you in what kind
or manner do the spirits use or vex men so little by
day, and so greatly by night ? Doctor Faustus
answered : because the spirits are by God forbidden
the light, their dwelling is in darkness, and the clearer
the Sun shineth, the further the Spirits have their
abiding from it, but in the night when it is dark, they
have their familiarity and abiding near unto us men.
For although in the night we see not the Sun, yet the
brightness thereof so lighteneth the first moving of
the firmament as it doth that on earth in the day, by
which reason we are able to see the Stars and Planets in
the night, even so the rays of the Sun piercing upwards
into the firmament, the Spirits abandon the place, and
so come near us on earth in the darkness, filling our
heads with heavy dreams and fond fantasies, with
screeching and crying in many deformed shapes : as
sometimes when men go forth without light, there
falleth to them a fear, that their hair standeth on end,
so many start in their sleep thinking there is a Spirit
by him, gropeth or feeleth for him, going round about
the house in his sleep, and many such-like fantasies :
and all this is for because that in the night the Spirits
are more familiarly by us than we are desirous of their
company, and so they carry us, blinding us and
plaguing us more than we are able to perceive.

CHAPTER XXVII

How Doctor Faustus was asked a question concerning the Stars that fall from Heaven

DOCTOR FAUSTUS being demanded the cause why the Stars fell from heaven, he answered : that is but our opinion ; for if one Star fall, it is the great judgment of God upon us, as aforewarning of some great thing to come : for when we think that a Star falleth, it is but as a spark that issueth from a candle or a flame of fire, for if it were a substantial thing, we should not so soon lose the sight of them as we do. And likewise, if so be that we see as it were a stream of fire fall from the firmament, as oft it happeneth, yet are they no Stars, but as it were a flame of fire vanishing, but the Stars are substantial, therefore are they firm and not falling : if there fall any, it is a sign of some great matter to come, as a scourge to a people or country, and then such Star falling, the gates of heaven are opened, and the clouds send forth floods, or other plagues, to the damage of the whole land and people.

CHAPTER XXVIII

How Faustus was asked a question as concerning thunder

IN the month of August, there was over Wittenberg a mighty great lightning and thunder, and as Doctor Faustus was jesting merrily in the market place with certain of his friends and companions being Physicians, they desired him to tell them the cause of that weather. Faustus answered : it hath been commonly seen heretofore, that before a thunder-clap fell a shower of rain or a gale of wind, for commonly after a wind followeth a rain, and after a rain a thunder-clap : such things come to pass when the four winds meet together in the heavens, the airy clouds are by force beaten against the fixed crystalline firmament, but when the airy clouds meet with the firmament, they are congealed, and so strike and rush against the firmament, as great pieces of ice when they meet on the water, the echo thereof soundeth in our ears, and that we call thunder, which indeed is none other than you have heard.

The third and last part of Doctor Faustus his merry conceits, shewing after what sort he practised Necromancy in the Courts of great Princes, and lastly of his fearful and pitiful end

CHAPTER XXIX

How the Emperor Carolus Quintus requested of Faustus to see some of his cunning, whereunto he agreed.

THE Emperor Carolus the fifth of that name was personally with the rest of his Nobles and gentlemen at the Town of Innsbruck where he kept his Court, unto the which also Doctor Faustus resorted, and being there well known of divers Nobles and gentlemen, he was invited into the Court to meat, even in the presence of the Emperor : whom when the Emperor saw, he looked earnestly on him, thinking him by his looks to be some wonderful fellow, wherefore he asked one of his Nobles whom he should be : who answered that he was called Doctor Faustus. Whereupon the Emperor held his peace until he had taken his repast, after which he called unto him Faustus, into the privy chamber, whither being come, he said unto him : Faustus, I have heard much of thee, that thou art excellent in the black Art, and none like thee in mine Empire, for men say that thou hast a familiar Spirit with thee and that thou canst do what thou list : it is therefore (saith the Emperor) my request of thee that thou let me see a proof of thine experience, and I vow unto thee by the honour of mine Imperial Crown, none evil shall happen unto thee for so doing. Hereupon Doctor Faustus answered his Majesty, that upon those conditions he was ready in anything that he could, to do his Highness' commandment in what service he would appoint him. Well, then hear what I say (quoth the Emperor). Being once solitary in my house, I called to mind mine elders and ancestors, how it was possible for them to attain unto so great a degree of authority, yea so high, that we the successors of that line are never able to come near. As, for example, the great and mighty monarch of the world, Alexander Magnus, was such a lantern and spectacle to all his successors, as the Chronicles make mention of so great riches, conquering, and subduing so many

Kingdoms, the which I and those that follow me (I fear) shall never be able to attain unto : wherefore, Faustus, my hearty desire is that thou wouldst vouchsafe to let me see that Alexander, and his Paramour, the which was praised to be so fair, and I pray thee shew me them in such sort that I may see their personages, shape, gesture, and apparel, as they used in their lifetime, and that here before my face ; to the end that I may say I have my long desire fulfilled, and to praise thee to be a famous man in thine art and experience. Doctor Faustus answered : My most excellent Lord, I am ready to accomplish your request in all things, so far forth as I and my Spirit are able to perform : yet your Majesty shall know, that their dead bodies are not able substantially to be brought before you, but such Spirits as have seen Alexander and his Paramour alive, shall appear unto you in manner and form as they both lived in their most flourishing time : and herewith I hope to please your Imperial Majesty. Then Faustus went a little aside to speak to his Spirit, but he returned again presently, saying : now, if it please your Majesty, you shall see them, yet upon this condition that you demand no question of them, nor speak unto them, which the Emperor agreed unto. Wherewith Doctor Faustus opened the privy chamber door, where presently entered the great and mighty Emperor Alexander Magnus, in all things to look upon as if he had been alive, in proportion a strong thick-set man, of a middle stature, black hair, and that both thick and curled head and beard, red cheeks, and a broad face, with eyes like a Basilisk, he had on a complete harness burnished and graven exceeding rich to look upon ; and so passing towards the Emperor Carolus, he made low and reverent curtsy : whereat the Emperor Carolus would have stood up to receive and greet him with the like reverence, but Faustus took hold of him and would not permit him to do it. Shortly after Alexander made humble reverence and went out again, and coming to the door his Paramour met him, she coming in, she made the Emperor likewise reverence, she was clothed in blue Velvet, wrought and embroidered with pearl and gold, she was also excellent fair like Milk and blood mixed, tall and slender, with a face round as an Apple, and thus she passed certain times up and down the house, which the Emperor marking, said to himself : now have I seen two persons, which my heart hath long wished for to behold, and sure it cannot otherwise be, said he to himself, but that the Spirits have changed themselves into these forms, and have not deceived me, calling to his mind the woman that raised the Prophet Samuel : and for that the Emperor would be the more satisfied in the matter, he thought, I have heard say, that behind her neck she had a great wart or wen, wherefore he took Faustus by the hand without any words, and went to see if it were also to be seen on her or not, but she perceiving that he came to her, bowed down her neck, where he saw a great wart, and hereupon she vanished, leaving the Emperor and the rest well contented.

153

CHAPTER XXX

How Doctor Faustus in the sight of the Emperor conjured a pair of Hart's horns upon a Knight's head that slept out of a casement

WHEN Doctor Faustus had accomplished the Emperor's desire in all things as he was requested, he went forth into a gallery, and leaning over a rail to look into the privy garden, he saw many of the Emperor's Courtiers walking and talking together, and casting his eyes now this way, now that way, he espied a Knight leaning out at a window of the great hall ; who was

fast asleep (for in those days it was hot) but the person shall be nameless that slept, for that he was a Knight, although it was done to a little disgrace of the Gentleman : it pleased Doctor Faustus, through the help of his Spirit Mephostophiles, to firm upon his head as he slept, a huge pair of Hart's horns, and as the Knight awaked thinking to pull in his head, he hit his horns against the glass that the panes thereof flew about his ears. Think here how this good Gentleman was vexed, for he could neither get backward nor forward : which when the Emperor heard all the Courtiers laugh, and came forth to see what was happened, the Emperor also when he beheld the Knight with so fair a head, laughed heartily thereat, and was therewithal well pleased : at last Faustus made him quit of his horns again, but the Knight perceived how they came, *etc.*[1]

CHAPTER XXXI

How the above-mentioned Knight went about to be revenged of Doctor Faustus

DOCTOR FAUSTUS took his leave of the Emperor and the rest of the Courtiers, at whose departure they were sorry, giving him many rewards and gifts : but being a league and a half from the City he came into a Wood, where he beheld the Knight that he had jested with at the Court with others in harness, mounted on fair palfreys, and running with full charge towards Faustus, but he seeing their intent, ran towards the bushes, and before he came amongst the bushes he returned again, running as it were to meet them that chased him, whereupon suddenly all the bushes were turned into horsemen, which also ran to encounter with the Knight and his company, and coming to them, they closed the Knight and the

[1] There seems to be no explanation for the *etc.* here and at the end of the following two chapters. Cf. also end of Chapter IV.

rest, and told them that they must pay their ransom
before they departed. Whereupon the Knight seeing
himself in such distress, besought Faustus to be good

to them, which he denied not, but let them loose,
yet he so charmed them, that every one, Knight and
others for the space of a whole month did wear a
pair of Goat's horns on their brows, and every Palfrey
a pair of Ox horns on their head : and this was their
penance appointed by Faustus, *etc.*

CHAPTER XXXII

*How three young Dukes being together at Wittenberg
to behold the University, requested Faustus to
help them at a wish to the town of Menchen
in Bavaria, there to see the Duke of Bavaria
his son's wedding*

THREE worthy young Dukes, the which are not here
to be named, but being students altogether at the

156

University of Wittenberg, met on a time altogether, where they fell to reasoning concerning the pomp and bravery that would be at the City of Menchen in Bavaria, at the wedding of the Duke's Son, wishing themselves there but one half hour, to see the manner of their jollity : to whom one replied, saying to the other two Gentlemen, if it please you to give me the hearing, I will give you good counsel that we may see the wedding, and be here again to night, and this is my meaning ; let us send to Doctor Faustus, make him a present of some rare thing and so open our minds unto him, desiring him to assist us in our enterprise, and assure ye he will not deny to fulfil our request. Hereupon they all concluded, sent for Faustus, told him their mind, and gave him a gift, and invited him to a sumptuous banquet, wherewith Faustus was well contented, and promised to further their journey to the uttermost. And when the time was come that the Duke his son should be married, Doctor Faustus called unto him the three young Gentlemen into his house, commanding them that they should put on their best apparel, and adorn themselves as richly as they could, he took off his own great large cloak, went into a garden that was adjoining unto his house, and set the three young Dukes on his cloak, and he himself sat in the midst, but he gave them in charge that in any wise they should not once open their mouths to speak, or make answer to any man so soon as they were out, no not so much as if the Duke of Bavaria or his son should speak to them, or offer them courtesy, they should give no word or answer again, to the which they all agreed. These conditions being made, Doctor Faustus began to conjure, and on a sudden arose a mighty wind, heaving up the cloak, and so carried them away in the air, and in due time they came unto Menchen to the Duke's Court, where being entered into the outmost court, the Marshal had espied them, who presently went to the Duke shewing his Grace that all the Lords and gentlemen were already set at the table, notwithstanding, there

were newly come three goodly Gentlemen with one servant, the which stood without in the court, wherefore the good old Duke came out unto them, welcoming them, requiring what they were, and whence : but they made no answer at all, whereat the Duke wondered, thinking they were all four dumb ; notwithstanding for his honour sake he took them into his court, and feasted them. Faustus notwithstanding spake to them, if any thing happen otherwise then well, when I say, sit up, then fall you all on the cloak, and good enough : well, the water being brought, and that they must wash, one of the three had so much manners as to desire his friend to wash first, which when Faustus heard, he said, sit up, and all at once they got on the cloak, but he that spake fell off again, the other two with Doctor Faustus, were again presently at Wittenberg, but he that remained, was taken and laid in Prison : wherefore the other two Gentlemen were very sorrowful for their friend, but Faustus comforted them, promising that on the morrow he should also be at Wittenberg. Now all this while was this Duke taken in a great fear, and stricken into an exceeding dump, wondering with himself that his hap was so hard to be left behind, and not the rest, and now being locked and watched with so many keepers, there was also certain of the guests that fell to reasoning with him to know what he was, and also what the others were that were vanished away, but the poor prisoner thought with himself, if I open what they are, then it will be evil also with me : wherefore all this while he gave no man any answer, so that he was there a whole day, and gave no man a word. Wherefore the old Duke gave in charge, that the next morning they should rack him until he had confessed : which when the young Duke heard, he began to sorrow and to say with himself, it may be that to-morrow, if Doctor Faustus come not to aid me, then shall I be racked and grievously tormented, in so much that I shall be constrained by force to tell more than willingly I would do : but he comforted himself with hope that his friends would entreat Doctor Faustus about his deliverance, as also it came to pass, for before it was day, Doctor Faustus was by him, and he conjured them that watched him into such a heavy sleep, that he with his charms made open all the locks in the prison, and therewithal brought the young Duke again in safety to the rest of his fellows and friends, where they presented Faustus with a sumptuous gift, and so they departed the one from the other, *etc*.

CHAPTER XXXIII

How Doctor Faustus borrowed money of a Jew, and laid his own leg to pawn for it

It is a common proverb in Germanie, that although a Conjurer have all things at commandment, the day will come that he shall not be worth a penny : so is it like to fall out with Doctor Faustus, in promising the Devil so largely : and as the Devil is the author of lies, even so he led Faustus his mind, in practising of things to deceive the people and blinding them, wherein he took his whole delight, thereby to bring himself to riches, yet notwithstanding in the end he was never the richer. And although that during four and twenty years of his time that the Devil set him, he wanted nothing ; yet was he best pleased when he might deceive anybody : for out of the mightiest Potentates' Courts in all those Countries, he would send his Spirit to steal away their best cheer. And on a time being in his merriment where he was banqueting with other Students in an Inn, whereunto resorted many Jews, which when Doctor Faustus perceived, he was minded to play some merry jest to deceive a Jew, desiring one of them to lend him some money for a time, the Jew was content, and lent Faustus threescore dollars for a month, which time being expired, the Jew came for his money and interest, but Doctor Faustus was never minded to pay the Jew again : at length the Jew coming home to his house, and calling importunately for his money, Doctor Faustus made him this answer : Jew, I have no money, nor know I how to pay thee, but notwithstanding, to the end that thou mayest be contented,

I will cut off a limb of my body, be it arm or leg, and the same shalt thou have in pawn for thy money, yet with this condition, that when I shall pay thee thy money again, then thou also give me my limb. The Jew that was never friend to a Christian, thought with himself, this is a fellow right for my purpose, that will lay his limbs to pawn for money, he was therewith very well content; wherefore Doctor Faustus took a saw, and therewith seemed to cut off his foot (being notwithstanding nothing so) well, he gave it to the Jew, yet upon this condition, that when he got money to pay, the Jew should deliver him his leg, to the end he might set it on again. The Jew was with this matter very well pleased, took his leg and departed : and having far home, he was somewhat weary, and by the way he thus bethought him, what helpeth me a knave's leg, if I should carry it home, it would stink, and so infect my house, besides it is too hard a piece of work to set it on again, wherefore what an ass was Faustus to lay so dear a pawn for so small a sum of money ; and for my part, quoth the Jew to himself, this will never profit me anything, and with these words he cast the leg away from him into a ditch. All this Doctor Faustus knew right well, therefore within three days after he sent for the Jew to make him payment of his sixty Dollars, the Jew came, and Doctor Faustus demanded his pawn, there was his money ready for him : the Jew answered, the pawn was not profitable or necessary for anything and he had cast it away : but Faustus threateningly replied, I will have my leg again, or else one of thine for it. The Jew fell to entreating, promising him to give him what money he would ask, if he would not deal straightly with him, wherefore the Jew was constrained to give him sixty Dollars more to be rid of him, and yet Faustus had his leg on, for he had but blinded the Jew.

CHAPTER XXXIV

How Doctor Faustus deceived an Horse-courser

IN like manner he served an Horse-courser at a fair called Pheiffring, for Doctor Faustus through his cunning had gotten an excellent fair Horse, whereupon he rid to the Fair, where he had many Chap-men that offered him money : lastly, he sold him for forty Dollars, willing him that bought him, that in any wise he should not ride him over any water, but the Horse-courser marvelled with himself that Faustus bade him ride him over no water (but quoth he), I will prove, and forthwith he rid him into the river, presently the horse vanished from under him, and he sat on a bundle of straw, in so much that the man was almost drowned.

The Horse-courser knew well where he lay that had sold him his horse, wherefore he went angrily to his Inn, where he found Doctor Faustus fast asleep, and snorting on a bed, but the Horse-courser could no longer forbear him, took him by the leg and began to pull him off the bed, but he pulled him so, that he pulled his leg from his body, in so much that the Horse-courser fell down backwards in the place, then began Doctor Faustus to cry with an open throat, he hath murdered me. Hereat the Horse-courser was afraid, and gave the flight,[1] thinking

[1] i.e. took to flight.

none other with himself, but that he had pulled his leg from his body ; by this means Doctor Faustus kept his money.

CHAPTER XXXV

How Doctor Faustus ate a load of Hay

DOCTOR FAUSTUS being in a Town of Germanie called Zwickaw, where he was accompanied with many Doctors and Masters, and going forth to walk after supper, they met with a Clown[1] that drove a load of Hay. Good even good fellow said Faustus to the Clown, what shall I give thee to let me eat my belly full of Hay ? The Clown thought with himself, what a mad man is this to eat Hay, thought he with himself, thou wilt not eat much, they agreed for three farthings he should eat as much as he could : wherefore Doctor Faustus began to eat, and that so ravenously, that all the rest of his company fell a-laughing, blinding so the poor Clown, that he was sorry at his heart, for he seemed to have eaten more than the half of his Hay, wherefore the Clown began to speak him fair, for fear he should have eaten the other half also. Faustus made as though he had had pity on the Clown, and went his way. When the Clown came in place where he would be, he had his Hay again as he had before, a full load.

[1] i.e. peasant.

CHAPTER XXXVI

How Doctor Faustus served the twelve Students

AT Wittenberg before Faustus his house, there was a quarrel between seven Students, and five that came to part the rest, one part being stronger than the other. Wherefore Faustus seeing them to be overmatched, conjured them all blind, in so much that the one could not see the other, and yet he so dealt with them, that they fought and smote at one another still, whereat all the beholders fell a-laughing : and thus they continued blind, beating one another, until the people parted them, and led each one to his own home : where being entered into their houses, they received their sight perfectly again.

CHAPTER XXXVII

How Faustus served the drunken Clowns

DOCTOR FAUSTUS went into an Inn, wherein were many tables full of Clowns, the which were tippling can after can of excellent wine, and to be short, they were all drunken, and as they sat, they so sang and hallowed, that one could not hear a man speak for them ; this angered Doctor Faustus ; wherefore he said to those that had called him in, mark my masters, I will shew you a merry jest, the Clowns continuing still hallowing and singing, he so conjured them, that their mouths stood as wide open as it was possible for them to hold them, and never a one of them was able to close his mouth again : by and by the noise was gone, the Clowns notwithstanding looked earnestly one upon another, and wist not what was happened ; wherefore one by one they went out, and so soon as they came without, they were as well as ever they were : but none of them desired to go in any more.

CHAPTER XXXVIII

How Doctor Faustus sold five Swine for six Dollars apiece

DOCTOR FAUSTUS began another jest, he made him ready five fat Swine, the which he sold to one for six Dollars a piece, upon this condition, that the Swine-

driver should not drive them into the water. Doctor Faustus went home again, and as the Swine had defiled themselves in the mud, the Swine-driver drove them into a water, where presently they were changed into so many bundles of straw swimming upright in the water : the boor looked wishly about him, and was sorry in his heart, but he knew not where to find Faustus, so he was content to let all go, and to lose both money and Hogs.

CHAPTER XXXIX

How Doctor Faustus played a merry jest with the Duke of Anholt in his Court

DOCTOR FAUSTUS on a time came to the Duke of Anholt, the which welcomed him very courteously, this was in the month of January, where sitting at the table, he perceived the Duchess to be with child, and forbearing himself until the meat was taken from the table, and that they brought in the banqueting dishes, said Doctor Faustus to the Duchess, Gracious Lady, I have always heard, that the great-bellied women do always long for some dainties, I beseech therefore your Grace hide not your mind from me, but tell me what you desire to eat, she answered him, Doctor Faustus now truly I will not hide from you what my heart doth most desire, namely, that if it were now Harvest, I would eat my belly full of ripe Grapes, and other dainty fruit. Doctor Faustus answered hereupon, Gracious Lady, this is a small thing for me to do, for I can do more than this, wherefore he took a plate, and made open one of the casements of the window, holding it forth, where incontinent he had his dish full of all manner of fruits, as red and white Grapes, Pears, and Apples, the which came from out of strange Countries, all these he presented the Duchess, saying : Madame, I pray you vouchsafe to taste of this dainty fruit, the which came from a far Country, for there the Summer is not yet ended. The Duchess thanked Faustus highly, and she fell to her fruit with full appetite. The Duke of Anholt notwithstanding could not withhold to ask Faustus with what reason there were such young fruit to be had at that time of the year ? Doctor Faustus told him, may it please your Grace to understand, that the year is divided into two circles over the whole world, that when with us it is Winter, in the contrary circle it is notwithstanding Summer, for in India and Saba there falleth or setteth the Sun, so that it is so warm, that they have twice a year fruit : and gracious Lord, I have a swift Spirit, the which can in the twinkling of an eye fulfil my desire in any thing, wherefore I sent him into those Countries, who hath brought this fruit as you see : whereat the Duke was in great admiration.

CHAPTER XL

How Doctor Faustus through his Charms made a great Castle in presence of the Duke of Anholt

DOCTOR FAUSTUS desired the Duke of Anholt to walk a little forth of the Court with him, wherefore they went both together into the field, where Doctor Faustus through his skill had placed a mighty Castle : which when the Duke saw, he wondered thereat, so did the Duchess, and all the beholders, that on that hill, which was called the Rohumbuel, should on the sudden be so fair a Castle. At last Doctor Faustus desired the Duke and the Duchess to walk with him into the Castle, which they denied not. This Castle was so wonderful strong, having about it a great and

deep trench of water, the which was full of Fish, and all manner of water-fowl, as Swans, Ducks, Geese, Bitterns, and suchlike. About the wall was five stone doors and two other doors : also within was a great open court, wherein were enchanted all manner of wild beasts, especially such as were not to be found in Germanie, as Apes, Bears, Buffs, Antelopes, and such like strange beasts. Furthermore, there were other manner of beasts, as Hart, Hind, and wild Swine, Roe, and all manner of land fowl that any man could think on, the which flew from one tree to another. After all this, he set his guests to the table, being the Duke and the Duchess with their train, for he had provided them a most sumptuous feast, both of meat and all manner of drinks, for he set nine messes of meat upon the board at once, and all this must his Wagner do, place all things on the board, the which was brought unto him by the Spirit invisibly of all things that their heart could desire, as wild fowl, and Venison, with all manner of dainty fish that could be thought on, of Wine also great plenty, and of divers sorts, as French wine, Cullin wine, Crabatsher wine, Rhenish wine, Spanish wine, Hungarian wine, Watzburg wine, Malmsey, and Sack: in the whole, there were an hundred cans standing round about the house. This sumptuous banquet the Duke took thankfully, and afterwards he departed homewards, and to their thinking they had neither eaten nor drunk, so were they blinded the whilst that they were in the Castle: but as they were in their Palace they looked towards the Castle, and behold it was all in a flame of fire, and all those that beheld it wondered to hear so great a noise, as if it were great Ordnance should have been shot off: and thus the Castle burned and consumed away clean. Which done, Doctor Faustus returned to the Duke, who gave him great thanks for shewing them of so great courtesy, giving him an hundred Dollars, and liberty to depart or use his own discretion therein.

CHAPTER XLI

*How Doctor Faustus with his company visited the
Bishop of Saltzburg his Wine-cellar*

DOCTOR FAUSTUS having taken his leave of the Duke,
he went to Wittenberg, near about Shrovetide, and
being in company with certain Students, Doctor
Faustus was himself the God Bacchus, who having
well feasted the Students before with dainty fare,
after the manner of Germanie, where it is counted
no feast except all the bidden guests be drunk, which
Doctor Faustus intending, said : Gentlemen and my
guests, will it please you to take a cup of wine with me
in a place or cellar whereunto I will bring you, and they
all said willingly we will : which when Doctor Faustus
heard, he took them forth, set either of them upon an
holly wand, and so were conjured into the Bishop of
Saltzburg his Cellar, for there about grew excellent
pleasant Wine : there fell Faustus and his company
to drinking and swilling, not of the worst but of the
best, and as they were merry in the Cellar, came down
to draw drink the Bishop's butler : which when he
perceived so many persons there he cried with a loud
voice, thieves ! thieves ! This spited Doctor Faustus
wonderfully, wherefore he made every one of his
company to sit on their holly wand and so vanished
away, and in parting Doctor Faustus took the Butler
by the hair of the head and carried him away with
them, until they came unto a mighty high-lopped
tree, and on the top of that huge tree he set the Butler,

171

where he remained in a most fearful perplexity, and Doctor Faustus departed to his house where they took their VALETE one of another, drinking the Wine the which they had stolen in great bottles of glass out of the Bishop's cellar. The Butler that had held himself by the hand upon the lopped tree all the night, was almost frozen with cold, espying the day, and seeing the tree of so huge great highness, thought with himself it is impossible to come off this tree without peril of death : at length he had espied certain Clowns which were passing by, he cried for the love of God help me down : the Clowns seeing him so high, wondered what mad man would climb to so huge a tree, wherefore as a thing most miraculous, they carried tidings unto the Bishop of Saltzburg, then was there great running on every side to see a man in a huge tree, and many devices they practised to get him down with ropes, and being demanded by the Bishop how he came there, he said, that he was brought thither by the hair of the head of certain thieves that were robbing of the Wine-cellar, but what they were he knew not, for (said he) they had faces like men, but they wrought like Devils.

CHAPTER XLII

How Doctor Faustus kept his Shrovetide

THERE were seven Students, and Masters that studied Divinity, Iuris Prudentia, and Medicina, all these having consented were agreed to visit Doctor Faustus and so to celebrate Shrovetide with him : who being come to his house he gave them their welcome, for they were his dear friends, desiring them to sit down, where he served them with a very good supper of Hens, fish, and other roast, yet were they but slightly cheered : wherefore Doctor Faustus comforted his guests, excusing himself that they stole upon him so suddenly, that he had not leisure to provide for them so well as they were worthy, but my good friends (quoth he) according to the use of our Country we must drink all this night, and so a draught of the best wine to bedward is commendable. For you know that in great Potentates' Courts they use as this night great feasting, the like will I do for you : for I have three great flagons of wine, the first is full of Hungarian wine, containing eight gallons, the second of Italian wine, containing seven gallons, the third containing six gallons of Spanish wine, all the which we will tipple out before it be day, besides, we have fifteen dishes of meat, the which my Spirit Mephostophiles hath fetched so far that it was cold before he brought it, and they are all full of the daintiest things that one's heart can devise, but (saith Faustus) I must make them hot again : and you may believe me, Gentlemen, that this is no blinding of you, whereas you think that it is no natural food, verily it is as good and as pleasant as ever you ate. And having ended his tale, he commanded his boy to lay the cloth, which done, he served them with fifteen messes of meat, having three dishes to a mess, the which were of all manner of Venison, and other dainty wild fowl, and for wine there was no lack, as Italian wine, Hungarian wine, and Spanish wine : and when they were all made drunk, and that they had almost eaten all their good cheer, they began to sing and to dance until it was day, and then they departed each one to his own habitation : at whose parting, Doctor Faustus desired them to be his guests again the next day following.

CHAPTER XLIII

How Doctor Faustus feasted his guests on the Ash-Wednesday

UPON Ash Wednesday came unto Doctor Faustus his bidden guests the Students, whom he feasted very royally, in so much that they were all full and lusty, singing and dancing as the night before : and when the high glasses and goblets were caroused one to another, Doctor Faustus began to play them some pretty jests, in so much that round about the hall was heard most pleasant music, and that in sundry places, in this corner a Lute, in another a Cornet, in another a Cittern, Gittern, Clarigolds, Harp, Horn pipe : in fine, all manner of music was heard there at that instant, whereat all the glasses and goblets, cups and pots, dishes, and all that stood on the board began to dance : then Doctor Faustus took ten stone pots, and set them down on the floor, where presently they began to dance and to smite one against the other that the shivers flew round about the whole house,

whereat the whole company fell a-laughing. Then
he began another jest, he set an Instrument on the
table, and caused a monstrous great Ape to come in
amongst them, which Ape began to dance and to skip,
shewing them many merry conceits. In this and such-
like pastime they passed away the whole day, where
night being come, Doctor Faustus bade them all to
supper, which they lightly agreed unto, for Students
in these cases are easily entreated : wherefore he

promised to feast them with a banquet of fowl, and
afterwards they would all go about with a Mask, then
Doctor Faustus put forth a long pole out of the window,
whereupon presently there came innumerable of
birds and wild fowl, and so many as came had not any
power to fly away again, but he took them and flung
them to the Students : who lightly pulled off the
necks of them, and being roasted they made their
supper, which being ended they made themselves
ready to the Mask. Doctor Faustus commanded
every one to put on a clean shirt over his other clothes,
which being done, they began to look one upon another,

it seemed to each one of them they had no heads, and so they went forth unto certain of their neighbours, at which sight the people were wonderfully afraid. And as the use of Germanie is, that wheresoever a Mask entereth, the good man of the house must feast them : so when these maskers were set to their banquet, they seemed again in their former shape with heads in so much that they were all known what they were : and having sat and well eaten and drunk, Doctor Faustus made that every one had an Ass's head on, with great and long ears, so they fell to dancing and to drive away the time until it was midnight, and then every man departed home, and as soon as they were out of the house each one was in his natural shape again, and so they ended and went to sleep.

CHAPTER XLIV

How Doctor Faustus the day following was feasted of the Students, and of his merry jests with them while he was in their company

THE last Bacchanalia was held on Thursday, where ensued a great Snow, and Doctor Faustus was invited unto the Students that were with him the day before, where they had prepared an excellent banquet for him : which banquet being ended, Doctor Faustus began to play his old pranks, and forthwith were in the place thirteen Apes, that took hands and danced round in a ring together, then they fell to tumble and to vaulting one over another, that it was most pleasant to behold, then they leaped out of the window and vanished away : then they set before Doctor Faustus a roasted Calve's head : which one of the Students cut a piece off, and laid it on Doctor Faustus his trencher, which piece being no sooner laid down, but the Calve's head began to cry mainly out like a man, murther, murther, but, alas, what doest thou to me ! Whereat they were all amazed, but after a while considering of Faustus his jesting tricks they began to laugh, and then they pulled in sunder the Calve's head and ate it up. Whereupon Doctor Faustus asked leave to depart, but they would in no wise agree to let him go, except that he would promise to come again : presently then Faustus, through his cunning, made a sledge, the which was drawn about the house with four fiery dragons : this was fearful for the Students to behold, for they saw Faustus ride up and down as though he should have fired and slain all them in the house. This sport continued until midnight with such a noise that they could not hear one another, and the heads of the Students were so light, that they thought themselves to be in the air all that time.

CHAPTER XLV

How Doctor Faustus shewed the fair Helena unto the Students upon the Sunday following

THE Sunday following came these Students home to Doctor Faustus his own house, and brought their meat and drink with them : these men were right welcome guests unto Faustus, wherefore they all fell to drinking of wine smoothly : and being merry, they began some of them to talk of the beauty of women, and every one gave forth his verdict what he had seen and what he had heard. So one among the rest said, I never was so desirous of anything in this world, as to have a sight (if it were possible) of fair Helena of Greece, for whom the worthy town of Troie was destroyed and razed down to the ground, therefore saith he, that in all men's judgment she was more than commonly fair, because that when she was stolen away from her husband, there was for her recovery so great bloodshed.

Doctor Faustus answered : For that you are all my friends and are so desirous to see that famous pearl of Greece, fair Helena, the wife of King Menelaus, and daughter of Tindalus and Læda, sister to Castor and Pollux, who was the fairest Lady in all Greece : I will therefore bring her into your presence personally, and in the same form of attire as she used to go when she was in her chiefest flowers and pleasantest prime of youth. The like have I done for the Emperor Carolus Quintus, at his desire I shewed him Alexander the great, and his Paramour : but (said Doctor Faustus) I charge you all that upon your perils you speak not a word, nor rise up from the Table so long as she is in your presence. And so he went out of the Hall, returning presently again, after whom immediately followed the fair and beautiful Helena, whose beauty was such that the Students were all amazed to see her, esteeming her rather to be a heavenly than an earthly creature. This Lady appeared before them in a most sumptuous gown of purple Velvet, richly embroidered, her hair hanged down loose as fair as the beaten Gold, and of such length that it reached down to her hams, with amorous coal-black eyes, a sweet and pleasant round face, her lips red as a Cherry, her cheeks of rose all colour, her mouth small, her neck as white as the Swan, tall and slender of personage, and in sum, there was not one imperfect part in her : she looked

round about her with a rolling Hawk's eye, a smiling and wanton countenance, which near hand inflamed the hearts of the Students, but that they persuaded themselves she was a Spirit, wherefore such fantasies passed away lightly with them : and thus fair Helena and Doctor Faustus went out again one with another. But the Students at Doctor Faustus his entering again into the hall, requested of him to let them see her again the next day, for that they would bring with them a painter and so take her counterfeit : which he denied, affirming that he could not always raise up her Spirit, but only at certain times : yet (said he) I will give you her counterfeit, which shall be always as good to you as if your selves should see the drawing thereof, which they received according to his promise, but soon lost it again. The Students departed from Faustus' home everyone to his house, but they were not able to sleep the whole night for thinking on the beauty of fair Helena. Wherefore a man may see that the Devil blindeth and enflameth the heart with lust oftentimes, that men fall in love with Harlots, nay even with Furies, which afterward cannot lightly be removed.

CHAPTER XLVI

How Doctor Faustus conjured away the four wheels from a clown's waggon

DOCTOR FAUSTUS was sent for to the Marshal of Brunswicke, who was greatly troubled with the falling sickness. Now Faustus had this use, never to ride but walk forth on foot, for he could ease himself when he list, and as he came near unto the town of Brunswicke, there overtook him a Clown with four horses and an empty waggon, to whom Doctor Faustus jestingly to try him, said : I pray thee, good fellow, let me ride a little to ease my weary legs ; which the buzzardly ass denied, saying : that his horses were also weary, and he would not let him get up. Doctor

Faustus did this but to prove the buzzard, if there were any courtesy to be found in him if need were.

But such churlishness as is commonly found among clowns, was by Doctor Faustus well requited, even with the like payment : for he said unto him, Thou doltish Clown, void of all humanity, seeing thou art of so currish a disposition, I will pay thee as thou hast deserved, for the four wheels of thy Waggon thou shalt have taken from thee, let me see then how canst thou shift : hereupon his wheels were gone, his horses also fell down to the ground, as though they had been dead : whereat the Clown was sore affright, measuring it as a just scourge of God for his sins and churlishness : wherefore all troubled, and wailing, he humbly besought Doctor Faustus to be good unto him, confessing he was worthy of it, notwithstanding if it pleased him to forgive him, he would hereafter do better. Which humility made Faustus his heart to relent, answering him on this manner, well, do so no more, but when a poor weary man desireth thee, see that thou let him ride, but yet thou shalt not go altogether clear, for although thou have again thy four wheels, yet shalt thou fetch them at the four Gates of the City, so he threw dust on the horses, and revived them again, and the Clown for his churlishness was fain to fetch his wheels, spending his time with weariness, whereas before he might have done a good deed, and gone about his business quietly.

CHAPTER XLVII

*How four Jugglers cut one another's head off, and
set them on again ; and how Doctor Faustus
deceived them*

DOCTOR FAUSTUS came in the Lent unto Franckfort
Fair, where his Spirit Mephostophiles gave him to
understand that in an Inn were four Jugglers that cut
one another's head off, and after their cutting off,
sent them to the Barber to be trimmed, which many
people saw. This angered Faustus (for he meant to
have himself the only Cock in the Devil's basket), and
he went to the place where they were, to behold them.
And as these Jugglers were together, ready one to cut off
the other's head, there stood also the Barbers ready to
trim them, and by them upon the table stood likewise
a glass full of distilled water, and he that was the
chiefest among them stood by it. Thus they began,
they smote off the head of the first, and presently
there was a Lily in the glass of distilled water, where
Faustus perceived this Lily as it were springing, and
the chief Juggler named it the tree of life, thus dealt
he with the first, making the Barber wash and comb his
head, and then he set it on again, presently the Lily
vanished away out of the water, hereat the man had
his head whole and sound again ; the like did they
with the other two : and as the turn and lot came to
the chief Juggler that he also should be beheaded, and
that his Lily was most pleasant, fair, and flourishing
green, they smote his head off, and when it came to

be barbed, it troubled Faustus his conscience, in so much that he could not abide to see another do anything, for he thought himself to be the principal conjurer in the world, wherefore Doctor Faustus went to the table whereat the other Jugglers kept that Lily, and so he took a small knife and cut off the stalk of the Lily, saying to himself, none of them should blind Faustus : yet no man saw Faustus to cut the Lily, but when the rest of the Jugglers thought to have set on their master's head, they could not, wherefore they looked on the Lily, and found it a bleeding : by this means the Juggler was beguiled, and so died in his wickedness, yet not one thought that Doctor Faustus had done it.

CHAPTER XLVIII

How an old man, the neighbour of Faustus, sought
to persuade him to amend his evil life, and to
fall unto repentance

A GOOD Christian an honest and virtuous old man, a lover of the holy Scriptures, who was neighbour unto Doctor Faustus : when he perceived that many Students had their recourse in and out unto Doctor Faustus, he suspected his evil life, wherefore like a friend he invited Doctor Faustus to supper unto his house, unto the which he agreed ; and having ended their banquet, the old man began with these words. My loving friend and neighbour Doctor Faustus,

183

I have to desire of you a friendly and Christian request, beseeching you that you will vouchsafe not to be angry with me, but friendly resolve me in my doubt, and take my poor inviting in good part. To whom Doctor Faustus answered : My loving neighbour, I pray you say your mind. Then began the old Patron to say : My good neighbour, you know in the beginning how that you have defied God, and all the host of heaven, and given your soul to the Devil, wherewith you have incurred God's high displeasure, and are become from a Christian far worse than a heathen person : oh consider what you have done, it is not only the pleasure of the body, but the safety of the soul that you must have respect unto : of which if you be careless, then are you cast away, and shall remain in the anger of almighty God. But yet is it time enough Doctor Faustus, if you repent and call unto the Lord for mercy, as we have example in the Acts of the Apostles, the eighth Chap. of Simon in Samaria, who was led out of the way, affirming that he was Simon homo sanctus. This man was notwithstanding in the end converted, after that he had heard the Sermon of Philip, for he was baptized, and saw his sins, and repented. Likewise I beseech you good brother Doctor Faustus, let my rude Sermon be unto you a conversion ; and forget the filthy life that you have led, repent, ask mercy, and live : for Christ saith, *Come unto me all ye that are weary and heavy laden, and I will refresh you.* And in Ezechiel : *I desire not the death of a sinner, but rather that he convert and live.* Let my words good brother Faustus, pierce into your adamant heart, and

184

desire God for his Son Christ his sake, to forgive you. Wherefore have you so long lived in your Devilish practices, knowing that in the Old and New Testament you are forbidden, and that men should not suffer any such to live, neither have any conversation with them, for it is an abomination unto the Lord ; and that such persons have no part in the Kingdom of God. All this while Doctor Faustus heard him very attentively, and replied : Father, your persuasions like me wondrous well, and I thank you with all my heart for your good will and counsel, promising you so far as I may to follow your discipline : whereupon he took his leave. And being come home, he laid him very pensive on his bed, bethinking himself of the words of the good old man, and in a manner began to repent that he had given his Soul to the Devil, intending to deny all that he had promised unto Lucifer. Continuing in these cogitations, suddenly his Spirit appeared unto him clapping him upon the head, and wrung it as though he would have pulled the head from the shoulders, saying unto him, Thou knowest Faustus, that thou hast given thyself body and soul unto my Lord Lucifer, and hast vowed thyself an enemy unto God and unto all men ; and now thou beginnest to hearken to an old doting fool which persuadeth thee as it were unto God, when indeed it is too late, for that thou art the Devil's, and he hath good power presently to fetch thee : wherefore he hath sent me unto thee, to tell thee, that seeing thou hast sorrowed for that thou hast done, begin again and write another writing with thine own blood, if not, then will I tear thee all to pieces. Hereat Doctor Faustus was sore afraid, and said : My Mephostophiles, I will write again what thou wilt : wherefore he sat him down, and with his own blood he wrote as followeth : which writing was afterward sent to a dear friend of the said Doctor Faustus being his kinsman.

CHAPTER XLIX

How Doctor Faustus wrote the second time with his own blood and gave it to the Devil

I, DOCTOR JOHN FAUSTUS, acknowledge by this my deed and handwriting, that sith my first writing, which is seventeen years, that I have right willingly held, and have been an utter enemy unto God and all men, the which I once again confirm, and give fully and wholly myself unto the Devil both body and soul, even unto the great Lucifer : and that at the end of seven years ensuing after the date of this letter, he shall have to do with me according as it pleaseth him, either to lengthen or shorten my life as liketh him : and hereupon I renounce all persuaders that seek to withdraw me from my purpose by the Word of God, either ghostly or bodily. And further, I will never give ear unto any man, be he spiritual or temporal, that moveth any matter for the salvation of my soul. Of all this writing, and that therein contained, be witness, my own blood, the which with mine own hands I have begun, and ended.

Dated at Wittenberg, the 25th of July.

And presently upon the making of this Letter, he became so great an enemy unto the poor old man, that he sought his life by all means possible ; but this godly man was strong in the Holy Ghost, that he could not be vanquished by any means : for about two days after that he had exhorted Faustus, as the poor man lay in his bed, suddenly there was a mighty rumbling in the Chamber, the which he was never wont to hear, and he heard as it had been the groaning of a Sow, which lasted long : whereupon the good old man began to jest, and mock, and said : oh what Barbarian cry is this, oh fair Bird, what foul music is this of a fair Angel, that could not tarry two days in his place ? beginnest thou now to run into a poor man's house, where thou hast no power, and wert not able to keep thine own two days ? With these and such-like words the Spirit departed. And when he came home Faustus asked him how he had sped with the old man : to whom the Spirit answered, the old man was harnessed, and that he could not once lay hold upon him : but he would not tell how the old man had mocked him, for the Devils can never abide to hear of their fall. Thus doth God defend the hearts of all honest Christians, that betake themselves under his tuition.

CHAPTER L

How Doctor Faustus made a marriage between two lovers

In the City of Wittenberg was a Student, a gallant Gentleman, named N. N. This Gentleman was far in love with a Gentlewoman, fair and proper of personage. This Gentlewoman had a Knight that was a suitor unto her, and many other Gentlemen, the which desired her in marriage, but none could obtain her : So it was that this N. N. was very well acquainted with Faustus, and by that means became a suitor unto him to assist him in the matter, for he fell so far in despair with himself, that he pined away to the skin and bones. But when he had opened the matter unto Doctor Faustus, he asked counsel of his Spirit Mephostophiles, the which told him what to do. Hereupon Doctor Faustus went home to the Gentleman, and bade him be of good cheer, for he should have his desire, for he would help him to that he wished for, and that this Gentlewoman should love none other but him only : wherefore Doctor Faustus so changed the mind of the Damsel by a practice he wrought, that she would do no other thing but think on him, whom before she had hated, neither cared she for any man but him alone. The device was thus, Faustus commanded this Gentleman that he should clothe himself in all his best apparel that he had and that he should go unto this Gentlewoman, and there to shew himself, giving him also a Ring, commanding him in any wise that he should dance with her before he departed. Wherefore he followed Faustus his counsel, went to her, and when they began to dance they that were suitors began to take everyone his Lady in his hand, and this good Gentleman took her, who before had so disdained him, and in the dance he thrust the Ring into her hand that Doctor Faustus had given him, the which she no sooner touched, but she fell immediately in love with him, beginning in the dance to smile, and many times to give him winks, rolling her eyes, and in the end she asked him if he could love her and make her his wife ; he gladly answered, he was content : and hereupon they concluded, and were married, by the means and help of Doctor Faustus, for which he received a good reward of the Gentleman.

CHAPTER LI

How Doctor Faustus led his friends into his Garden at Christmas, and shewed them many strange sights in his nineteenth year

In December, about Christmas in the City of Wittenberg, were many young Gentlewomen, the which were come out of the Country to make merry with their friends and acquaintance ; amongst whom there were certain that were well acquainted with Doctor Faustus, wherefore they were often invited as his guests unto him, and being with him on a certain time after dinner, he led them into his Garden, where he shewed them all manner of flowers, and fresh herbs, Trees bearing fruit and blossoms of all sorts, in so much that they wondered to see that in his Garden should be so pleasant a time as in the midst of summer : and without in the streets, and all over the Country, it lay full of Snow and Ice. Wherefore this was noted of them as a thing miraculous, each one gathering and carrying away all such things as they best liked, and so departed delighted with their sweet-smelling flowers.

CHAPTER LII

How Doctor Faustus gathered together a great army of men in his extremity against a Knight that would have injured him on his journey

DOCTOR FAUSTUS travelled towards Eyszleben, and when he was nigh half the way, he espied seven horsemen, and the chief of them he knew to be the Knight to whom he had played a jest in the Emperor's Court, for he had set a huge pair of Hart's horns upon his head : and when the Knight now saw that he had fit opportunity to be revenged of Faustus he ran upon him himself, and those that were with him, to mischief him, intending privily to shoot at him : which when Doctor Faustus espied, he vanished away into the wood which was hard by them. But when the Knight perceived that he was vanished away, he caused his men to stand still, where as they remained they heard all manner of war-like instruments of music, as Drums, Flutes, Trumpets, and such-like, and a certain troop of horsemen running towards them. Then they turned another way, and there also were assaulted on the same side : then another way, and yet they were freshly assaulted, so that which way soever they turned themselves, he was encountered : in so much that when the Knight perceived that he could escape no way, but that they his enemies laid on him which way soever he offered to fly, he took a good heart and ran amongst the thickest, and thought with himself better to die than to live with so great an infamy. Therefore being at handy-blows with them, he demanded the cause why they should so use them : but none of them would give him answer, until Doctor Faustus shewed himself unto the Knight, where withal they enclosed him around, and Doctor Faustus said unto him, Sir, yield your weapon, and yourself, otherwise it will go hardly with you. The Knight that knew none other but that he was environed with an host of men (where indeed they were none other than Devils) yielded : then Faustus took away his sword, his piece, and horse, with all the rest of his companions. And further he said unto him ; Sir, the chief General of our army hath commanded to deal with you according to the law of Arms, you shall depart in peace whither you please : and then he gave the Knight an horse after the manner, and set him thereon, so he rode, the rest went on foot until they came to their Inn, where being alighted, his Page rode on his horse to the water, and presently the horse vanished away, the Page being almost sunk and drowned, but he escaped : and coming home, the Knight perceived his Page so bemired and on foot, asked where his horse was become ? Who answered that he was vanished away : which when the Knight heard, he said, of a truth this is Faustus his doing, for he serveth me now as he did before at the Court, only to make me a scorn and a laughing stock.

CHAPTER LIII

How Doctor Faustus caused Mephostophiles to bring him seven of the fairest women that he could find in all those countries he had travelled in, in the twentieth year

WHEN Doctor Faustus called to mind, that his time from day to day drew nigh, he began to live a swinish and Epicurish Life, wherefore he commanded his Spirit Mephostophiles, to bring him seven of the fairest women that he had seen in all the time of his travel : which being brought, first one, and then another, he lay with them all, in so much that he liked them so well, that he continued with them in all manner of love, and made them to travel with him in all his journeys. These women were two Netherlanders, one Hungarian, one English, two Wallons, one Francklander : and with these sweet personages he continued long, yea even to his last end.

CHAPTER LIV

How Doctor Faustus found a mass of money when he had consumed twenty-two of his years

To the end that the Devil would make Faustus his only heir, he shewed unto him where he should go and find a mighty huge mass of money, and that he should have it in an old Chapel that was fallen down, half a mile distant from Wittenberg, there he bade him to dig and he should find it, the which he did, and having digged reasonable deep, he saw a mighty huge serpent, the which lay on the treasure itself, the treasure itself lay like a huge light burning : but D. Faustus charmed the serpent that he crept into a hole, and when he digged deeper to get up the treasure, he found nothing but coals of fire : there also he heard and saw many that were tormented, yet notwithstanding he brought away the coals, and when he was come home, it was all turned into silver and gold, as after his death was found by his servant, the which was almost about estimation, a thousand gilders.

CHAPTER LV

How Doctor Faustus made the Spirit of fair Helena of Greece his own Paramour and bedfellow in his twenty-third year

To the end that this miserable Faustus might fill the lust of his flesh, and live in all manner of voluptuous pleasures, it came in his mind after he had slept his first sleep,[1] and in the twenty-third year past of his time, that he had a great desire to lie with fair Helena of Greece, especially her whom he had seen and shewed unto the Students of Wittenberg, wherefore he called unto him his Spirit Mephostophiles, commanding him to bring him the fair Helena, which he also did. Whereupon he fell in love with her, and made her his common Concubine and bedfellow, for she was so beautiful and delightful a piece, that he could not be one hour from her, if he should therefore have suffered death, she had so stolen away his heart : and to his seeming, in time she was with child, and in the end brought him a man child, whom Faustus named Justus Faustus : this child told Doctor Faustus many things that were to come, and what strange matters were done in foreign countries : but in the end when Faustus lost his life, the mother and the child vanished away both together.

CHAPTER LVI

How Doctor Faustus made his Will, in the which he named his servant Wagner to be his heir

DOCTOR FAUSTUS was now in his twenty-fourth and last year, and he had a pretty stripling to his servant, the which had studied also at the University of Wittenberg : this youth was very well acquainted with his knaveries and sorceries, so that he was hated as

---

[1] The German text has " at midnight, when he awoke."

well for his own knaveries, as also for his Master's :
for no man would give him entertainment into his
service, because of his unhappiness, but Faustus : this
Wagner was so well beloved with Faustus, that he used
him as his son : for do what he would his master
was always therewith well content. And when the
time drew nigh that Faustus should end, he called
unto him a Notary and certain masters the which
were his friends and often conversant with him, in
whose presence he gave this Wagner his house and
Garden. Item, he gave him in ready money one
thousand six hundred gilders. Item, a Farm. Item,
a gold chain, much plate, and other household stuff.
This gave he all to his servant, and the rest of his time
he meant to spend in Inns and Students' company,
drinking and eating, with other jollity : and thus he
finished his Will for that time.

CHAPTER LVII

*How Doctor Faustus fell in talk with his servant
touching his Testament, and the covenants
thereof*

Now when this Will was made, Doctor Faustus
called unto him his servant, saying : I have thought
upon thee in my Testament, for that thou hast been
a trusty servant unto me and a faithful, and hast not
opened my secrets : and yet further (said he) ask of
me before I die what thou wilt, and I will give it unto
thee. His servant rashly answered, I pray you let

me have your cunning. To which Doctor Faustus answered, I have given thee all my books, upon this condition, that thou wouldst not let them be common, but use them for thine own pleasure, and study carefully in them. And dost thou also desire my cunning ? That mayest thou peradventure have, if thou love and peruse my books well. Further (said Doctor Faustus) seeing that thou desirest of me this request, I will resolve thee : my Spirit Mephostophiles his time is out with me, and I have nought to command him as touching thee, yet will I help thee to another, if thou like well thereof. And within three days after he called his servant unto him, saying : art thou resolved ? wouldst thou verily have a Spirit ? Then tell me in what manner or form thou wouldst have him ? To whom his servant answered, that he would have him in the form of an Ape : whereupon presently appeared a Spirit unto him in manner and form of an Ape, the which leaped about the house. Then said Faustus, see, there hast thou thy request, but yet he will not obey thee until I be dead, for when my Spirit Mephostophiles shall fetch me away, then shall thy Spirit be bound unto thee, if thou agree : and thy Spirit shalt thou name Akercocke, for so is he called : but all this is upon condition that thou publish my cunning, and my merry conceits, with all that I have done (when I am dead) in an history : and if thou canst not remember all, thy Spirit Akercocke will help thee : so shall the great acts that I have done be manifested unto the world.

CHAPTER LVIII

How Doctor Faustus having but one month of his appointed time to come, fell to mourning and sorrow with himself for his devilish exercise

TIME ran away with Faustus, as the hour-glass, for he had but one month to come of his twenty-four years, at the end whereof he had given himself to the Devil body and soul, as is before specified. Here was the first token, for he was like a taken murderer or a thief, the which findeth himself guilty in conscience before the Judge have given sentence, fearing every hour to die : for he was grieved, and wailing spent the time, went talking to himself, wringing of his hands, sobbing and sighing, he fell away from flesh, and was very lean, and kept himself close : neither could he abide to see or hear of his Mephostophiles any more.

CHAPTER LIX

How Doctor Faustus complained that he should in his lusty time and youthful years die so miserably

THIS sorrowful time drawing near so troubled Doctor Faustus, that he began to write his mind, to the end he might peruse it often and not forget it, and is in manner as followeth.

Ah Faustus, thou sorrowful and woeful man, now

197

must thou go to the damned company in unquenchable fire, whereas thou mightest have had the joyful immortality of the soul, the which thou now hast lost.] Ah gross understanding and wilful will, what seizeth on my limbs other than a robbing of my life ? Bewail with me my sound and healthful body, wit and soul, bewail with me my senses, for you have had your part and pleasure as well as I. Oh envy and disdain, how have you crept both at once into me, and now for your sakes I must suffer all these torments ? Ah whither is pity and mercy fled ? Upon what occasion hath heaven repaid me with this reward by sufferance to suffer me to perish ? Wherefore was I created a man ? The punishment that I see prepared for me of myself now must I suffer. Ah miserable wretch, there is nothing in this world to shew me comfort : then woe is me, what helpeth my wailing.

CHAPTER LX

Another complaint of Doctor Faustus

OH poor, woeful and weary wretch : oh sorrowful soul of Faustus, now art thou in the number of the damned, for now must I wait for unmeasurable pains of death, yea far more lamentable than ever yet any creature hath suffered. Ah senseless, wilful and desperate forgetfulness ! O cursed and unstable life ! O blind and careless wretch, that so hast abused thy body, sense, and soul ! O foolish pleasure, into what a weary labyrinth hast thou brought me, blinding mine eyes in the clearest day ? Ah weak heart ! O troubled soul, where is become thy knowledge to comfort thee ? O pitiful weariness ! Oh desperate hope, now shall I never more be thought upon ! Oh, care upon carefulness, and sorrows on heaps : Ah grievous pains that pierce my panting heart, whom is there now that can deliver me ? Would God that I knew where to hide me, or into what place to creep or fly. Ah, woe, woe is me, be where I will, yet am I taken. Herewith poor Faustus was so sorrowfully troubled, that he could not speak or utter his mind any further.

CHAPTER LXI

*How Doctor Faustus bewailed to think on Hell, and
of the miserable pains therein provided for him*

Now thou Faustus, damned wretch, how happy wert thou if as an unreasonable beast thou mightest die without soul, so shouldst thou not feel any more doubts? But now the Devil will take thee away both body and soul, and set thee in an unspeakable place of darkness : for although others' souls have rest and peace, yet I poor damned wretch must suffer all manner of filthy stench, pains, cold, hunger, thirst, heat, freezing, burning, hissing, gnashing, and all the wrath and curse of God, yea all the creatures that God hath created are enemies to me. And now too late I remember that my Spirit Mephostophiles did once tell me, there was a great difference amongst the damned ; for the greater the sin, the greater the torment : for as the twigs of the tree make greater flame than the trunk thereof, and yet the trunk continueth longer in burning : even so the more that a man is rooted in sin, the greater is his punishment. Ah thou perpetual damned wretch, now art thou thrown into the everlasting fiery lake that never shall be quenched, there must I dwell in all manner of wailing, sorrow, misery, pain, torment, grief, howling, sighing, sobbing, blubbering, running of eyes, stinking at nose, gnashing of teeth, fear to the ears, horror to the conscience, and shaking both of hand and foot. Ah that I could carry the heavens on my shoulders, so that there were time at last to quit me of this everlasting damnation ! Oh who can deliver me out of these fearful tormenting flames, the which I see prepared for me ? Oh there is no help, nor any man that can deliver me, nor any wailing of sins can help me, neither is there rest to be found for me day nor night. Ah woe is me, for there is no help for me, no shield, no defence, no comfort. Where is my hold ? knowledge dare I not trust : and for a soul to Godwards that have I not, for I shame to speak unto him : if I do, no answer shall be made me, but he will hide his face from me, to the end that I should not behold the joys of the chosen. What mean I then to complain where no help is ? No, I know no hope resteth in my groanings : I have desired that it should be so, and God hath said Amen to my misdoings : for now I must have shame to comfort me in my calamities.

CHAPTER LXII

*Here followeth the miserable and lamentable end
of Doctor Faustus, by the which all Christians
may take an example and warning*

IN the twenty-fourth year Doctor Faustus his time
being come, his Spirit appeared unto him, giving him
his writing again, and commanding him to make preparation, for that the Devil would fetch him against
a certain time appointed. D. Faustus mourned and
sighed wonderfully, and never went to bed, nor slept
wink for sorrow. Wherefore his Spirit appeared again,
comforting him, and saying : My Faustus, be not thou
so cowardly minded ; for although that thou losest
thy body, it is not long unto the day of Judgment, and
thou must die at the last, although thou live many
thousand years. The Turks, the Jews, and many
an unchristian Emperor, are in the same condemnation:
therefore (my Faustus) be of good courage, and be
not discomforted, for the Devil hath promised that
thou shalt not be in pains as the rest of the damned are.
This and such-like comfort he gave him, but he told
him false, and against the saying of the Holy Scriptures.
Yet Doctor Faustus that had none other expectation
but to pay his debts with his own skin, went on the
same day that his Spirit said the Devil would fetch
him, unto his trusty and dearest beloved brethren
and companions, as Masters, and Bachelors of Arts,
and other Students more the which had often visited
him at his house in merriment : these he entreated

that they would walk into the Village called Rimlich, half a mile from Wittenberg, and that they would there take with him for their repast part of a small banquet, the which they all agreed unto : so they went together, and there held their dinner in a most sumptuous manner. Doctor Faustus with them (dissemblingly) was merry, but not from the heart : wherefore he requested them that they would also take part of his rude supper : the which they agreed unto : for (quoth he) I must tell you what is the Victualler's due : and when they slept (for drink was in their heads) then Doctor Faustus paid and discharged the shot, and bound the Students and the Masters to go with him into another room, for he had many wonderful matters to tell them : and when they were entered the room as he requested, Doctor Faustus said unto them, as hereafter followeth.

CHAPTER LXIII

An Oration of Faustus to the Students

MY trusty and well-beloved friends, the cause why I have invited you into this place is this : Forasmuch as you have known me this many years, in what manner of life I have lived, practising all manner of conjurations and wicked exercises, the which I have obtained through the help of the Devil, into whose Devilish fellowship they have brought me, the which use the like Art and practice, urged by the detestable provocation of my flesh, my stiff-necked and rebellious will, with my filthy infernal thoughts, the which were ever before me, pricking me forward so earnestly, that I must perforce have the consent of the Devil to aid me in my devices. And to the end I might the better bring my purpose to pass, to have the Devil's aid and furtherance, which I never have wanted in mine actions, I have promised unto him at the end and accomplishing of twenty-four years, both body and soul, to do therewith at his pleasure : and this day, this dismal day, those twenty-four years are fully expired, for night beginning my hour-glass is at an end, the direful finishing whereof I carefully expect : for out of all doubt this night he will fetch me, to whom I have given myself in recompense of his service both body and soul, and twice confirmed writings with my proper blood. Now have I called you my well-beloved Lords, friends, brethren, and fellows, before that fatal hour to take my friendly farewell, to the end that my departing may not hereafter be hidden from you, beseeching you herewith courteous, and loving Lords and brethren, not to take in evil part anything done by me, but with friendly commendations to salute all my friends and companions wheresoever : desiring both you and them, if ever I have trespassed against your minds in anything, that you would all heartily forgive me : and as for those lewd practices the which this full twenty-four years I have followed, you shall hereafter find them in writing : and I beseech you let this my lamentable end to the residue of your lives be a sufficient warning, that you have God always before your eyes, praying unto him that he would ever defend you from the temptation of the Devil, and all his false deceits, not falling altogether from God, as I wretched and ungodly damned creature have done, having denied and defied Baptism, the Sacraments of Christ's body, God himself, all heavenly powers, and earthly men, yea, I have denied such a God, that desireth not to have one lost. Neither let the evil fellowship of wicked companions mislead you as it hath done me : visit earnestly and oft the Church, war and strive continually against the Devil with a good and steadfast belief on God, and Jesus Christ, and use your vocation in holiness. Lastly, to knit up my troubled Oration, this is my friendly request, that you would to rest, and let nothing trouble you : also if you chance to hear any noise, or rumbling about the house, be not therewith afraid, for there shall no evil happen unto you : also I pray you arise not out of your beds. But above all things I entreat you, if you hereafter find my dead carcass, convey it unto the earth, for I die both a good and bad Christian ; a good Christian, for that I am heartily sorry, and in my heart always pray for mercy, that my soul may be delivered : a bad Christian, for that I know the Devil will have my body, and that would I willingly give him so that he would leave my soul in quiet : wherefore I pray you that you would depart to bed, and so I wish you a quiet night, which unto me notwithstanding will be horrible and fearful.

This oration or declaration was made by Doctor Faustus, and that with a hearty and resolute mind, to the end he might not discomfort them : but the

Students wondered greatly thereat, that he was so blinded, for knavery, conjuration, and such-like foolish things, to give his body and soul unto the Devil : for they loved him entirely, and never suspected any such thing before he had opened his mind to them : wherefore one of them said unto him ; ah, friend Faustus, what have you done to conceal this matter so long from us, we would by the help of good Divines, and the grace of God, have brought you out of this net, and have torn you out of the bondage and chains of Satan, whereas now we fear it is too late, to the utter ruin of your body and soul ? Doctor Faustus answered, I durst never do it, although I often minded, to settle myself unto godly people, to desire counsel and help, as once mine old neighbour counselled me, that I should follow his learning, and leave all my conjurations, yet when I was minded to amend, and to follow that good man's counsel, then came the Devil and would have had me away, as this night he is like to do, and said so soon as I turned again to God, he would dispatch me altogether. Thus, even thus (good Gentlemen, and my dear friends) was I enthralled in that Satanical band, all good desires drowned, all piety banished, all purpose of amendment utterly exiled, by the tyrannous threatenings of my deadly enemy. But when the Students heard his words, they gave him counsel to do naught else but call upon God, desiring him for the love of his sweet Son Jesus Christ's sake, to have mercy upon him, teaching him this form of prayer. O, God, be merciful unto me, poor and miserable sinner, and enter not into judgment with me, for no flesh is able to stand before thee. Although, O Lord, I must leave my sinful body unto the Devil, being by him deluded, yet thou in mercy mayest preserve my soul.

This they repeated unto him, yet it could take no hold, but even as Cain he also said his sins were greater than God was able to forgive; for all his thought was on his writing, he meant he had made it too filthy in writing it with his own blood. The Students and the others that were there, when they had prayed for him, they wept, and so went forth, but Faustus tarried in the hall: and when the Gentlemen were laid in bed, none of them could sleep, for that they attended to hear if they might be privy of his end. It happened between twelve and one o'clock at midnight, there blew a mighty storm of wind against the house, as though it would have blown the foundation thereof out of his place. Hereupon the Students began to fear, and got out of their beds, comforting one another, but they would not stir out of the chamber: and the Host of the house ran out of doors, thinking the house would fall. The Students lay near unto that hall wherein Doctor Faustus lay, and they heard a mighty noise and hissing, as if the hall had been full of Snakes and Adders: with that the hall door flew open wherein Doctor Faustus was, then he began to cry for help, saying: murther, murther, but it came forth with half a voice hollowly: shortly after they heard him no more. But when it was day, the Students that had taken no rest that night, arose and went into the hall in the which they left Doctor Faustus, where notwithstanding they found no Faustus, but all the hall lay besprinkled with blood, his brains cleaving to the wall : for the Devil had beaten him from one wall against another, in one corner lay his eyes, in another his teeth, a pitiful and fearful sight to behold. Then began the Students to bewail and weep for him, and sought for his body in many places : [lastly they came into the yard where they found his body lying on the horse dung, most monstrously torn, and fearful to behold, for his head and all his joints were dashed in pieces.]

The forenamed Students and Masters that were at his death, have obtained so much, that they buried him in the Village where he was so grievously tormented. After the which, they returned to Wittenberg, and coming into the house of Faustus, they found the servant of Faustus very sad, unto whom they opened all the matter, who took it exceeding heavily. There found they also this history of Doctor Faustus noted, and of him written as is before declared, all save only his end, the which was after by the Students thereto annexed : further, what his servant had noted thereof, was made in another book. And you have heard that he held by him in his life the Spirit of fair Helena, the which had by him one son, the which he named Justus Faustus, even the same day of his death they vanished away, both mother and son. The house before was so dark, that scarce anybody could abide therein. The same night Doctor Faustus appeared unto his servant lively, and shewed unto him many secret things the which he had done and hidden in his lifetime. Likewise there were certain which saw Doctor Faustus look out of the window by night as they passed by the house.

And thus ended the whole story of Doctor Faustus his conjuration, and other acts that he did in his life ; out of the which example every Christian may learn, but chiefly the stiff-necked and high minded may thereby learn to fear God, and to be careful of their vocation, and to be at defiance with all Devilish works, as God hath most precisely forbidden, to the end we should not invite the Devil as a guest, nor give him place as that wicked Faustus hath done : for here we have a fearful example of his writing, promise, and end, that we may remember him : that we go not astray, but take God always before our eyes, to call alone upon him, and to honour him all the days of our life, with heart and hearty prayer, and with all our strength and soul to glorify his holy name, defying the Devil and all his works, to the end we may remain with Christ in all endless joy : Amen, Amen, that wish I unto every Christian heart, and God's name to be glorified.   Amen.

FINIS

P

FRESCO FROM AUERBACH'S CELLAR IN LEIPZIG

1525

VIVE. RIBE. OBSREGARE . MEMOR FAVSTI HVIVS . ETHVIVS POENÆ : ADERAT CLAVDOHÆC ASTERAT AMPLA . GRADV 1525 . "

FRESCO FROM AUERBACH'S CELLAR IN LEIPZIG

THE
SECOND REPORT

of DOCTOR JOHN FAUSTUS, containing his appearances, and the deedes
of *Wagner*.

VVritten by an English Gentleman
student in VVittenberg an Vniuersity of Germany in Saxony.

PVBLISHED₁ FOR THE DELIGHT
of all those which desire Nouelties by a frend
of the same Gentleman.

LONDON.
PRINTED by ABELL JEFFES, for CUTHBERT
Burby, and are to be sold at the middle Shop at Saint
Mildreds Church by the Stockes. 1594.

UNTO THEM WHICH WOULD KNOW THE TRUTH

I

IT is plain that many things in the first book[1] are mere lies, for proof mark this : it is said that it is translated, so it is, and where it is word for word : But I have talked with the man that first wrote them, having them from Wagner's very friend, wherein he saith many things are corrupted, some added *de nouo*, some cancelled and taken away, and many were augmented. As for addition to the Copy is there where Mephostophiles disputeth of the numbers of Hells, and some other disputations : And let a man mark them duly, they shall find them I will not say childish, but certainly superficial, not like the talk of Devils, where with foldings of words they do use to dilate at large, the more subtle by far. But as for his Obligation[2] and the most part, it is certain they are most credible and out of all question.

II

For to take away a doubt, whether there were such a man, which is generally a thing not believed, I assure them this, that there was, and it is proved thus, nor is Germany so unknown but that the truth of these things following may be found if any suspect.

[1] i.e. *The English Faust Book* which is printed in the present volume.

[2] i.e. Faust's compact with Mephisto.

THE SECOND REPORT

III

First there is yet remaining the ruins of his house, not far from Melanchthon's house as they call at the town's end of Wittenberg, right opposite to the Schools.

IV

Secondly, there is yet to be seen his tree, a great hollow Trunk, wherein he used to read Nigromancy to his scholars, not far from the Town in a very remote place, which I think is sufficient testimony to any reasonable ear. And enquire of them which have been there, see if they will not affirm it. Notwithstanding I do not go by these means, to entreat men to believe, for I care not whether they do or no, but only to certify you of the truth as I myself would be.

V

Next, his tomb is at Mars' Temple, a three miles beyond the City, upon which is written on a Marble stone by his own hand, this Epitaph, which is somewhat old by reason of his small skill in graving.

Hic iaceo Johannes Faustus, Doctor diuini iuris indignissimus, qui pro amore magiae Diabolicae scientiae vanissime cecidi ab amore Dei : O Lector pro me miserrimo damnato homine ne preceris, nam preces non iuuant quem Deus condemnauit : O pie Christiane memento mei, & saltem vnam pro infiducia mea lachrymulam exprime, & cui non potes mederi, eius miserere, et ipse caue.

216

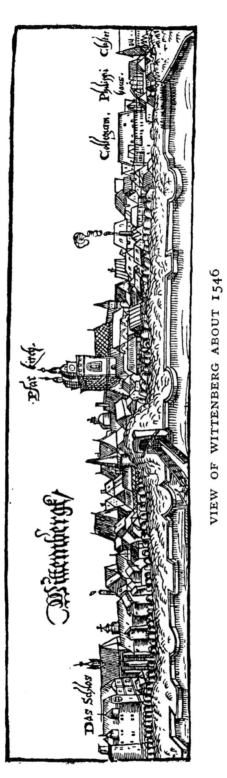

VIEW OF WITTENBERG ABOUT 1546

After a woodcut by Lucas Cranach the Elder

THE SECOND REPORT

The Stone was found in his study, and his will was fulfilled, and he lieth betwixt a heap of three and thirty fir trees in the fort of the Hill in a great hole where this is erected.

VI

If these will not serve, then shall you hear the testimony of a learned man John Wierus, *cap.* 4. *libro* 1. *de magis infamibus.*[1] Which I have translated.

John Faustus, born at Kundling, a little village, learning Magic at Gracovia, where he was openly taught, and exercised it. In sundry places of Germany, with the admiration of many and with manifold lies, fraud, and illusions, with vain vaunting and promises but could do nothing : one example I will shew to the Reader, upon this condition, that he will pass his faith first to me that he will not imitate him : Then rehearseth he one of his knaveries, how he took upon him to make no hair grow upon a man's face, and took away with a powder which I will not name, both the beard that he had and all the skin, causing such inflammations in his face that it burned all over cruelly. This he committed being taken at Batoburg upon the bank of the river Mosa hard upon the bounds of Gelderland : Another (saith this learned Physician) not unknown to me, having a black beard, the rest of his face somewhat dark and swarthy, witnessing melancholy (for he was splenetic) when he came to Faustus, who readily said : Truly I thought you had

[1] V. Introduction.

been my Familiar, straightway marking your feet, whether long and crooked nails stuck out of them : So likening this man to the Devil, which he thought had come unto him, which Devil he was wont to call Sorarius.

VII

For his death in the same place, thus saith he : At length he was found in a Village of the Duchy of Wittenberg by his bedside stark dead, and his face turned backwards, and the midnight before, the house was shaken as it is reported. Thus far he, an Author not to be doubted of, and approved through Christendom of singular and exact judgment, as appeareth by his writings of the like argument confutation.

VIII

More in the same place he saith : That a schoolmaster amongst the Goslaryens, instructed of Faustus the Magician, or rather Infaustus his evil doctrine, learned a way how the Devil might be bound by spell on a glass, who as you may there read was so affrighted, that lying one whole year speechless, at the end he spake of his fear and Devil's appearance, and then having received his Christian rites died.

As for the Author this Doctor Wier, doubt you not of his credit, for he is alleged of the very singularest scholars, as the best that ever wrote in that argument. We have a Gentleman of our own country, master Reignold Scot, Esquire,[1] that doth universally quote

[1] Author of *Discovery of Witchcraft,* 1584.

him as his chief and especial help in his discovery of Witchcraft, yea and he testifieth of him not without good desert, saying : J. Bode[1] in his lawyerly Physic reasoneth contrarily, as though Melancholy were farthest off from these old women whom we call Witches. And the most famous and noble Physician John Wier for his opinion in that behalf : Lo, where he calleth him the most famous Physician as he was then certainly, in the discovery of Witchcraft, *lib.* 3. *Cap.* 7.

IX

Thus far I have set down that you may know and persuade yourselves so far as you see just cause by the reasons.

VALE.

[1] Jean Bodin, author of *Démonomanie des Sorciers*, 1580.

THE SECOND REPORT OF DOCTOR JOHN FAUSTUS

In nomine aeterne & semperuiuae maiestatis, Amen.
Spectatum admissi risum teneatis amici.

CHAPTER I

DOCTOR JOHN FAUSTUS, whose parentage howsoever
hitherto informed, is known to be base, his father
when he was at the best, but the son of a poor Farmer,
his Mother the daughter of one of the same condition,
born in a small village called Kundling in Slesia,
brought up in literature at Gracovia, after at Wittenberg, whose life made him famous, and death notorious:
being thus tormented and torn in pieces, at the time
appointed betwixt the Devils and him, moved by this
example woeful and lamentable enough, the hearts
of the Students and Scholars which were witnesses
of his distraughture, that with an inward terror of
conscience vexed and tormented, they departed and
declared the whole volumes of his detestable life,
which afore his Tragedy was thus acted, were not
known. Christopher Wagner, his familiar servant
unto whom he had committed the secrets of his bosom,
and had intimated unto him whatever his four and
twenty years' familiarity with the black Art, and more

black Devils had taught him : He after the death of
his thus slain Master musing at everything thus done,
everything thus done being wonderful : (as men do
whom fear makes passionate and meditation of former
loss urgeth a latter augment of fresh sorrows) : in
a distraughtful fury (the Company of Students being
departed, which were eye witnesses of the Doctor's
lamentable end) conveyed himself unto his Master's
Library, viewing with sorrowful eyes the only Monuments of his life, the disputations betwixt him and
Mephostophiles, his answers and demands, and else
whatsoever questions moved or disputed of betwixt
the Devils and him, and memorials of his Heavens and
Hells voyages, his conveyance with many the like
comical journeys. The boy of a sudden fell into
a deep considering of his former merriments, sports
and delights, in so much that in this conceit he flung
out of this study, as if he meant to bury the remembrance of these matters by contempt and negligence :
coming into the same Hall wherein his Master's latest
Tragedy was performed, sighing for his want, he
remembered (for as then he lately read it) how that
one Article to the which his Master had bound
Mephostophiles was, that after his death he should be
a Spirit in nature and essence as others were. The Wag
at this began to smile (oh how such things seeming
pleasant make fools' hearts merry) conceiving with
himself how to make his once Master become his man,
and to have the number of his spiritual followers
doubled, scorning the alonely attendance of one servant. To this therefore he determined a time for the
raising of his Master's spirit : and therewith he fell

to read earnestly of other matters, so long that he began
to leave as wearied and wearied began to muse.
Suddenly the air began to receive an alteration and
change with a thick foggy mist, as if it would have
shut up the desired day from man's view, the winds
raged, the thunder lifted up his voice above the
common strain, hail and rain immediately following,
and all these but the ordinary presages of an appearing
Spirit. At this Kit began to tremble, not as afraid
of that which came, but struck with inward horror of
conscience, thinking that no other time had been
appointed to be his doomsday. Suddenly (for always
such haps are sudden) the doors flew open as if they
would have fled from flying, and in all pomp entered
as it were the Prologue of a Comedy, a fellow so short
and little as if he should be of one year, and yet not
so brief as ill-favoured, in his hands a Club, on his
head a Crown of Laurel, riding upon a low Mule,
his name was Gomory, a strong and mighty Duke,
the ruler of six and twenty Legions : and next in
bravery appeared Volac, a great Governor, in the shape
of a Boy with wings like an Angel of Hell, seeming
to be of old rusty iron, riding upon a Dragon with
four heads, in his hands he held a flaming Torch to
give light to the after-comers and beholders : next
after him appeared Asmoday, a King mighty and puissant, ragged and bristled like a Boar on foot, bearing
a banner or a lance. After him issued Lucifer the
King of the Orient with the four Monarchs of his
dominions, betwixt them were two mighty Spaniels
which drew in a fiery Cart Doctor John Faustus,
whom if reason had not better ruled Wagner would

have saluted, for so natural was his semblance, so lively his countenance, as if it had either been a new Faustus, or not the old murdered Faustus, but the fear which his Master's harm put him in, cast him besides the renewing of his old acquaintance, after these came divers others with trumpets and excellent melody.

This right marvellous triumph thus presented, each one did his humble obeisance, the best beginning (though good there were none) and in the end with huge tumult and echoing of trumpets they crowned him a King, which when they had done, with the like ceremonies they conveyed out again the Doctor whom his wretchedness made a King, and his new King-ship nothing. Wagner started as if he had now begun to marvel, amazed at this merry Interlude, having recovered his memory again, he began softly to speak to himself in such-like manner. Is this (quoth he) the honour my Master hath in Hell? Is this the reverence with which the Fiends infernal use to entertain such guests? O ye Spirits of Hell, and ye even now revived Emperors of great Limbus, from whence have you drawn this extraordinary humanity, is it to scorn poor Faustus or to mock Wagner that you shew such reverence to a vile object, what then would they do to Wagner who is worthy to have a fitter servant than their King? At these words he blushed exceedingly, and began to rage very grievously with his conscience's terror, and with some few tears repenting his irreligious conclusion, rose up from the ground, and supposing it to be but an illusion, dream, or a temptation, or else some conceit proceeding from his moist and melancholic fantasy, overpressed with too many vapours, raised up by continual thought into his Pores : wherefore he went forthwith into the streets (so much he distrusted himself) and demanded whether it rained, hailed, or thundered, and it was answered that it neither rained, hailed, nor thundered. Wagner, albeit he was newly revived from a fear, and scarcely thoroughly wakened from this his great terror, yet with this comical jest his decayed spirits began to recover their old strength and power, turning these great braveries of Devils into a merriment, and his conceived fear into a mere fancy. This was the first time that ever Faustus appeared unto his servant Wagner, who recited this unto his companions as a matter of great truth and little moment.

CHAPTER II

How certain drunken Dutchmen were abused by their own conceit and self-imagination, of seeing the grand Doctor, Doctor Faustus

IT shall not be impertinent (my very good friends) to declare as I am bound by a Translator's duty, to shew what these my Dutch friends and Students have imparted unto me, not for that I will be a King of your hearts to command you to believe, but that you may with the rest of the History conceive the common opinion of him in the vulgar's belief here in Germany, as concerning such the like illusions before pretended. About the same time, the next year wherein Faustus was thus handled betwixt six and seven o'clock in the morning, the five and twentieth day of June, 1539, there chanced certain Scholars to the number of nine, and five other Merchants (called of them Copfhmen) two being English, to walk abroad to a little village within four English miles (which is about one of theirs) of Wittenberg called Shaftsburg to the intent to make merry, whither being come they were exceeding pleasant, as Dutchmen are, especially when they be at their good Beer, for they are men very impatient of thirst, wherewith the Italian mocks them saying :

Germani multos possunt tolerare labores,
O vtinam possint tam bene ferre sitim.
Unto which they merrily answer :
Vt nos dura sitis, sic vos Venus improba vexat,
Lex lata est Veneri Iulia, nulla mero.

So long they drank, that at last they came to be within a little of drunk, fetching over the *Green nine Muses*[1] so often at sundry draughts, till they began to be exceeding merry and pleasant, till it being time to depart, so they set out for Wittenberg, and being within a mile or such a matter of the City, they came to a thick Grove called of them the Phogelwald which is Bird's Wood in English, a place somewhat delightsome above any thereabouts, situated upon a top of a very high Hill, but the arms of it spread themselves somewhat lower into the neighbour valleys and meadows, full of very fine Crystalline brooks and springs, which running through the large ranks of trees empty themselves into the Elve, a River which keeps his current

[1] Perhaps a toast.

by Wittenberg ; in this place in a fair Summer sun-shine day, gather together a great number of country maids, servants, and other of the female sex, which they call Phogels (Birds) ; unto them there resort in such-like days, a great number of scholars to meet with these Birds, which exercise Venery either for pleasure, but indeed seldom but for gain, with whom when they have danced a great while (after some odd tune, as after that which they call Robinson's delight, but more truly a jest, though somewhat tolerable) some twenty or thirty or forty couples together, then here steps out one couple, and here another, and get them to such odd corners, as their continual practice doth make known ; on the same day wherein this merry company were wandering, who if I should not much err, I durst say they were most deeply drunk, being a Sun-shining day and having no other way to pass to Wittenberg, but only by this Phogelwald, where they determined to be lusty with some of the Phogels, they came at length to these fore-named places, where as to them it seemed sundry Women dancing, and amongst them divers Scholars, and verily they deemed Magister Doctor Faustus likewise, and seeing diverse maids standing idle, so many as would fit their many, they went to take them by the hands, and as their order is saluting them, to hop a bout or two (for all the high Dutchmens' dances stand upon hopping, turning, winding, and such odd gesture) and as they seemed, they danced at great leisure till this said Faustus came to them, requesting them not to be amazed, for that it was reported he was dead, assuring them in very deed he was not in this

227

World, but had changed it for a better, which if it did please them he would shew unto them, where betwixt their delights and his were no comparison, at his request they were all contented, and he leading the foremost, brought them down into a fair pleasant green, whereon instead of certain flowers grew Pots full of ye best beer, which they tasted on, finding them as good as any that ever they drunk in their whole lives, and farther into a most rich and sumptuous palace, wherein as they seemed they dwelt many days with great mirth and pleasure, till at length one more full of courtesy than the rest thanked Master Faustus for his good entertainment, at which words suddenly was heard so great a noise and howling especially of the poor Doctor, who was immediately reared up into the Air, accompanied with such a sort of black clouds and mists, as therewith not only the sky, but also their eyes were mightily darkened, and they brought into a deep Cavern, wherein besides most soft beds they had nothing to comfort themselves, in which they wallowed and slept till they snorted, some of the Scholars that were present at their departure being in a soberer conceit than the rest, desirous to see whither they would go, followed them fast after, till they espied them on this dirty ease, for instead of beds they were all bewrapped, and some more than half sunk in deep and yielding mire by the river's banks. Whom when they saw in this more than miserable case, moved with pity, conveyed them in Waggons home : and being demanded in the morning (for then they were a little wiser) the occasion of their so great and seldom seen disorder, they declared it from the beginning to the ending, which they were so far from believing, that they counted it as canonical, which when some Students reported unto me, I could not abstain from hearty laughter, not only to see how they had abused themselves, but also others by so fond belief. For I said that in drunkenness, so thick a vapour as riseth from so thick a matter as their Beer, clambering up and spreading itself so universally in the fantasy, maketh it conceive no other impression, but that which the mind, afore it came to be overpressed, was conversant about, and it was evident that in all the talk they had, there was nothing mentioned but only Faustus, and Faustus' merriments, and where a thing is amongst so many so agreeingly talked of, it is likely it should take effect as well in all as in one. Well, I was content to subscribe to their folly rather to satisfy their self-willed conceits, than mine own thought. Many odd pranks Faustus is made the father of, which are either so frivolous as nobody can credit but like frivolous people, or so merely smelling of the Cask, that a man may easily know the child by the Father.

CHAPTER III

Wagner's conference with Doctor Faustus, and how miserably they broke up their disputations

WAGNER one morning arose betimes and departed to Wittenberg, but a small mile from the house, and having purveyed himself of all necessaries, was admitted for a scholar (immediately after his Master was departed out of this World) into the University. Where, for that he was Faustus' true and familiar servant, he was both well and manifoldly acquainted, wherein he remained in all solace amongst a great number of his companions, who then rather frequented his company, not only for that he was Faustus his servant, whose memory was very freshly continued among them, but that they were verily assured that he had a great part of his Master's skill and science, which they honoured with more than lawful reverence.

Upon a day Christopher Wagner (as many times he did) separated himself from his other companions and friends, to ruminate upon his melancholic conceits, erring far in a place full of Trees and the fulness of Trees gave it the name of a Grove, suddenly like as all such chances hap, Faustus or Faustus' Spirit clapped him upon the shoulder, saying: Wagner, good morrow. Wagner availed[1] his Scholar's Bonnet, thinking verily that he was some other Student, but beholding his Master Faustus, he was most terribly affrighted, and stepping aside he began to mumble to himself a *Benedicite*, and crossing himself, rehearsing and saying *CONIVRO TE IN NOMINE PATRIS ET FILII ET SPIRITUS SANCTI*, etc. making Circle, etc.

Faustus rolling his eyes and for mere fury and anger stamping, bound (for so he seemed) with the vehemency of the Exorcism ran about most terribly the brims thereof, that therewith the neighbour ground

[1] Doffed.

did seem to tremble, casting out a blackish slomy[1] sulphury smoke out of his mouth, wherewith the bright air was much darkened, at length appeased, either forced with necessity or knavery, he spake and that very distinctly. Wagner (qd. he) art thou afeared of me as of a Spirit, or infernal Ghost, am not I (ungrateful rascal) Faustus, am not I thy Master Faustus ? quoth Wagner very confidently, what thou wert I know, what also thou art who knows not ? Though once my Master, now thou shalt be my servant, though once my friend and familiar, now I may justly term thee neither, the Laws of Devils hath not made me secure from thy tyranny, and how may thy friendship avail me ? For how can that help which is not ? affections are not amongst Fiends, nor passions amongst Spirits.

Wherefore Faustus if thou wilt that I be thy Master, as whether thou wilt or no, I will Conjure thee, etc. to answer directly and truly to all my questions. Ah Wagner (quoth Faustus) is this the duty of a servant ? dost thou mistrust that in me, which neither I mean nor thou of honest thought and duty oughtest imagine ? And as for affections in Spirits, certainly there is none, but I am none, feel me my good Wagner, behold flesh, blood, and bones, and Spirits have neither flesh, blood, nor bones. Believe me I shall teach thee the nature and essence of Devils, I will teach thee that which neither thou canst desire of me or think *Extra captum humanum*. Then my good Boy Wagner come to me, and use me not as a

[1] Sluggish, or gloomy.

Spirit whose body is nothing but a Spirit, and as Logicians say *Substantia incorporea*, and I will open unto thee the secrets of the World, and Hell, and else whatsoever in the works of Nature. Come my Wagner my son, my darling, my sweet delight, and rejoicing, the only hope of my labours, boldly, lovingly, courteously above all, which am the very same matter and substance I once was, and if thou doubtest as well thou mayest reach thy hand to me, for I cannot mine to thee, and feel whether I am not as I say I am, flesh, blood, and bones : Wagner half astonished at this his fervent speech, yet rather hearing it than believing it : Why Faustus, let me speak to you somewhat more considerately, thou sayest thou art substance, and all substance is heavy, and no heavy thing can ascend upwards, and as thy conference with Mephostophiles doth plainly declare, the place of Spirits is in the Air, in which nothing that is heavy can remain, and therefore thou art not substance or not Faustus. Quoth Faustus, that no heavy things is in the Air is plainly false, for thou seest that material bodies are in the Air, as hail, snow, and other meteors : Whereto Wagner answered : Faustus, they truly are in the Air, not of the Air, and you know the causes of them are terrestrial vapours drawn from the earth by the attractive virtue of the Sun, and therefore they fall down because they are heavy, for were they of the Air as are Spirits, then should they still remain in it, but briefly no violent motion may be called natural, as that heavy material Dew is carried from the earth by a violent and contrary motion : the Sun therefore leaving the Zenith of any Horizon, and coming to the

Nadir oppositely, the material bodies of Dew (as the causes always fail with the effects), and nextly the concretion of Snow and Hail, because they are substance, cannot remain in the light and unheavy Air : Wherefore I have answered thee that thou art either a Spirit or not substance. I wondered when I read this discourse, with what patience the Doctor could endure so long an argument, but it proved otherwise, for the Doctor brake forth into these speeches, unable to contain himself any longer. Wagner, thou seemest to gather natural arguments of Metaphysical effects, I say unto thee Wagner sith thou art thus far entered into a Philosophical discourse, that I being as I am Faustus, may be, for so I am, a dweller in the profound Abyss of the Air, whose compass is measurable in this, that it is not measurable : For let us speak according to men naturally, the rather to fit thy capacity, we see that in the regiment of man's body, the man is of quality like to the predominant complexion and Element, as if Choler abound, the man is light, nimble, and for a while furious, seldom strong, ready to meddle, and carried away with phanatick illusions : If Blood abound, he is ruddy, fair, gentle, etc. *Et sic de reliquis.* If therefore the predominant Element is able so much to change the nature of man, as to make it above the rest capable or incapable, the same reason maketh that this body of mine which thou seest, being governed and predomineered by that quick and ready spirit and soul which makes a man immortal, is no hindrance why this corporal reality of me should accompany my Spirit, not as a body, but as a part of the same Spirit ; and otherwise *Wagner,* the whole world is in the Air, and as it were the centre of the Heavens, and what substances soever is made, Fishes which dwell in the deep Seas except (and yet not always) are moved in the Air, Kit, believe me I am as thou seest Faustus and the same very same.

Wagner almost at the last cast, said, we dispute not what you are Faustus, but what by reason you may be. Well, answered Faustus, seeing thou wilt not believe, nor give any credit to my sayings, and which I prove by arguments, I hope thou wilt believe thine own eyes, and if thou seest what I say unto thee, thou wilt neither be obstinate nor incredulous, and rather than Wagner (whom I do love as myself) should be carried away with so palpable an Heresy, behold Wagner and believe, and straightways he drew his knife, the Prologue of his knavery, and looking first upon Wagner, and next on the weapon which he had in his hand, as if with his eyes he would have moved him to some pity, and moved them to be witnesses of the truth, he struck himself into his thigh twice or thrice, and after his strokes followed blood so hastily, as if it would have overtaken the injurious worker of his effusion : which blood Faustus received in a silver Bowl, and staunching his wound, but not until the blood might be seen over the Cup-brims, then Faustus lifted the blood on high saying : See here the witness of the truth, Wagner take it, look how fresh it is, it is not that which comes from a Spirit, it is blood both in nature and colour, and if this be not enough to make thee believe that which I do tell thee, it boots not, there is not any truth at all.

I thought it enough for an extemporal Dis[1] and controversy, I thought the scholar had heard as well and as long as the Doctor had taught, but yet he had not ended. Wagner receiving the Cup and looking on the blood, beheld him without saying anything, shewing by his silence his meaning. Faustus minding to revenge and recompense Wagner his unbelief, nay further (quoth he) feel my hand, tell me whether it hath not the natural heat and essential solidity : then immediately he stretched forth his arm. Wagner with sudden ecstasy of joy carried away, ran to embrace his old Master, as his new friend, whom when Faustus had encircled he fell to beating the poor Scholar most miserably, that Wagner's pitiful roaring seemed to be an Echo to the Doctor's blows, now (quoth Faustus) hereafter be learned either to be more wary or less mistrustful, and therewith laughing effusedly vanished away, leaving Wagner to be a witness (yet almost half dead with his buffeting) of their conference, and that he was a good substantial Burgess of Hell : Wagner, poor Boy, for the space of seven hours not able scarce of himself to stir or to take breath, and without much stirring either of hand or foot, whereby any able life might be conjectured : At length lifting up his head and sighing a little (for a little was as much as he could do at that time), he reared himself up, and laying his head upon his hand and his hand upon the ground, he after sighs sent out most sorrowful groans, and after groans some feeble words, as he after reported it to his companions and familiar acquaintance : to accuse either his Master's

---

[1] Possibly *discourse* or *disputation*.

rigour or his own folly, he thought as merely vain as little prevailing : Wherefore comforting himself with his misery, because he was comfortless, rose up, and looking for the cup of blood (for the gain of the silver moved him) : In place whereof he found his Cap full of piss, and all beraied,[1] sore ashamed and sore withal, so well as he might, which was sorely enough, he rose up, and what by creeping and going he got home to his Chamber, where he abode till he had recovered his health again.

Thus was his Philosophical incredulity recompensed with rustical cruelty, such was the good love of the Spirit that for a long space after he was not able to walk out his Chamber. This did he affirm for most certain truth, and to his saying added his beaten skin, a testimonial and witness to his familiarly beloved acquaintance, one of the which recounted it all summarily in a Letter from Wittenberg to me, where I was at Lyptzig, knowing that I intended to certify my friends in England of a matter so notable and strange, and worthy of memory, and augmented by Fame more than of very deed, for the idle-headed fellows having gotten such a notable fellow as Faustus to Father their lies upon, ceased not daily and hourly to beget new children, but they cost very little nursing and bringing up, they had the wide World, a very good Grandam where they might feed their fill : As for the disputations betwixt those two in this place, and those which you shall find in other places likewise abundantly, consider from whose brains they proceed, for you must give the German leave to shew

[1] Dirtied.

236

his Art, for wit for the most part they have very little, but that which they toil for like Cart Horses. But in all their doings you shall easily perceive if anything be in them excellent, either with how much liking and urging they bring it forth or how it is wetted over with dropping of the Tap exceedingly.

CHAPTER IV

Wagner's cozenage committed upon the sellers of his Master's goods

ACCORDING to the Law of the country the goods of Faustus were to be confiscate and applied to the Treasury, by an Edict published against Conjurers by Sigismund, Duke of Saxony. According to the tenor thereof Faustus' goods were to be alienated, but Wagner so handled the matter that the spear being stuck up,[2] and his goods set to be sold, Wagner had provided bidders and money of his own, the one were such as never were seen more, and the other but round counters. The Messengers being thus cozened by Wagner, durst not for shame report it, nor he for fear of further punishment vaunt of it : the one contented to put up the loss quietly, and the other to enjoy them without further contradiction.

[1] The sign of an auction in ancient Rome.

CHAPTER V

The description of Vienna

FAME had so far carried the report of Faustus' death, as it had the memory of his life, and for by continual motion rumours increase, as saith the Heroical fountain of Latin verse Virgil,

Mobilitate viget viresque acquirit eundo.

In Austrich these news were very frequent, being a Province mightily replenished with people, and marching upon the hems of the Hungarian, is a near neighbour to the most cruel Dog and tyrant the Turk. In Vienna, a City of the same, by which, as the Thames by London, the great and often but never enough praised River of great Danuby keeps his current, the City itself (being every way bigger then the fair City of London) within the Walls, the head of the City resteth upon the mountain of Orstkirken, the front displayeth the wide plains upon the descendant of the same Hill, but she washes her feet in the River : her body and her breast covering the large valley lying betwixt Hill and Hill, not far into the City the Danuby is derived into two arms, which by running about a certain Hill, of some half mile and more, meet at length again in the same Channel : in this Island is the Duke's Court, out of which are two and thirty marvellous goodly stone Bridges, intending to either side of the City : at the very promontories' ends, stands two no less fair, than high and strong Castles, in this place did the Duke keep his Court, with very great royalty, unto whom when this was reported, hearing of a certain that Wagner had great store of his Master's skill and whatsoever, he caused one that in such matters is commonly commanded, to ride to Wittenberg, to the intent to hear the truth, for many things more than the truth were certified unto him : the messenger without delay (because the journey was long) departed and left the Court, and we him a while.

CHAPTER VI

A long discourse betwixt the Devil and Wagner, and ended with a good Philosophical repast

WAGNER solitary musing in his Chamber and conversing with many multitudes of thoughts, suddenly appeared Mephostophiles, his master's Familiar, after him Akercocke, which was Wagner's, and after all Faustus : Quoth Mephostophiles, what cheer ? Sirrah such as you see, we are as we were and never the better : and welcome Akercocke, but my very good Faustus, that you come at this time I rejoice. So then they all sat down, and sat right against him. Then entered in divers delicate viands, and there not then to be ended, with unseen Symphonies of Music. Then spake Wagner and said *Claudite iam riuos*, now we have satisfied our appetite with meat, I pray you hear me with patience, for I have a thing in my mind of which I would fain be resolved, but because you so foully, and so often foully entreated my Master, for demanding some questions, you shall ratify this Article with me again. I. *That in my demands you shall answer truly and patiently*, for what hurt can redound to you by answering of a question, seeing if you are sure of anything you may hold fast, a question cannot take it away : Without delay these good fellows confirmed the Article with a great oath : but he would take their simple word without surety, he knew their honesty so well. Then Wagner pulling down his Cap into his eyes, and leaning upon his elbow a while, and throwing up his eyes to heaven, and then sighing, at length folding his arms within themselves, sat still a little time, then spitting a little and fetching a hearty hem, with a good courage spake unto them thus.

Sirs, it is not unknown unto you how dear I have always accounted of my Master, whose condition is as far from that it was as mine from yours, for which I have more often lamented his departure than mine own misery, being once every way a man, so thoroughly instructed with the weapons of all Sciences, that in all the world hardly his peer could be found, so that your victory over such a man is more to be wailed than over many a thousand such as I am. To be short, that you may understand whither I will go without further Oration. Wherefore I desire you, I pray you, nay I by your Article command you, that you declare unto me truly without collusion, whether that Faustus here present in that state wherein he now is, may come again to be a living man amongst us, either his old shape renewed, or he in a new : For some Philosophers

LUTHER'S HOUSE AND SURROUNDINGS IN THE YEAR 1611

THE CASTLE OF WITTENBERG IN THE YEAR 1611

say, and some Divines, as Origenes and Tertullian, and whether they say truly or no I know not, that no sooner the soul of man departeth from one but that it both enter into another. Wherefore I considering with myself thus much, and often for his cause that he may not only be Faustus, but also a living man and dweller upon the earth, to enjoy not only those graces which through his great deserts he had lost, but also according to his infinite knowledge, multiply them through God's favours again and again abundantly. And though you shall perhaps deny that the same Individual cannot be again so resuscitated, yet that Numero it may in spite of you all, I know it may : for we do not doubt that the same Individual may Numero be again regotten, because that after seven and thirty thousand years, the heavenly constellation shall be in every point *per totum* the same then that now it is, according to Plato and the Astronomers. And therefore we shall be ye same in Numero, and shall sit in this or that school or place as now we do, that is in that *Magno anno*, in that great year : Whereupon Plato said, that after the great year he should return to Athens, and should there read : Because the constellation shall happen so, therefore that returning, the same effects shall with them likewise return. Now having heard my resolution, answer me to my first proposition in full and amply, as that I may be satisfied. At the conclusion of this speech Faustus turned his head aside laying it betwixt his hands hiding it, so sat a great while. Akercocke he frisked up and down, for he had neither clog nor chain, because he was in the number of the wild ones, and over the table and back

242

again. Akercocke was the familiar which Faustus gave to Wagner who asked him in the fashion of an Ape. Such cranks, such lifts, careers and gambalds,[1] as he played there, would have made a horse laugh. Mephostophiles who as it seemed was the speaker of ye Parliament in hell, rose and walked about very hastily, at length he came to the table and striking his fist on it (the print was seen two years after, and was carried to S. Marget's church for a relique, to shew what a hot fellow the Devil is in his anger) and again beating said, thou, and then left, and came and went, and came and went again, here he takes me one book and hurls it against a Cupboard, and then he takes the Cupboard and hurls it against the wall, and then he takes the wall and throws it against the house, and the house out at the Window. Pacifying his rage at the length, rolling his eyes, and seeming to beat his teeth together, sat down further off, and thus quietly spake with a loud voice. Were it not Wagner that our solemn vow forbiddeth to disturb or torment thee for any demands, this thy fond pride should be rewarded with most intolerable punishments : As for the question, I will answer thee more substantially than such a foolish doltish one doth require. And for that we have day enough before us, I will travel further in it then ye gravity of the argument can require, if it be but that thou mayest see how great an Ass thou art, which canst imagine so gross a matter in thy more gross head : As for thy great Peer,[2] be it as you expect it you, in the mean we will enjoy him and thee at our pleasure in despite of God and

---

[1] Gambols.   [2] i.e. Faust, or perhaps *Year*.

Heaven and all his imperial armies of saints. Thy question is this : *Whether the Spirit of a damned man can return into the body of another man.* To which I answer Negatively, it cannot.

1. If this were to them granted, then they should observe and keep the Embryons in the Womb of the mother, that they might constitutively unite themselves to it, to have at the leastwise, sensual consolation and delectation.

2. Then secondly, because it is common to reasonable creatures to fashion and informate the body, and to perfect it with some natural delightment, not to vex it.

3. Then thirdly, because of the law and order of Nature, the souls from the places in their departure to them allotted, assigned and deputed of God, neither do nor can depart at any time : for it is written : For the soul is a Spirit going and returning. And they which do otherwise hold opinion are to be accused, nay condemned in this with Pythagoras, who did abstain from all living Animals and creatures, believing that in some the souls of some men did dwell and abide. Thus far the Arrogonian named Bartholomew Sybilla,[1] a Monopolitan, who writ upon this question being at Wittenberg, at the request of him that did set forth the Dutch Copy, shews himself to be a good Philosopher and no worse Divine. But mark what follows, this is written according to men in faith : the Devil was out of the first street of Coany when he was past this last period. For that Pythagorical opinion, if that were : this absurdity would follow : (I will

[1] Author of *Speculum Peregrinarum Questionum,* 1493.

speak plainly the rather to fit thy capacity), and if the soul should pass out of the dead into the living, then should mortality be the cause of the soul's immortality (this is prettily spoken) and by that means make it corruptible, which cannot be. And seest thou Wagner ? for I will teach thee by demonstrations, and therewith he took a coal of fire, and held it to him so long that it came to be but a coal, now thou seest Wagner, that so long as fire was in this subject it had life, but the quality being removed from the quantity, neither is the quality found or seen or known whither it vanisheth, nor can the same fire though fire may return into another body or subject albeit the quantity remaineth. Thus may the soul of man be compared to the fire in the coal, as concerning his entrance and departure, but not re-entrance, for that coal may take life again, that is fire, but so cannot human body, because one spirit can be united but to one body, and not two to one, nor one spirit to two bodies : Wherefore that Spirit being departed, it is irrevocable because of the unity, and the impossibility of returning in the one, in the other of receiving any other. As for other reasons directly by circumstance, if the Soul goeth either to joy or pain immediately, then I am certain that that hope which thou hast is so merely vain, as anything which may hap under that title : For proof behold, and then through the Wainscot door of Wagner's study entered in two Kings, which drawing their swords did there in presence combat together fiercely and courageously, one of them shortly after fainting under the adversary's strokes fell down, the other victorious, yet wounded, very canonically as a man may say, staggered immediately, as if he would fain have not fallen, yet for all that, he fell; then entered two men carrying Torches with the snuffs downwards, with great solemnity (more than is needful to be recapitulated, for I see nothing but that this might have been very well left out for anything worthy the gravity of the matter) which when they had carried out the first slain combatant, with armed men, and a dying stroke of the Drum, clothed all in the colour which best notes by his external hue the internal sorrow. Then next there entered two Pages all in silver white, crowned with Bays, carrying their Torches aloft declaring the height of their glory by the height of their flames: next to them divers Trumpeters and all in white, urging forth into the vast air their victorious flourishes, next a great standard bearer, and I cannot tell what, but the conclusion was, that the triumph was exceeding great and pompous, adorned with as many ceremonies as such a victory might or could be, the Spirit when they were all gone began to speak and said, this was the battle which was fought for the great Realm of Asia, by Hercules and Orontides, where Orontides was slain, and Hercules sore wounded, but yet recovered, after which he achieved his twelve labours, and the thirteenth of which the Poet speaketh, the hardest of all.

> *Tertius hinc decimus labor est durissimus, una*
> *Quinquaginta simul stuprauit nocte puellas.*

This History is as I do think in the Chronicle of Hell, for I did never hear of it before, nor anybody else, I appeal to all the Histories. Marry it may be this was when Hercules was a little Boy, and then peradventure indeed the records make no mention of it, but yet we have that recorded which he did when he was less than a little Boy, as his killing of a Serpent in his Cradle, and such a History as I do remember is enrolled in the golden Book of the seven wise Masters of Rome, an authentical author. But let that pass and let us draw more near unto the cause : For as the Devil was afore our days, so by authority he may allege experience, and we must of necessity believe that it is either true or a lie. Mephostophiles continued his speech for all this parenthesis, declaring to Wagner his meaning in this point for (quoth he) as you see these two champions contending for the title of victory, one of them must needs, if they try the extremest as they did, receive the dishonour, the other the glory, so in the combat wherein the dying body battleth with the lively soul, the soul, if grace hath made acceptable, shall enjoy those everlasting pleasures of Paradise, and dwell in heaven blessed and glorious amongst the beautiful Angels, but if it be counted as reprobate and outcast of God, then according to that punishment which his great sins did deserve, he can have no other place but the continual horror of hell, wherein we miserable dwell, and the ugly company of black Devils and his frightful Angels. There is no other mean but honour or dishonour in this case, no other mean but joy or pain, no other mean but heaven or hell perpetually : there is no place left for a third. I could more copiously dispute of this matter, but that I will not be too tedious in so exile[1] a question. For where it is said in an author

[1] Poor, attenuated.

to which I am witness, for I stood by his elbow when he writ the lines. *Animae sunt in loco certo et expectant iudicium neq; se inde possunt commouere.* Which place as appeareth in the precedent chapter is heaven or hell: again it is said *Anima quae pecauerit ipsa morietur.* Of necessity then the soul to whom the Lord imputeth not his sin shall live, for they are immediate oppositions, for the soul that is in joy will not come to these troubles, nor that which is in torment cannot: therefore it is said: *Et reuertatur puluis in terram quemadmodum erat, et spiritus reuertatur ad Dominum qui dedit illum,* so there is no mention in any scripture of the soul's returning, but to a certain place deputed of God to him. But before I go any further in ye declaring of that which is here to be set down, I know they that have their consciences more of the precise cut, will say, that here was a learned Devil, true it is he is learned, strong, and above all human conceit, subtle and crafty: and if they say it is blasphemously done to have the word spoken to the world by so vile a mouth, first they know how mightily the Devil is conversant in holy writ, in anything to overthrow a Christian thought, knowing that as ye word of God is a word of power to attain salvation to whom grace is given: and to work eternal damnation where that gift is wanting, knowing it is the only means to debel[1] and conquer the Christian thought, for as a man is governed by a law and by it lives, so if anything be evidently directed against him in it, it slays his heart, it overthrows him, it takes away his power for ever, nor is it more blasphemous to be spoke to us men, than

[1] Subdue.

to God himself, as it is in S. Alathero, where the Devil was not afeard, to assail his creator with most terrible arguments of the divine letter. They which have right minds can persuade themselves accordingly : but otherwise they may cavil as long as they will, which they may do to their small profit, assuring them this that in coveting by fault finding to seem learned, they make themselves the notes and reproach not only of the learned, but even of the absurd and barbarous rude fools, and that they are the only spirits of error and contention, and the chief causes of unbelief by vain reasonings and questions to the unresolved Christian. But as for this speech which is but *Humile dicendi genus* in very truth, let them thus think, that if there were any such controversy betwixt Wagner and his Spirit, as is here mentioned, that those are not the words which were spoken, but that they do proceed from a young Scholar who gave me this copy, and not of a Devil, of whose familiarity and frequency and of other circumstantive causes, I will God willing in the Catastrophe and conclusion of this Book deliver unto you my poor opinion. In the meanwhile I will follow the matter into which we are fallen, my good friends, and without further ado I pray without any more excusive phrase, patiently expect the good hour wherein the death of this volume is prepared : Mephostophiles taking breath a little, presented his speech saying : it is said likewise. *Factum est autem vt moreretur mendicus, etc. And it came to pass that the beggar died, and was carried away of Angels into Abraham's bosom, and that rich man died and was buried, and he being in Hell lifted up his eyes,*

249

when he was in torments, and saw Abraham afar off and Lazarus in his bosom. Nor nothing doth that impugn which is said of the Papist, that he cannot come into God's presence nor be one of the elect unless they be purified from their sins, for which purification, they ordain a place so terribly stuck with pins, needles, daggers, swords, nails, etc., so soultring[1] with hot burning furnaces, and so every way formidable with material sulphury fires, that no tongue can express, nor any heart imagine, wherein the sinful soul must be many times and often cleansed, but I hope if this were true then Lazarus should have been likewise so dressed in their terrible imagined terrors, which he was not, unless they will be so impudent to say that he had no sin. I shall not need to dispute how absurd it is to say that the sin of the soul in the body committed, must be extirpated and purified by a material substance and rigour, nor of the matter of the like argument. And hereupon he seemed to sigh as if some sudden thought had overpressed his stomach. I can, quoth he, largely discourse of all divine and human propositions, but as the unlearned Parrot who speaketh oft and much, and understandeth never anything to profit himself. Ah that unto us Spirits no secrets are secret, no doings of man unhid, and yet we Devils cursed of God are incapable of any of God's mercies, though through them we were created. We know repentance is the way to attain the celestial favour : we know God's mercies how great they are, and that we ought to despair of nothing, yet there is nothing (such is our seeing blindness) so it

---

[1] Sweltering.

appertain to God and godliness, of which we do not despair. No, Wagner, we are so far from living again, as we are from certainty to be saved. But instead of that we are crossed with all kind of vexation, for since the first time that I with my Master and fellows fell down from heaven, being of the most royal order of Angels, Potestates, Cherubins, and Seraphins, riding upon the wings of the Wind in all bright shining Majesty, and enjoying the most glorious and divine presence of our Creator, till for our heart-swelling pride, and haughty insolency, within as little space of time as we were created in, with his dreadful lightning threw us down headlong into the bottomless Abysses of the Air, wherein we endure these tortures and like wicked souls with us, as our manifold deserts have brought upon us. And for that we know that the way to mercy is utterly denied, and that we are as much hated of ourselves as of God, we think it the sweetest remedy in these manifold miseries to have partakers of our common woe with us. Wherefore it is most expedient for us to be thus enviously malicious against all mankind, making them too as far in God's dreadful curse as ourselves.

Wagner melting at these words, his eyes undid the great burthen of his sorrow, straining himself so long that he wept, and yet could say nothing, but only a small volley of sobs hastily following : Mephostophiles seeing how Wagner was drowned in so deep a melancholy, told him pulling him by the sleeve, that he would be still demanding of such foolish questions which will profit him so little as mought be. Knowest thou not (quoth he) that all the Rhetorics are the servants of my tongue, or that we can move pity or hatred when we please, fool as thou art, forget these vain conferences, persuade thyself that they are but the effect of speech, long canst thou not live, and yet dost thou live as if thou didst not long : youthly should be thy thoughts, and fraught with the rank lustiness of conceit and amorous delight, if thou wilt ask questions, let them be such as appertain to love and wealth, to pleasure, to pastime, and to merriment. How sayest thou to such a one, naming a Gentlewoman, the most beautiful Lady under the cope of Heaven ? Thou shalt enjoy her, nay, anyone so she be one whom thou lists to call beautiful, whosoever thy eyes shall lay their delight upon. And presently Music was heard so sweet, so plenteous, and so ravishing, as if on Music depended all sweet, all plenty, all ravishment. The doors conveying themselves aside, as giving place to so divine a fairness, entering in a blue Velvet Gown raised, and thickly beset in the gards[1] with most pure Ooches[2] of gold, not altogether ignorant of precious stones, furred with royal Ermines, loose about her : her head's ornament (though greater ornament to her head than her head there could not be) was a kind of attired Caul (such as I have seen none in England according to their description) raised up at the corners with stiff square wires of beaten gold, on that a Chaplet or frontier of Roses, on the Chaplet a veil of Lawn, which covered all her fair body denying the sight of such an Angel, but only through a shadow : In brief

---

[1] Ornamental border, or trimming.
[2] *Ouch* or *nouch* was a kind of brooch.

she was such a one as would have roused the basest desire in the whole World to attempt wondrous enterprises, in her hands silken soft, she held a Lute, discoursing sweetly upon the solemn strings with her nimble fingers. A maid carrying a blue waxen Taper in a silver white Candlestick made in the fashion of a Censer, but it was derived into two several branches, in whose ends were curiously wrought two most beautiful places to pight[1] tapers on. The maid by her Lady would have well contented a reasonable proper Squire, it was a pretty rank lass, round about as plump as a Bladder, which being yet smoking new is blown up with Wind : well I will not trouble you with these rude descriptions any longer, but desire you to conceive the excellency of this fair Lady, for it is far more copious in the Dutch Copy than is here necessary to be recapitulated. Wagner's heart leaping at this sight looked about him, as if he would have nobody privy to himself but himself, and so it was indeed, for Faustus, Mephostophiles, and Akercocke were gone, and thereupon with a boon courage advancing himself upon his toes, and weeding himself in the best German fashion, as he could very well, began to travel unto her, but remembering his bad apparel stepped back and blushed, and hid his face, but suddenly returning again as if he had known now how rather to become his weeds, began to fewter[2] himself, but, O wonder, his habit was changed with his thought, and he was now no more Wagner but Armisuerio the Lady's Lord. And to be short this new Armisuerio and old Wagner met with the Lady,

---

[1] To pitch.   [2] Brush up.

and saluting her in the best kind of *Bon noche*,[1] used her as he would do his Lady, and she him as her Lord. So passing over their weary night in such pleasure as I could find in my heart to enjoy, or any Man (unless an Eunuch beside).

CHAPTER VII

The arrival of the Messenger at Wittenberg, and the description of Wagner

IT is time to wind about another furrow with our sweating Team and bring our speech to another matter, entering out of one into another, for change is sweet. Not forgetting by the way the Pursuivant, or, as we may better call him, a Messenger, who lately departed from Vienna in Austria, and I think by that time this disputation was finished, had almost overtaken all the way betwixt him and home, which was some fifteen days' travel, after five German miles to the day's labour, and arrived at Wittenberg, by enquiry came to Wagner's chamber, which was in the way as ye go to the Public Schools, as ye go from Melanchthon's house, a pretty house and of a reasonable large size built of hewn stone, and environed with a good thick Wall, of some three foot and a half thick and twenty high, at the bottom guarded about with a good broad Mount of seven yards over, and round about very large and secret walks, far from all company and resort, and there

---

[1] Good night (Spanish).

he might talk without fear with the Devil and his Dam too, thither this fellow coming, knocked peremptorily at the door, Wagner was even now gone to his study and rising up in a Pedlar's chafe,[1] that he should go to his book, especially if it were goodness not once in a month, and yet then to be troubled, he swore a little thing would make him never study more, it should not, but putting on his cloak and his hat, came down and unbolted the door : Unto whom the Messenger seeing such a pretty jolly fellow did some little of reverence, Wagner as yet scarce having let down his choler, stepped back, and perceiving him wear such a Weed as Serjeants there do use to wear, thinking with himself that some had come from the prince for cozening of his servants, shut the door upon him and went pouting and swearing and pitifully chafing, that if the knave offered to sue him, he would surely kill him at the least, down he fetched a good Bastinado and set it behind the door and opened it again, and demanded somewhat mildly what he had to say unto him, to whom the Messenger said, that he came from the Arch-Duke of Austria from Vienna, who willing to hear some certainty of his Master, did send for him assuring himself, that not only he could satisfy his desire in that matter, but also shew him as much skill as ever his Master had. Wagner hearing the purpose of his message with good effectual words, thanked him again, and rendered most serviceable reverence to his good Lord and Master for remembering so gently of his poor servant, etc. Desiring him to tarry until he might set everything in

[1] Rage, temper.

due order and he would not fail to go with him. The Messenger did not deny him, and so they went up together into their Chamber, whom ever after the Messenger loved dearly for his proper behaviour and personage, for indeed Wagner was a very goodly young man, being about the common stature, straight and reasonably slender, well trussed, his hair very yellow and his face fair, his beard which did but now express the blossoms of his lusty courage of ye like yellow, well-mannered, as having been brought up amongst the finest and best sort of Devils : having a pleasant filed tongue, and would make the dainty Rhetoric come as smoothly out of his mouth as an arrow out of a piece of paper, well could he talk of amorous devices, and entreat the bravest Ladies with sweet entertainment, in truth by report he was a Gentle-like man, and accomplished with as many fine parts as a better man than he might justly vaunt of : he could play upon any fine Instrument, and was not ignorant of any laudable exercises, carrying a brave lusty conceit even to his death : and furnished with many proportions of art, there was nothing wanting in the man but a Godly mind.

CHAPTER VIII

The Tragedy of Doctor Faustus seen in the Air, and acted in the presence of a thousand people of Wittenberg. An. 1540

IN a brave summer Sunshine day, the whole people of Wittenberg being gathered together, to behold certain matches for the Garland who could drink most, and also to see a match shot at a pair of Butts with Harquebusiers, as their order is, in a low meadow hard by the Elve : which now being on his freshest pride was full of fine and sweet flowers, being in the latter end of the month, wherein the Sun departs from the last embracings of *Gemini.* On a sudden there was seen a marvellous bright and glorious Rainbow, spreading the wide arms over the wide World, and straight was there heard a noise of Trumpets, sounding a short flourish, and then another, and by and by another, all alike short, at the which the assembly was wondrously affeard, and listened, desirous to see the effect of this wonder and strange miracle, some of them fell to their *Ave Maries* lustily, thinking that the universal Doom had been at that instant, as thus they beheld with admiration, they might distinctly perceive a goodly Stage to be reared (shining to sight like the bright burnish gold) upon many a fair Pillar of clearest Crystal, whose feet rested upon the Arch of the broad Rainbow, therein was the high Throne wherein the King should sit, and that proudly placed with two and twenty degrees to the top, and round about curious wrought chairs for divers other Potentates, there might you see the ground-work at the one end of the Stage whereout the personated Devils should enter in their fiery ornaments, made like the broad wide mouth of an huge Dragon, which with continual armies of smoke and flame breathed forth his angry stomach's rage, round about the eyes grew hairs not so horrible as men call bristles, but more horrible as long and stiff spears, the teeth of

S   257

this Hell's mouth far outstretching, and such as a man might well call monstrous, and more than a man can by words signify: to be short his hue of that colour which to himself means sorrow, and to others ministers like passion: a thick lamp-black, blacker then any paint, any Hell, blacker than its own self. At the other end in opposition was seen the place wherein the bloodless skirmishes are so often performed on the Stage, the Walls not (so pleasant as old wives would have their tales adorned with) of Pasty crust, but Iron attempered with the most firm steel, which being brightly filed shone as beautifully over the whole place as the Pale shining Cynthia, environed with high and stately Turrets of the like metal and beauty, and hereat many in-gates and out-gates: out of each side lay the bended Ordnance, shewing at their wide hollows the cruelty of death: out of sundry loops many large Banners and Streamers were pendant, briefly nothing was there wanting that might make it a fair Castle. There might you see, to be short, the Gibbet, the Posts, the Ladders, the tiring house, there everything which in the like houses either use or necessity makes common. Now above all was there the gay Clouds *Vsque quaque* adorned with the heavenly firmament, and often spotted with golden tears which men call Stars: There was lively portrayed the whole Imperial Army of the fair heavenly inhabitants, the bright Angels, and such whose names to declare in so vile a matter were too impious and sacrilegious. They were so naturally done that you would have sworn it had been Heaven itself or the Epitome of it, or some second Heaven, and a new Heaven it was, from thence like dewy drops wherein the Sun lays his golden shine, making them to appear like small golden tears, the sweet odours and comforting liquor streamed, and seemed always to rain from thence, but they never fell, but kept a beaten path from down on high wherein the descending Angel might rejoice. I should be too long if I should express this rare Stage, especially in such sort and suchlike words as the like occasion in a more worthy subject would require, but of necessity we must barely apply our descriptions to the nature of the whole History. We must not fail in the first principle of Art, according to that of Horace.

> Humano capiti ceruicem pictor equinam
> Iungere si velit, & varias inducere plumas
> Vndique collatis membris, vt turpiter atrum
> Desinat in piscem mulier formosa superne :
> Spectatum admissi risum teneatis amici ?
> Credite Pisones isti tabulae fore librum
> > Per similem.
> Non vt placidis coeant immitia.

I shall not need to turn back to declare the deep astonishment of the people, who are always in most small manners induced easily to wondering, but now this excellent fair Theatre erected, immediately after the third sound of the Trumpets, there entereth in the Prologue attired in a black vesture, and making his three obeisances, began to shew the argument of that Scenical Tragedy, but because it was so far off they could not understand the words, and having thrice bowed himself to the high Throne, presently vanished. Then out of this representance of Hell's mouth,

259

issued out whole Armies of fiery flames, and most thick foggy smokes, after which entered in a great battle of footmen Devils, all armed after the best fashion with pike, etc., marching after the stroke of the courageous Drum, who girded about laid siege to this fair Castle, on whose Walls after the summons Faustus presented himself upon the battlements, armed with a great number of Crosses, pen and ink horns, charms, characters, seals, periapts,[1] etc., who after sharp words defied the whole assembly, seeming to speak earnestly in his own defence, and as they were ready to rear the Ladders, and Faustus had begun to prepare for the counterbattery, determining to throw down upon the assembly's heads so many heavy charms and conjurations, that they should fall down half way from the ascendant, whilst these things began to wax hot from the aforesaid Heaven, there descended a Legion of bright Angels riding upon milk-white Chariots, drawn with the like white steeds, who with celestial divine melody came into the Town, to the intent to fight for the Doctor against his furious enemies, but he wanting pay-money, and void indeed of all good thoughts, not able to abide their most blessed presence, sent them away, and they returned from whence they came, sorrowfully lamenting his most wilful obstinacy, whilst he had all benointed the Walls with holy Water, and painted with blood many a crimson Cross. At length the Alarm was given, and the Ladders cleaved to the Walls, up the assailants climbed, up they lifted their fearful weapons. Faustus not able (destitute of help) to withstand them, was taken prisoner, and his

---

[1] Charms, amulets.

Tower razed down to the earth, with whose fall both the large Heaven and World shook and quaked mightily, whom, when they had fettered, they left there, they marching out and the fore-named Chairs were presently occupied with all the Imperial rulers of Hell, who clothed in their holiday apparel sat there to give Judgment upon this wilful Faustus, whom two Hangmans of Hell unloosed, and there in presence of them all the great Devil afore his chief peers, first stamping with his angry foot, and then shaking his great bush of hair, that therewith he made the near places and the most proud Devils' courages to tremble, and with his fire-burnt sceptre, and his like-coloured Crown, all of gold, setting one arm by his side, and the other upon the pommel of his Chair, shook a pretty space with such angry fury, that the flames which proceeded from his frightful eyes did dim the sight of the Wittenbergers below. There was in this said Wittenberg a gallant fair Lady and a virgin, which now following her mother, accompanied with sundry gallant German Gentlemen, had even now entered out of their Barge, and seeing the whole world of people as they thought gazing up into the Heaven so very strangely, were partly struck with wonder, some with fear, and some with sudden merriment, and hasting down the hill more than a round pace, asked some what was there to do, and they bid them look up (for here is to be noted that they looked up afore but could see nothing, but as always they were wont until they shewed them it), which they did, and at the same time wherein the great Devil was in his red-hot anger, this young Gentlewoman looked up, whose most ugly shape so feared her, that even then there she fell down in a swoon, whom they conveyed away very speedily, yet ere they could come home she was well-nigh dead, and so she lay for two years without hope of life, or certainly of death : great sorrow to her parents, and as cruel pain to her : But she at length recovered her Spirit, and if by your patience I may, I will tell you how. There was a most learned and excellent Doctor dwelling in the town who had great knowledge in the black Art, who being requested to use some Physic to aid her in her great extremity, being promised for reward five thousand Dollars. This Doctor perceiving the cause of her malady was not caused of any distemperature of her body, but only of the aforesaid fear, knew that Physic might well make her body sound, but her mind never. Wherefore not only for the reward, but also to become gracious and famous at once, proceeded in his cure on this manner. One night having made his Orisons and nine times combed his hair with tears of a pure maid, and nine times gone about a fire made all of pure Heben[1] coal, and thrice nine times called upon the name of the most dreadful Hecate, he laid himself to sleep upon a pure white and clean unspotted maiden's smock, and covered himself over with the ashes of a white Hind roasted and burned altogether, he slept, and the next morning apparelled in white robes, having often and often called, recalled and exorcised the three Fairies Millia, Achilya, and Sybilla, at length the ground opened, and with them they brought a milk-white Steed, and did put upon his finger the

[1] Ebony.

ring of invisibility; when they were vanished, he
mounted up upon his Horse, who with more swift
flight then the winged Pegasus carried him through
the wide Air so fast and so long, that having passed
over Bohem, Hungary, Thracia, all Asia Minor,
Mesopotamia, and at length to Arabia Felix, where
he alighted upon a most high Mountain, all the way
from the top to the bottom of a just breadth and steep-
ness, so that he that were on that would think himself
not in the world, and they beneath would deem him
to be in Heaven, upon the brims of it round about
grew the high Pines, the stately Cedars, and always
so green as the most fresh Meadow : the height of
this huge rock was two and twenty miles in even
altitude and half a mile of just circuit all the way :
there he tied his Horse to a Tree and knocked at
the Castle gate, where afore was never seen any, so
that no path could there be seen, so that a man might
justly have called it the house of little Hospitality, to
him there came Neglectment, an old Lady, and
demanded what he would, who told her his errand,
and withal a ring of fine gold from the three Fairies ;
she knew the ring and his errand, and conveyed him
into many a fair room, wherein she shewed him many
a worthy Knight's memorials, many an antique
Monument heaped up, but inner rooms so monstrous
dark and nightly, that no human eye could perceive anything, and forth she brought him unto a Garden, out
of the midst whereof rose a little Hill, from the summit
whereof there was a paved way of pure Crystal stone,
from along whose bosom trilled a small Water : This
water an old man held, and indeed he had it as a

Patrimony, for therefore he could shew many an ancient evidence, and worn Charter, his hair was all fled to his front, as if some enemy had scared the hinder locks from his scalp, on his back hung a pair of Wings which flagged down, as if either they had been broken or he weary, and thus he overstrode a round World, from out of every part whereof gushed out this small River which was conveyed down in this Crystal pipe, in his hand he held a long scythe, and in the other an hour-glass, here the Doctor seeing the old ruins of this sumptuous house, and all the fair Walls and buildings overgrown with a deadly Moss, was much amazed, but because he could not tarry, he dipped a small Vial in the spring and departed, and for because he was so peremptorily warned not to tarry, he could not behold the most stately Galleries, in which he might see the World's chief pleasures and Monuments, some wholly worn away, some half, and some even now beginning, and some wholly quite over-grown with a thick earthy fur, for as he came by an old Wall he chanced with his elbow to rub off the thick Moss, and then might he see a fair piece of Parchment gilded and painted curiously, wherein was truly described the ancient tokens of a most brave and worthy Gentleman, so having sped of his journey he came by the same way again as he went, Neglect-ment shut the doors upon him, whilst he mounted upon his white swift-footed Horse and by the like time arrived at his own house, where having with the blood of a new-slain heifer, thrice anointed the feet of his Cavallo, and tying at his ear with a string of fine silk spun by the hands of a pure maid, the received ring of invisibility unto his ear, with many a Cross, and many an open *Ave Maria*, dismissed him, who in the same moment returned to the place from whence he came. With this water the Doctor came to the maid, and having used a certain incantation, gave her to drink of the water of deep Oblivion, which she had no sooner tasted of, but straightways she had forgotten the terrible picture of the Devil, and was revived out of all her infernal fears, the Doctor called, winning him credit, favour, and fame, and richly rewarded for his medicine, departed, and running home threw his Vial into the deep River burying oblivion with oblivion, the parents of the young Lady rejoicing exceedingly at their daughter's recovery, for ever after caused the place wherein their daughter was thus scared, to be inaccessible for man or beast, compassing it in with a high wall, and overthrowing the banks, so that now there is no mention of the meadow nor of the Wall.

The Devil, the great Devil Lucifer having finished his brief Oration, descended down out of his Judgment seat, and pointing unto all his Nobles, took Faustus by the hand, and placed him just before him, taking him by the chin, seemed to them to bid him speak freely, he mounted up again unto his high Throne, and with a more mild madness expected the speech of the Doctor, who having bowed himself submissively unto these damnable company, he began to speak, and yet not long, then he began to walk up and down and to shew strange gestures, when suddenly for some bug's-words[1] escaped by Faustus, all the Devils

[1] Swaggering, or threatening language.

there rose up, and with their swords drawn threatening with them the poor Doctor, turning all their bodies and directing their faces to the King, who with a stern countenance commanded silence. When Faustus having long raged, of a sudden howling loud, and tearing his hair, laid both his arms upon his neck, and leaped down headlong off the stage, the whole company immediately vanishing, but the stage, with a most monstrous thundering crack followed Faustus hastily, the people, verily thinking that they would have fallen upon them, ran all away, and he was happiest that had the swiftest foot, some leaped into the River and swam away, and all of them with great affright ran into the City and clapped the City gates together, straight, and to increase this fear they thought they heard a thing fall into the river as if a thousand houses had fallen down from the top of Heaven into it. But afterwards this was known to be Wagner's knavery, who did this to shew the Pursuivant some point of his skill.

CHAPTER IX

THE messenger had not tarried above three days, when as Wagner had trussed up his baggage, and was now ready to depart, when on the third day at night he caused his boy Artur Harmarvan (who was the son of a wealthy boor, witty above many, and praised for his notable waggery: his father dwelt at Malmesburg a town hard by Wittenberg in Saxony in high Dutch-land, with whom Wagner being acquainted had obtained him of his father to serve him, and he to be taught of Wagner), him he caused to go to divers scholars of his acquaintance, to sup with him at his departure, who being invited to this hated farewell, came speedily, where they had a banquet and other courtesies which in such a time both custom and laws of their fellowship do prescribe : In the supper time the scholars moved many questions, and amongst the rest, one desired the Pursuivant to describe unto them his Lord and master, for they heard say that the Duke Alphonsus was a marvellous qualified Gentleman : The Pursuivant not willing to refuse their request told them that seeing their demand proceeded of a common good zeal, he could not but wrongfully refuse to satisfy : notwithstanding the truth might be better known of another than of him, when duty bids to be partial, if any defect might breed partiality, but so much as I will tell you, the enemy will not disdain to affirm : And there he told them the very stature, proportion, and particular lineaments, concluding that he shewed the uprightness of his mind by the proportion of his body, and keeping in his outward shape, the virtue which philosophers would have kept in the mind. There he told them the feature of his countenance, the colour of his hair, eyes, face, cheeks, etc. He told them his stature, favour, and strength, which was such, that with pure cleanness of his force, he hath foiled a gentleman in wrestling, who beside whiteness of body, was very firm without affection, not as some do which in performing anything will with such a ridiculous sourness act it, as if the force of the body must be personated upon the Theatre of his face : He declared unto them that the gifts of his mind were such as then he could not for the number reckon up, but even as occasion should serve might meet with them, being all such as were more ready to be admired than imitated, as if all virtues were gathered in him together, magnanimity, magnificence, affability, modesty, etc., briefly (he said) there were in him all those Graces, which adorn the subject with the title of Virtuous. He likewise recounted unto them his studies, unto which he accommodated himself at vacant hours, were partly the Poetry. A Poem of his he said he had by chance gotten (and by greater chance had it there at that instant) which he had made in praise of his excellent Lady when he was but of young years, his Father living, I dare say he would not for ten thousand florins have it seen, being such a one as on a dreaming passion he had let fall from his pen, and of many the most abject, but such as this is deserves commendations, because a Prince made it, but if you saw his real devices, you would then say they were Prince-like. And then he read it, which I was loath, my good friends, either to translate or translated to present it here, for that it was not worthy your censure, considering the nice buildings of Sonnets nowadays, but according to Ariosto's vein you shall find it very conformable, as also for that I knew that if I should have left it out, it would have been more wished for than now admired. Yet for that I prefer your well-known good wills afore any vain fear, take this with the rest, if they be any with such favour, as if I were by you at the reading.

OF DR. JOHN FAUSTUS

A mio solemente amandona
  Madonna : Donna non parelia.

L'Angelico sembiante e quel bel volte,
  Fal'odio, el'ira va in oblivione,
  Ch'a l' etc.

Thus have I harshly Englished them verbally.

Angellike semblaunce beauties ornament,
Whose Vertue quels all wrath and rancor deepe,
Whose life Heauens grace and death would monument
Vertue thy life aie.[1]
How many wounded hearts thou makst to tremble,
And I of many one cannot dissemble,
How farre into in   *that eie-sore.*

So were thy beauty but deseruing praise,
So were thy beauty but as feminine,
Then could my quill his straine so high arrayse,
Then could with it compare the masculine,
Thy beauty praise thy bounty past diuine,
No straine no quill such wonderments assaies,
Then Poets pen shall to thy power his power resigne.

What words may wel expresse such excellence,
No humane thought thy beauties may comprise
And wordes may tell al humane insolence
All humane words and witte thy gifts surprise.
To satisfie my selfe in my pretence,
Our pen vnto the heauens must wander hence.
And fill it selfe with dew of heauenly Sapience.

And I my life shall to your hands resigne,
  Which liue to serue a humane Sainct so past deuine.

  Se dacolei.
  Che poco ingegno adhor adhor mi lima.

[1] The Letters were worn out in this place.—[*Translator's Note.*]

THE SECOND REPORT

This Sonnet was ended with as much praise as it began with desire, and one of them copied it out, and so it was made common to the rest, and made a good sort of them Poets, rectifying their gross conceits, with so sweet a matter. He told them that this was but a preparative to wondering in respect of his choice makings. Then he shewed them this Epigram, which he made when as before the Duke his Father, a brace of fair English Greyhounds fell down at the Hart's heels stark dead (the Hart also lying not above six yards off dead too) with chasing, having outstripped the rest of the dogs above half a mile.

Then he reckoned unto him the delight he took in Limning, and shewed them very many fine devices of his own handiwork. The scholars singularly delighted with the view of the reliques of so great a Prince, approved by silence that excellency which by speech they could not. In fine there he reckoned up enough to be praised, and peradventure more than was true, but not more than is desired. There he set forth with great and ardent Emphasis other qualities, as his skill and hardy demeanour at the Tilt tourney, how he could manage the sturdy steed, leap, run, vaunt, dance, sing, play on divers Instruments, and talk with amiable speech amongst fair Ladies which we call courting, in all his actions full of gentle familiar affability, still reserving to himself the due honour belonging to his personage. He concluded in fine that he was the most qualified Prince and absolute Gentleman that day in all Christendom : saying if they knew his humanity, justice and liberality, you would say in him were all humanity, justice and liberality;

And as the greatest thing that the world can shew is beauty, so the least thing that is to be praised in him is beauty, you would say no less than I have spoken could be in his person, if you did but see him. Thus far the digression came in the commendations of this Alphonsus, which truly I was weary of, fearing the great insufficiency of the description, but yet he had not done. I would to God (quoth he) you would come to Vienna and I promise you such lodging and entertainment, that next to the sight of him should be worthiest of your thanks. Wherefore you shall not sorrow that your friend Wagner departeth unless you will seem to envy rather his felicity than his departure. I would we were even all of us as we sit at the Table in the Duke's Court, and here again with a wish, and herewith there knocked one at the door, Wagner craftily feigning that he himself would rise to see him that knocked so, desiring them all to sit still in any case, and opening therewith the door, there entered two young Lords of Tergeste and Moravia, bearing torches, and next there came the Duke of Austrich, as they thought, and Wagner talked with him bare-headed (the Pursuivant, thinking verily it had been his Master, would have done his duty unto him, but that the rest hindered him): on his head he wore a little Hat of blue velvet, with a rich band of pearl, stone and gold, and a long white feather, his cloak of blue velvet, round guarded with gold lace, edged with Orient pearl, and betwixt the gards oylet[1] holes where-out hung by small silk threads long bugles, all the sleeves in the like order : by his side a golden-hilted

[1] Eyelet.

Rapier, and on his Rapier his hand, his Buskins of
the fine Polonian leather, richly embroidered on the
turnings down with costly Goldsmith's work, all his
apparel whatsoever most beautiful and princely, he
had no sooner passed by (which was not until he was
distinctly viewed of them) but that Wagner spake
unto them in such manner : saying that that Honourable, this man's Lord had sent for him, whose commandment I will in no wise repugn. Wherefore I
beseech you to take it as you would my greatest advancement. This his description of his feature,
judge how rightly he hath said, for my part I confess
that they are rather less than the truth, than not as he
hath reported, and herein to satisfy you the more,
I have caused my spirit Akercocke to take his shape
upon him.

Now (quoth he) it is time to depart, but because it
shall be the last night of our meeting, none of you shall
depart, for I have lodging enough for you all, and for
you shall not be forgetful of Wagner when he is gone,
let every man wish his woman, and so to bed my
masters. They began all to laugh merrily, not as
hoping or wishing, but as if they had heard a merry
purpose, and therefore they laughed because it was
merry, and such mirth they always liked of. Wagner
was almost angry, and yet for that he was almost,
he was not angry, sending out a great oath as the
Prologue of his Comedy, bidding his Boy go prepare
their beds and chambers, and bid them wish
whom they would, he would their wishes should be
performed. Then rose up one of the scholars persuading himself of Wagner's earnest, and yet doubting,

because he feared he was not in earnest. Why (quoth he) if you mean in very deed, my friend Kit, I would I had such a woman, I believe beside herself there is none fairer then the fairest in this town. Why weenest thou I jest (quoth Wagner), go thy ways, yonder she is upon pain of my head, and so it was indeed : then everyone strove who should wish first, and he that wished last had his first wish, so everyone took his Damsel and for that night departed to their beds, who are witnesses of that night's great pleasures, and in the morning they arose wishing that every morning were the morrow of such a night. Every one gat him a Hackney, and brought him on the way a day's journey, where they with great grief left him, who rode till he came to Vienna, and they till they arrived at Wittenberg. Thus still you see these Pot-meetings are ended amongst these puffed-cheeked Hannikins[1] with bed dalliances, rightly describing their lives most bestial and Epicure-like.

CHAPTER X

A lamentable history of the death of sundry students of Wittenberg

Not long after it was reported and blazed abroad that Wagner was departed, divers Scholars guessing that he had left his Books or the most part behind, determined to send for Harmarvan, which they did, who by

---

[1] German *Hänschen.*

no persuasions could be won to let them have his
master's Keys, so they devised amongst themselves to
bind the Boy as he should go home to his Inn, whereat
his Master had put him to board till his return. And
night drawing on, Harmarvan went to his lodging,
by the way Scholars to the number of seven met him
and bound him, and beat him sore until he gave them
all the Keys, which he carefully carried about him
sewed in a wide German slop,[1] which when they had
(they being all muffled and disguised strangely with
vizards) they loosed, and then they ran hastily to
Wagner's house, as if they had fled from followers, or
else followed some hastily flying, where being come,
they opened the gates, and being entered shut them
again, this being about eleven of the clock in ye night,
and in they went, where they found two Barrels of
mighty strong March English Beer of two years old,
which they broached, and sat so long drinking till
they were all well drunk. And then down they get
into a back Court, and having lighted Tapers, having
injuriously framed all the circles, squares, triangles,
etc., and apparelled with all the conjuring robes that
the Art requireth, there they begin in a most dreadful
confusion of hellish syllables to inform the Fiend, and
after these words followed as if there needs must such
things follow after such words, a terrible roar, and then
so bright a smothering thick fiery fume ascended out
of the earth as if it would have made an eternal night,
then a vehement flame followed which with continual
motion, ran about the brims of the circle, until as
weary it left moving (all this while they continued

[1] Baggy breeches.

reasonably constant, and continued their invocations without any fear), then from beneath was heard most lamentable outcries, from above huge trembling, thunder, and round about nothing but fear and death in a thousand diverse shapes, then they began to quail a little, but yet by encouragement grew hardy by reason of the number, then round about was sounded alarms with drums, and on set with Trumpets, as if there all the World had conflicted, then ye flame which all this while ran about the circle became a body, but such a body, as, if it had been but a Picture, would have madded anyone. At whose sight they wholly overcome with deadly fear forgot the use of their Pentacles or any such gear, but even submitted themselves to the small mercy of the Fiend, who with great violence rent them and tore them most lamentably. Harmarvan who had raised a great many to the intent to follow them suspecting that which indeed was, was after long wandering (for they had caused a Devil descryer to void all within a certain circuit) with his company brought to the house, where round about they might see in the Court wherein these seven were conjuring, huge flames as if some great pile had been made to the burial of a noble Hero, climbing up in huge volumes up into the Air, or if some great store of stubble had been fired, so vehemently furious was the flame that no man there (and there were above thirty) was able once to draw near to any part of ye House, the cry was carried into the City of this fire, whereupon the whole town was assembled with hooks, buckets, ladders, etc., where in vain they emptied many a large Well, till divers

275

learned Preachers falling down submissively on their knees, with good faith appeased this seeming fire which indeed was none, but a mere diabolical illusion, then they entered into the house, where they found the Barrels brought a bed and delivered, the cups, the whole furniture clean destroyed, broken, and thrown about the House, but drawing near unto the most rueful and lamentable spectacle of all, coming into the yard or grove which was moated about and enclosed with a thick Wall of trees very exceeding high, as Fir trees are, so very thick that no light was pierceable into it, in the very midst whereof was a round plot of some one hundred foot any way from the Centre, there found they the religious Circles, there the strange Characters, names of Angels, a thousand Crosses, there found they the five cross hilted Daggers for the five Kings of Hell, there many a strong bulwark builded with rows of Crosses, there found they the surplices, the stoles, pall, mitres, holy water pots broken, their periapts, seats, signs of the Angels of the seven days, with infinite like trash and damnable roguery, the fruits of the Devil's rank fancy. But the most lamentable sight of all, the seven Scholars utterly torn in pieces, their blood having changed the colour of the ground into a dark Crimson, all their bodies as black as any coal, as if they had been scorched with a material fire, their flesh violently rent from the bones, and hanging down in morsels like the skirts of a side-coat, their bones all broken, their veins cut in sunder, and their bowels broad shed upon the earth, their brains poured out and covering the red grass all over, their noses stumped, their eyes thrust out, their

GORGONEVM CAPVT.
Ein new seltzam Meerwunder auß den Newen erfundenen Inseln/von ettlichen
Jesuitern an ire güte günner geschickt.

Gleich wie der Heilig ist/   Also steht er gerüst.

A CARICATURE OF THE PÒPE

mouths widened and slit up to the ears, their teeth dashed out, and their tongues starting out betwixt their gums, their hair clean singed off, in brief imagine with yourselves in your minds, and propound a picture in your thought, the most deformed, torn, and ill-favoured that you can think on, yet shall it not compare to the most lachrimable sight and shew of them, surpassing as much all credit as my skill duly to describe them, whom when they had buried without tarriance, razed the house to the ground, and filled up the moats with earth, heaping upon the place of this murther the stones of the house defaced, then they returned home discoursing with lamentable judgment upon the high and severe revenge of God's indignation upon them which durst presume to tempt his glorious Majesty. And finally, unless repentance breed a more speedy remorse, such is the fatal end of such proud attempts. And surely this is most true, for I myself have seen the ground where the house stood, and yet the moats dammed up and the Water breaking through the stones even to this day, there did I see a skull and a shank bone of them not yet rotten : and there did I see the huge heap of stones wherewith they are covered, a fearful example of God's wrath and justice against such infidel Christians.

CHAPTER XI

THE great Turk called Soldan, Alias Chan, comprehending as many victories in his sword as some Emperors in their thoughts, arrived at length afore

Vienna, having made his preamble with the destroying and burning of the country before him, thinking upon the ancient politic rule, *Better it is to have a spoiled country than a lost*, with a brave prepared Army of two hundred thousand Saracens, horse and foot, and so many it is certain he had, because they doubted not but there were 300,000. The mighty Cham having erected his royal Pavilions, and entrenched himself to besiege the noble Vienna, munified his camp with Artillery and deep ditches, and then he sent a Letter of defiance unto the honourable Alphonsus, as being principal in his own City, who was environed within the walls of the City expecting the day of battle, for to this intent the states of Italy and the Emperor of Germany, with the Dukes of Saxony, Bavaria, and the other Provinces near assembled (for now necessity bred unity) with a brave company of Soldiers to exterminate this monster out of their confines : unto the Duke of Austrich only (for he had no intelligence of their assembled forces) he directed his Letters with defiance, meaning to conclude his long travails with a certain victory ; fearing neither the peril which so many gallant soldiers thoroughly resolved might bring, nor that ever God or fortune (as they call it) would once shew him any disfavour, whose only favour is only in show. Nor yet that the heaven's great God would not with severe revengement chastise the Leviathan's insolency and slaughter of so many Martyrs, rather deferring than forgetting so just a punishment.

THE SECOND REPORT

CHAPTER XII

ABOUT this time the Messenger and Wagner arrived at
Vienna very late in the night and passed through
the Turkish Sentinels, and arriving at the City, and
for that night they lay at the Pursuivant's house; no
sooner had the approaching Sun sent afore him the
Marshals of the morrow light, and a new morning
ministered occasion of new matter, but up those two
arose and being ready departed for the Court, and now
the day was almost in the greatest beauty, when the
Messenger was admitted into the Duke's presence,
unto whom he recited whatever was seen and done
in that time of his absence (only I forgot to tell you
how Wagner raged and stormed, and thundered,
when Akercocke brought him word of the destruction
of his House at Wittenberg as he was in the way to
Austria), wherewith the Duke was wonderfully both
delighted and astonished. And having welcomed
Wagner very graciously and accordingly rewarded,
he dismissed them till further leisure, commanding
the Pursuivant to shew him all the pleasure he mought.

CHAPTER XIII

AFTER all these most excellent Princes were come into
the counsel chamber, the Herald sounded his trumpet
after the Turkish summons, then did all the states
draw into the Great Hall, wherein a high Imperial
throne richly ordered with shining cloth of Gold,

every noble and estate placed correspondently to his degree, where in presence of them all the Herald was admitted, who coming with his coat of Arms lying upon his right arm into the bottom of the Hall, made three obeisances down with the right knee unto the ground, with a loud and distinct voice spake unto the Duke only, telling him that his sovereign and Master Sultan Alias Chan, the son of Murad Chan, the son of Rabeck Chan, the son of Mahomet Chan, and so upwards till he came to their great Prophet Mahomet, God on the earth, and Emperor of all the East. And then he began to reckon five hundred titles, with a long etc. . . . . Unto thee Alphonsus Arch-Duke of Austrich, and there he declared the whole effects of his message, and at last with a great Bravado ended, and then he did on his gay coat of Arms, expecting their answer. When as the Duke craving licence of the Emperor to speak, answered ye Herald in most gallant and triumphing terms, commanding him to say unto the proud Turk his Master, that ere five days came about, he would trample his victorious horns under his feet, and ride in triumph upon his stubborn neck, and that in defence of himself and of brave Christendom he would leese[1] the uttermost drop of his blood, and to make it good he would not be in quiet till he had met his Master in the midst of the field, and therewith he drew out his sword, and all they with him, crying God and Saint Michael for the right of Christendom : then stood up the Emperor and avowed all that they had said afore him, commanding moreover the Herald to say to the proud Usurper, that seeing the quarrel

[1] Lose.

would breed great effusion of blood, and yet he never the nearer, that he a man every way equal to himself, not only for the speedier advance of his battles, but also to have a certain end to such an uncertain enterprise, he would fight with him body to body, armed at all points after their own guise at any time within this fortnight, and Herald, bring me word (quoth he) that he will so do, and by my Honour I promise to give thee for thy tidings 10,000 Ducats. Then the Herald being highly rewarded was dismissed, and reported their brave answers unto the Turk, with all the great majesty of the Christian Princes, who presently went to counsel together, and so continued till other like necessary business called them away.

CHAPTER XIV

IN this Chapter (Gentlemen) part of the Dutch copy was wanting, and the other part so rent that it could not be read, yet by some circumstances I conjecture that the Duke of Austrich had divers and dangerous conflicts with the Turk, yet being supported by the English men and other Christians, with the help of Wagner, who standing in a high tower to see the conflicts, caused by his Magic such a storm to arise that no man was able to abide, the Turk was still discomfited.

CHAPTER XV

The gifts of Wagner to the Duke, and three Devils retained for Soldiers to the same Prince

IN the next morning Wagner presented himself to the Duke in presence of all the whole Princes of the Christians, whom very graciously he entertained as he might for his good service, and there in presence of them all he desired the Duke to take at his servant's hands a small gift, which he condescended unto, and then Wagner caused a Chest to be brought in of fine Iron, wrought and enamelled with gold and colour most curiously, then he opened it and took out a whole armour of fine bright steel so light as a common Doublet, but so subtly and excellently framed, that it passed all comparison of hardness, there was a Musket shot at every piece whereon remained no great notice of a blow, but as of a little touch, plain without any broider work or otherwise carved, but so exceeding bright as would well have dazzled the long beholder's eyes, a shield of the same fashion, made like a tortoise shell, a sword of the like fine temper, with all the furniture of a soldier, then took he out a Plume which he had no sooner put into the crest, but he that stood behind could not see no part of his back, nor he that stood before of his breast, so that thus it made him invisible, there he told him it was fetched out of the great Turk's armoury, which they say was Mahomet's, but I say more truly Alias Chan's, which for himself caused it to be made, having called together the most excellent Philosophers and workmen that were to be found in all his wide Empire. The great rewards the Duke would have given him for it he refused, he was only contented with thanks and favour. And then might they see from the door of the chamber three most gallant men to enter, which were his three Familiars, whom Wagner taking by the hands presented unto the whole assembly of Princes, but more directly to the Duke, assuring them that they were the most fortunate, most valiant, strong, hardy, and puissant men that in the World were to be found, and indeed they seemed to be as goodly swart men as any eye beheld, he told their several names : Mephostophiles he termed Mamri, Akercocke he termed Simionte, Faustus he called Don Infeligo, shewing that they were born in those fortunate Islands, wherein the Poets feigned the Elysian fields to be, joining by West upon the end of Barbary, being from Vienna to those fortunate Islands 35 degrees of longitude and eight minutes, and 48 degrees and 22 minutes from the Equator or Equinoctial, in latitude not then found out. So were they most graciously entertained of all the Nobles, and entertained in the Duke's most Honourable pay. Wagner said that they three left their country and sought adventures, and by chance coming this way, I knowing of it by secret intelligence, met them and certainly assured of their high valours, thought good to shew them to you, for he that first had spoke to them had been first served, nor cared they whether to serve us or the Infidel.

CHAPTER XVI

I SPAKE before of a challenge made by the Emperor
unto the Turk, which when the Herald had reported
unto the Sultan (who certainly was a very honorable
Soldier) but there he vowed to perform it, and to set
the Emperor's head upon the highest pavilion in view
of all the City. And thereupon the next day after this
skirmish, he sent the same Herald with purpose and
commandment to declare in excellent gallant terms
the acceptance of the combat, knowing that it depended
upon his honour to shew his small fear, in not refusing
so equal a Foe, whose proffer proceeded from a most
Honourable resolution : when it was reported unto the
Emperor that the same Herald returned, he caused the
Hall to be adorned with most brave furniture, his high
Chair of estate placed, and all about seats for the other
Princes. The Emperor having seated himself, full
of brave thought and gallant hardihood, expecting the
answer of the enemy in such sort as it was in very deed.
In all brave manner the Herald in proud phrase uttered
the purport of his message, requesting that a peace
being concluded on both parties for the space of three
days, and free egress and regress for the Nobles on
both parties, the one to view the Camp, the other the
Court, and on the third day he would, armed in his
country manner, meet him in the lists, to shew that
he never refused the combat of any Christian Emperor,
albeit he knew his calling far superior to that of his.
So then the message was accepted, the Herald had his
10,000 Ducats carried to the Turk's camp on horse,

285

and they in the City began to keep feasts, and entertained the Turkish Nobles in exceeding bravery, and they theirs in the like without damage or thought of treason.

CHAPTER XVII

DURING the time of this truce, these four companions, Infeligo, Wagner, Mamri, Simionte, cast how to abuse the great Turk most notably, and Akercocke otherwise called Simionte he would begin first, and lead them the dance. Then he leaves them and gets me up unseen to the Turk's Camp, and in his Camp to his own Pavilion, and so into the place where the great Infidel himself sat, he being then gone into the Lavatory, which is a place wherein he three times a day doth bathe himself, which by so doing he doth verily believe that all his sins are remitted and washed away, be they never so horrible, Devilish, or wicked, then Akercocke or Simionte, which ye will, goes invisibly into the Lavatory where the great Villain was bathing himself amongst three of his most fair Concubines stark naked, swimming as much in their dalliance as in the water, mingling his washing with kisses and his cleansing with voluptuousness, Akercocke in the shape of a bright Angel appears unto him, and with a proud *magnifico* presented himself unto the slave, who straightways very reverently fell down upon his knees, and with his hands high lifted up, worshipped towards him in great humility, whilst Akercocke with good devotion fell aboard the Concubines, and there acted them before his face one after another : when he had so

286

done, he takes the great slave by the tip of his picke-devant,[1] and shaking him fiercely (who all this while with great dread and fear lay half astonished and all naked on the ground), told him that he had prepared a more braver place for his so good a servant than so base a bath, and no fairer Concubines. (Now the Turk had seen how like a lusty rank fellow this Simionte had behaved himself, at which he wondered not greatly, because Faustus whom he thought to have been Mahomet, as well as he did think Akercocke, had also shewed the virtue of so great a God as Mahound, twenty times more beauty than Jupiter.) Then the Turkish Emperor with half-dying hollow voice, as if his breath had been almost gone or else but now coming, said that he was all at his command-ment, and so followed Simionte stark naked as he was born, who led him by the hand round about, and through every Lane and place of his Camp, to the great wonderment and laughter of his people, who verily thought Mahound had commanded him to do penance before he fought with the Christian Emperor. But for all this the people fell into such laughter that some had wellnigh given up the Ghost at the same instant, divers Christian Nobles saw him all this while, who effusedly laughed at so apparent foolery. The Turk for all this not moved, for indeed he heard all and saw nothing, went about wonderfully mannerly : like as you shall see a Dutch Frow, with a handkerchief in her hand, mince it after ye hopping German. Could a man devise a more notorious kind of abuse, than to make that man which will not be seen but in great

[1] Peaked beard.

secrecy, and abundantly and richly clad, to be not only seen openly but also stark naked, and become their laughing-stocks whose terror he is always, but Aker-cocke had not yet so left him, but down he runs to Danuby, (where there was ready Mamri or Mephos-tophiles to receive him), and there having turned himself and the vilest part of himself to the Turk's mouth, making him kiss and kiss it again, he took him and hurled him violently into the Water, and then Akercocke vanished away.

CHAPTER XVIII

The second Mocking

No sooner was he in but he saw then apparently how he had been misled and abused, and there for very shame would have drowned himself in very deed, had not Mamri come swiftly flying over and gave him a terrible blow on the noddle with a good Bastinado, that he almost made his brains fly out, and rapt him up by his long hair out of the water unto the land, where he buffeted him so long till at length he came to himself again, then Mamri fewtered himself to abuse him kindly, and there with sweet and compassionative speech comforted him, desiring his reverend Majesty not to take any grief seeing it was done in the sight of all his men, in the knowledge of none. And therewith to shew ye more pity of his misery, he seemed to shed abundance of tears, desiring him to go with him

LUTHER AS A SEVEN-HEADED MONSTER

A caricature of Luther, 1529

and he would put upon him his soft raiment. The Turk (who then had his crown upon his head or else it had not been half in the right Qu[1]), seeing one lamenting his case so affectionately, condescended unto him and promised him most large honourable promotion and reward. Mamri set him upon his legs and led him to a little muddy place by the river-side, and there varnished the Emperor over with most thick, terrible, and excremental mud, not sparing either his face, nose, eyes, mouth, nor any thing, whilst he miserable man thought he had been in most divine contentment. Thus he led him in the view of five thousand people (for here is to be noted that all that ever saw him both knew him to be the great villain Turk, and could not but laugh most entirely at him, nor his own men could do any other, nor once think of any rescue or remedy, by the working of infernal instinct), until he came to Vienna, and in Vienna to the most fair gates and where greatest resort of people are always together, there at the City gate he drew out a long tabor and a pipe and struck up such a merry note, as the foolish ornament of all London stages never could come near him, no not when he waked the writer of the news out of Purgatory with the shrill noise. There at the gate stood a Carpenter, who was then carrying a Coffin to a certain house to bury one in, him Mephostophiles beat till he lay on the cold ground, and took the Coffin and caused the Turk to hold it in his hand. *Memorandum* that none of all these Spirits were seen of any one, but felt of them which saw them. Then from the gate

[1] Cue (a theatrical term).

he began to play, the Turk and the Coffin skipped and turned, and vaulted, and bounded, and leaped, and heaved, and sprung so fast and so thick together, that the Coffin rapping the miserable man sometime on the shins, breast, thighs, head, face, that the dirty colour was almost wiped away with the streams of blood. At this strange sight and the unheard noise of that kind of Instrument, all the boys, girls, and rogues in the town were gathered with this troupe, and with this mirth he conveyed them round about the streets, and all the way as they went, such eggs, such chamber-pots' emptyings, such excrements, odoure,[1] water, etc., were thrown down on their heads, that it seemed all those vile matters were reserved for that Tempest, until such time (then it being about two of the clock in the afternoon when everyone is busied in some pleasant pastance[2]), as all this fair company came to the Court, whereout at divers windows lay the chiefest of all the Nobility, and the most brave Gentlewomen, who seeing such a huge crowd of Boys, the great Turk and a Coffin dancing, and a tabor and pipe played upon, they were almost amazed, thus he marched finely round about the whole Court, till coming to the Court gate he entered in (but the Boys were excluded), with this merry Morris there in presence of them all, the Turk fell down dead, whom Mamri laid in the Coffin, and then vanished away.

[1] Ordure. [2] Pastime.

CHAPTER XIX

The third

THEN came Infeligo or Faustus and touching him revived him to the great wonder of the beholders, and covering him somewhat shamefastly, went into his chamber with him, and there benotted[1] him round upon the head and the beard, which is the foulest reproach and disgrace that can be offered to the Turk, which done he conveyed him into the presence of the Emperor, where he made them such sport, that unneath[2] they could recover their modesty in three hours' space, to see the proud Villain plastered over with such muddy mortar, all over his head and face, his teeth and eyes shewing like black Moors, or as a pair of eyes, looking through a Lattice, or as they call it a Periwig, wherein if the eyes had feet they might be set in the stocks : All his lineaments were lineamented with this pariet,[3] he stood quivering and shaking either for cold or fear like an Aspen leaf (as they say) whilst every man buffeted him, he standing with a scourge stick and an old shoe, as they do at blind man buff to see who he could hit. Thus long he made them sport, till one told the Emperor that it was the great Turk, at which he was exceeding wroth and sorry.

[1] Cropped close. [2] Scarcely. [3] Plaster.

CHAPTER XX

The fourth and last

WHEN Wagner seeing him grieved, came and kneeled down before him, declaring that he would undertake to heal all his wounds and other grievances whatsoever, yea and make him utterly forget all that was passed as if it had never been, and promised more to carry him home himself safe and sound, which the Emperor thanked him highly for, requesting him to perform it presently, for he would not for half his revenues that his Foe should have any occasion to allege against him, for to excuse the Combat. Then went Wagner up into his chamber, and apparelled himself in white taffeta made close to his body, and there where they use to wear round hose half a foot deep, stuck with swans' feathers, like the skirts of a horseman's coat, his hose, shoes (for all were together) of the same white taffeta, and within with white leather, at his heels two fine silver wings, and on his shoulders two marvellous large bright silvery wings, and on his head an upright little steeple hat (with a white feather of two or three ranges) of white taffeta, and in his hand a Caduceus or a Mercurial Rod in the same white silver colour, he entered into the Presence Chamber afore all the assembly to their singular contentation, for in his Personated garments he seemed to be a very Angel, for it was in doubt whether Mercury was half so beautiful or no. And there opening a large casement (as there they are very large) with a brave R'ingratio[1] departed from them taking up his flight

[1] Ringrazio (Ital.)=I thank.

in the view of them all into the air, as if he would have beaten the Azure firmament with his vast wings. Thus he carried him lower and lower till he did light upon a great Elm, and there he opened his sight to see in what plight he was. The Turk seeing in what a trance he had been, began to swear, to ban and curse, and was even then ready to have thrown himself down headlong, but Mercury he stepped to him and bade him be of good cheer, for it had pleased the great God Jupiter, whose servant Mahomet was, to shew him those great abuses, to the intent he should be more wary in his actions, and take heed how to tempt the Christians with vain battles and such-like speech, but now (quoth he) come and give me thy hand, and then will I lead thee to thy Pavilion, where as yet thou art not missed of the Nobles, for in the place where thou wast taken away, hath Jove sent one to bear thy shape. Then again he took his flight and all the way as he went he rapped his heels against the tops of the high trees, and beat him pitifully upon the shins all the journey, upon the tents' tops. Now they arrived in the same place from whence he was taken, and there he laid himself down who presently recovered his former strength in full perfectness, and not only not felt it but utterly forgot it. Then he continued his wonted solace and prepared himself to the battle, whilst he was made a laughing-stock of the world, Wagner returned through ye same path which he had made in the air before, came not yet to the Court before they had done laughing, for there the matter from the beginning to the end was rehearsed.

CHAPTER XXI

The process to the Combat

THE two days of the truce were passed and the third morning was come, in which time many gallant feats of arms and activity were performed on both parts. Now the time of the combat was come. There was in the River of Danuby a pretty Island of a quarter of a mile long or more, as even as ground might be all the way, in this place were the lists prepared, and a scaffold richly hanged for the Judges to determine in. In the evening about four of the clock (being then reasonably cool) the Christian Emperor issued out with above 100,000 Christians, the rest being above 60,000 were left to defend the City (for both the Christian and especially the Turks were increased) where he entered into the wide plain, and coming to the bank's side he entered into a broad Ferry boat leaving his whole Army on the other side of the River whilst he laboured to attain to the Island. The Duke of Austria with his attendants Mamri, Simionte, Infeligo, and Wagner, the Dukes of Cleve, Saxony, Campany, and Brabant, with the like number all bravely and gloriously mounted : The Duke of Austria in his bright armour marshalled the field, and of the Christians sat as Judges the kings of Lusitany and Arragon with their Heralds : Now the Emperor is landed in the Island and is mounted into his rich saddle, armed in armour so costly, strong, curious, and resplendescent, that it seemed all the beauty in the world had been gathered together in it, his courser so firm, nimbly jointed, tall and large, such a one might have been the son of Gargantua's mare for his Giant-like proportion. Then took he his strong and large Ashen lance, bearing in his steel head Iron death, at the top whereof hung a fair and rich pennon, the whole shaft of the spear double gilded over and curiously enamelled, about his neck hung his horn shield, artificially adorned with his own achievements, the belt whereon his sword hung of beaten gold, his caparison of pure cloth of gold, whereon the rich stones were so ordinary that they took away ye glittering of the metal only as if it had been the Sunbeams, trailed along betwixt precious gutters. On his helmet was fixed a rich Crown of the most excellent metal. In brief, for I would fain have made an end of this idle news, there was all the richness in his Empire, in that all the beauty of his richness, in them all ye desire of each eye : when he had saluted ye judges he trotted twice or thrice about the lists, and then lighted at his Pavilion which was there erected of cloth of gold, where he sat with convenient company and refreshed himself. Now in the mean the Turk he set forward with an army double the Christian, and 100,000 and above still left in the Camp. And here I must needs leave to tell you of his exceeding preparation unless I should make a whole volume, for beside the wondrous furniture of his Soldiers, the most rare choice of ornaments, there was nothing could be devised, nay more than of set purpose could be devised was there. But briefly I will turn to the Turk himself, where if I had art according, I should sooner weary you with delight than words : But

100,000 of his men having marched before to the banks and there embattled themselves by the river all along, with such hideous noise of Trumpets, horns (for so they use), drums of brass, flutes, etc., that there was more heard than seen by far, then approached the great Turk himself, before him rode 4000 Janissaries armed in their fashion, with a long Gown of Scarlet-red laced with gold lace, and long sleeves of a very narrow breadth, which was girt close unto him, under that a good armour, with a long high cap like a milk-pail for all the world, of white Satin or some such-like gear, with a long feather enough to come down to a tall man's hams, very thick laced in the brims with gold and pearl, in his hand a short Javelin, at his side his Scimitar, at his back a great Quiver of broad arrows, and by a string of silk hung his steel bow, over every one hundred of these is a Boluch Bassa, a Centurion as we call him, and these be of the Turk's guard, and are called Solaquis Archers, and they rode fifty in a rank, then came following them about two hundred Peicher or Peiclers, all in one livery of very rich tissue after their fashion, and these are of the Turk's Laqueis[1] which have a sharp teen[2] Hatchet sticking at their girdles, and the haft of Brasil,[3] with this they will stand thirty paces off and cleave a penny loaf or hit it somewhere, they will commonly stick an inch and half deep into a very tough Ashen wood, or a Brasil, or such-like hard wood : there in great triumph upon an Elephant richly trapped, stood a Tower of two yards and a half high of pure silver, in the top whereof stood an Image of beaten gold, representing

---

[1] A kind of foot-soldier. [2] Keen. [3] Brazil wood.

their Mahomet, round about which upon Mules Azamoglans or Jamoglans, who are children of tribute exacted upon the Christian captives, and contributary, fine, sweet, and the most choice picked Gentlemen brought up to sundry dainty qualities, who with heavenly melody followed this Elephant, the religious men going round about singing sweetly together : afore all these next to the Janissaries went above two hundred Trumpets, and as many followed the great Turk, who then approached, having his Chariot of pure silver of above 20,000 pound weight, drawn with eight milk-white Elephants, round about rode and went bare-headed, Azamoglans Peyclers most gorgeously and resplendescent apparelled, under the Turk's feet lay a pillow of clear Crystal embossed at the ends with huge golden knobs, on his head a wreath of purple with a most rich diadem as it is commonly known the order of it, the stage can shew the making of it, but other things they differ mightily in. Here you must suppose the exceeding glory of his apparel, there he sat upright in the Chair with such a majestical, proud, severe, war-like countenance, as justly became so high a throne, before him went Aga which is the great Captain of his Janissaries, with the Hali Bassa, the Captain of his naval expeditions, Bianco Bassa, the Captain of his Janissarie Harquebusiers, the Zanfyretto Bassa Captain of his Guard, with others of great authority bare-headed. After his Chariot came sweet melody, and then five Elephants of War (an Elephant is well-nigh as big as six Oxen gaunt and slender like a horse in ye flanks, and of more swift foot than a man would think for, his fashion is like no beast in England, but the ridge of his back is like that of an horse, his feet hath five great horny toes, and a very long snout of above two yards in length, with which he will draw by only snuffing up a good pretty big lad, and deliver him to the Rider ; this long trunk falls down betwixt a large pair of teeth or tushes[1] of above an Ell and a half long (as ye may commonly see at the Comb-makers in London) bending like a Boar's upward, his ears well-nigh from the top to the nether tip of the hanging down above seven feet long). And after these five Elephants, saddled and ordered for a man to ride on, came trumpets, and all in the like manner as before, and then marched 500 in a rank, 100,000 footmen, and by their sides for wings 40,000 horsemen, so that he came to the combat with 240,000 fighting-men, well accomplished in arms : then was the great Turk carried under a goodly canopy upon a black Waggon on men's shoulders into the Ferry, which was richly prepared, where in the view of both Camps he landed, whilst the warlike instruments echoed wide in the Air. In the Island for Judges sat (in armour as did the others) the king of Rhodes and the king of Pamphilia, now called Alcayr. When the Turk was landed, there was brought to him by the hands of two kings a great Elephant of an Ash colour, white embossed very glitteringly, whereon the great Turk mounted by a short ladder of silver, armed very strongly and most beautifully, then took he his Javelin in his hand and vibrated it in great bravery (as he could handle his weapon well) and hung his quiver of long Darts at his Back, then his

[1] Tusks.

Scimitar, etc., and so having saluted the Judges retired unto the uttermost part of the field, then mounted up the brave and puissant Emperor so lightly in his heavy armour, as if either his gladness had lessened his weight, or the goodness of his cause, to the great rejoicing of the Christian and amazement of ye Turk, at whom the Christians yelled so universally and hallooed, and other infinite kinds of gladsome tokens, that the Turk astonished stood stone still till the Christian had done, and then as men new risen to life, with such an horrible shout, that their voice rebounded to the air, at which same time the Christian shouted again with them, as if they would have committed a battle with voices, and surely their voices did fight in the wide coasts and shores of the air. This done the Emperors prepared themselves to the fight.

CHAPTER XXII

The Combat

AND when they were sworn that neither of them had any magic herb, charm or incantation whereby they might prevail in their fight on their adversary, and had solemnized the accustomable ceremonies in like matters of combat. The Heralds gave their words of encounter, then with loud voice and shrill Trumpets' courageous blast, whilst all the people were in dead night expecting the demeanour of these renowned Princes. Now we have brought you to behold these

two champions, arrived thither with their brave
followers, ready to prove their valiance in the face of
so great a multitude. Now if you will stand aside
lest their ragged spears endamage you, I will give
you leave to look through the Lattice, where you shall
even now see the two Emperors, with their brave shock,
press Doubt betwixt their cruel encounterings. Now
you may see the two combatants, or but as yet champions, coming from the ends of the field, the excellent
Christian Emperor with incomparable valour, visiting
his Horse sides with his spurs, carrying his spear in
the rest with an even level, so that the thundering of
the brave Steed presaged ye dint[1] of the great thunder-
clap. When Ali Chan, gently galloping with his huge
beast, came forward with more swift pace still as he
drew nearer to the Emperor. All this while you may
behold them hastening in their course, like as you see
two great waves galloping from the corners of the sea
driven by contrary winds, meeting together by long
random, to make the neighbours' shores to quake and
dimmed with their boisterous career. The Emperor
being now with his greatest fury ready to fasten his
lance upon his adversary, and his adversary ready
to fasten his Javelin on him, when the Turk
suddenly stepped aside, and the Emperor thrusted
his void lance into the Air, (for he mought easily
do it), for though the Elephant be but low, yet
he was higher than his horse by a yard, and yet
his horse was the fairest and tallest to be found
in all Christendom, so that needs he must lay his spear
in an uneven height to break it on him. Suddenly ye

---

[1] Force.

THE SECOND REPORT

Turk stopped and with his nimble Beast followed the Emperor as he had fled, whereat all the whole army of Turks shouted horribly clapping their hands, and the Christian stood still in great silence, struck with just wonder of this strange Quiddity[1] in combat, and ere the Emperor could make his stop with a short turn, the Turk had hit him upon the shoulder with his Javelin, which being denied entrance, for very anger rent itself in forty pieces, and chid[2] in the Air till they broke their necks on the ground : and had not then the Horse started, the monstrous Elephant had overthrown him with his rider to the earth. But then the Horse incensed with ire for this injury, and his master more hotly burning with disdain and furious gall, leaped, bounded, and sent out at his mouth the foamy arguments of his better[3] stomach, but so fast the vile Turk followed, that he had spent three long Darts upon the barbed flanks of the Horse, which all in vain returned to their Master. The beholding Turks so eagerly pursuing the strokes with shouting, as if with a hidden Sympathy their training[4] had augmented the violence of the blows. At length the good Emperor sorely ashamed came now to make him amends for his pretty falsery : and with great scope thronging[5] his lance forward just upward upon the Turk's face, and when he was almost by him, the Infidel, as if he but make a sport of the fight, stepped aside very delivery,[6] thinking that he should have made him run in the like order as before, but he, more

---

[1] Subtlety, trick.
[2] Applied to sounds suggesting angry vehemence.
[3] Bitter ?   [4] Enticing.
[5] Forcing, pressing.   [6] Nimbly.

cautelous marking of purpose which way he meant to decline, turned with him, and his learned Horse could well do it, and indeed desire of revenge had so seated itself in his brave courageous breast, that now he even followed him as he had been drawn with Cart-ropes, the Turk seeing how he was circumvented, fetched a pretty compass and trod a round, the Elephant flying from ye horse and the horse following the Elephant, as you might see Seignior Prospero lead the way in Mile end Green in the ringles,[1] this was a pretty sport to see the matter turned to a play. Now the Christians having like occasion to shew their gladness, gave such an *Applaudite* as never was heard in any Theatre, laughing so effusedly that they dashed their adversaries clean out of countenance, tickling again with the long loud laughter : When they had run not passing twice about, the Turk, seeing his time, conveyed himself out of the ring, and then got again on his back, spending his cowardly Darts upon his strong enemy's armour, and so fast he followed and so quickly the good Emperor turned back again, that his horse's barb of Steel out-sticking in his front, met just upon the outside of the right eye of the Elephant, that it sticking out a foot entered in above an inch, which ye horse perceiving made the rest follow into his head up to the hilts (as to say) laying out his fore feet out straight, and his hinder legs in like manner, went poking, and crowded himself forward still gathering upon the Elephant, so that not so much with the Horse's force as the great beast's cruel pain, the Elephant swayed back above one hundred feet. Now

[1] Ring, or circle.

was the Emperor glad, and with both his hands lifting himself upon his stirrups, took his lance and struck with the point the Turk full on the vizard so thick and so many times, that some blood followed, with an hue and cry out of the windows of the Helmet, to find the worker of his effusion : till the villian slave drawing his fine sword smote the lance very bravely in two, and casting his shield afore him, received the last stroke on the truncheon of it, which the gentle Emperor with fell fury threw at him, that he made him decline almost to the fall. The Turk sitting on the Elephant's back could not with his Scimitar reach the Christian, nor he the Turk with his Curtilax,[1] so that now they sat and looked one upon the other, and the people at them, and all at this strange coping.[2] The good Horse Grauntier by chance being gored a little under the mane betwixt the bendings of the barbs with the sharp tusk of the Elephant, neighed with great stomach, and leasing[3] from the beast which he had well-nigh forced to the lists' end, being thereto forwarded with the sharp spurs with so exceeding fury, that it was not only a marvel how the good Prince could sit him so assuredly, and also that he spoiled not himself, and with more eager fury began to gallop upon the Elephant again, his mouth wide open, and horrible with the salt fume[4] which in abundance issued from his great heart : for by how much the more a thing is gentle and quiet, by so much the more being moved he is iracund[5] and implacable. But the Emperor turning his reins carried him clean contrary

[1] Cutlass. [2] Encounter. [3] Releasing.
[4] Smoke, vapour. [5] Irascible.

304

to the lists' end, where stood lances for the same purpose as the manner is, of which he chose the two stiffest, longest, and rudest for their stature and came softly pacing to the Turk : who stood even there still where he was, the Elephant bleeding in such abundance, that by the loss of so much blood his meekness turned into rage, and began to rise and bray, and stamp, and with an uncertain sway to move, so that with much ado the Slave stayed and appeased him, then the brave Emperor, lifting up his vizor not only to take breath but the more freely that his speech might have passage, he told the Turk that he had in a base cowardly manner by false fraud and unequal fight dishonoured himself and endangered him, for which he told him *Malgrado suo*[1] he would be gloriously revenged : and now that they had spent a good time in uncertain Fortune, he had brought two lances, choose which he would, and either begin the fight anew or make an end of the old, promising upon his Honour that if he refused so to do, he would fasten one in his beast and another in his heart. And if he dared to do that, he bade him come down on foot and there break a staff with him. The Turk, as he was an Honourable soldier, then presently slipped off his Elephant, bravely answering that he came to conquer him in sport, and not meaning to make a purposed battle, but sith he was so presumptuous as to dare him to his face, he should soon perceive how lightly he weighed his proud words, and then skipping to him straight a Lance out of his hand, and went one hundred paces backwards, so did the Emperor very joyfully, when they were come so far as they

---

[1] In spite of himself ; reluctantly (Ital.)

thought, they might trust to their breath, holding their Lances in both their hands, began to run very swiftly, and desire brought them together so fast and outrageously, that their Lances somewhat too malapert[1] not suffering them to come together, hurled the Turk above seven feet of the Lances' length, so that not one there but thought he had been either slain, or his wind dashed out of his belly : the Prince reeled backward above two paces and yet fell down much astonished. The people on both sides exceedingly amazed and affrighted, especially the Turks, who sent out such a doleful *Sauntus*[2] that it would have moved the stones to ruth, but the dolour of the Christian was not so great, for the moving of the Emperor revived their spirits much. In a cause on which the beholders' safeties do depend, the ill-success is much feared, for it may be seen by this, that they will with a certain alacrity and Sympathy seem to help or pity as the cause requires. On a sudden the Emperor lifted up his head, at which the Christians gave such an universal shout, as if even now they would have frayed[3] the mountains adjacent. The two courageous beasts having lately heaped up red-hot rancour in their disdainful stomachs, assaulted the one the other with all the weapons of nature, that it had been enough for to have delighted anyone, but the Horse had some small advantage by reason of the Elephant's right eye was covered with the trailing down of the blood. By this time the Emperors rose again, and the one went to his Horse, the other to his Elephant, having first splintered their

[1] Impudent.   [2] A form of *sanctus ;* an outcry.
[3] Frightened.

spears, and fenced so long as any virtue remained in the slaughtered Lances. When each had gotten to their beasts, they began to forward them, who with equal ire moved needed no encouragement, then did the Emperor coming with full scope upon the Turk, smite the Elephant just upon one of the teeth, while with great rage the Horse had fastened his pike again in the Jaw bone, so that the Elephant still swayed back, but neither of them being able to reach the one the other, the excellent Prince, casting his golden shield before him and drawing his glittering Curtelax, leaped upon the neck of his Horse, and laying one hand upon the one tooth of the Elephant, with the other hand upon the thong, that went across his forehead, vaulted up, and settling his feet upon the tusks and his hand on the head of the beast, cast up himself, and laid his sitting place where his hands were, and there rode by little and a little till he might buckle with the insedent.[1] No sooner came he within the reach of the Turk, but he smote the Turk so freely, who was ready prepared for him, that he made him decline a little, there they fought so long that the Elephant driven through pain was thrust up to the lists, hereupon all the people Christian in a more free manner than ever at any time before, all the while their hard-metalled swords played upon each other's shield, so that the glory of their rare fight was so wonderfully pleasing to the eye, and so honourable to the combatants, that if they had jested, one would well have been contented to view all the long day : but the good Prince was too hard for

---

[1] A person sitting on something (in this case, the elephant's rider).

the other, for with his ready blows he urged the great Slave out of his cell, and made him sit behind the arson[1] of the saddle, and if this chance had not happened, he had surely made him sit behind the arson of his Elephant's Tail. For as soon as the Elephant had but touched the lists, the Christian Marshals of the field came galloping and parted the Combatants, holding the Turk as vanquished, whilst betwixt the contrary and adverse part there was four Negatives,[2] so that well-nigh they had fallen to blows, for ye case seemed to the Christian plain, to the Turk unjust. That because the Beast whereon he rode went to the Lists' end, therefore the stopper should be blamed. Well, Heralds whose office it is to deal in such royal matters, had the discussing of it, and it was deferred to arbiters, with this condition, that if the Turk was found vanquished, he should be yielded as recreant (and miscreant he was). So the matter was posted off whilst it never was concluded, and both the parties departed, the one to ye camp, the other to the city, in no less solemn pomp than they entered accompanied into the sands, where so rare a chance fortuned betwixt so puissaunt Emperors. And because the matter was as strange as true, I have sojourned a little too long in it. But in the next Inn you shall have a better refreshment or a newer choice.

CHAPTER XXIII

BY chance a Knight smote Faustus a box on the ear in the presence of a great company of brave Ladies,

---

[1] Saddle-bow.   [2] i.e. The Turkish umpires.

wherefore he swore to be egregiously revenged on him, giving him the Field, which the Knight refused not, so the weapons, the place, the time were ordained, and Faustus went out to the field, and no sooner was Faustus gone out of the presence but Signior di Medesimo, who was well-known to be a valorous and courageous man in his kind as any was about the Court, on a sudden fell down on his knees before all the Ladies, shaking and quivering, with a face as pale as him which was new risen from a month's burying, desiring them if ever they tendered any Gentleman's case, to entreat Monsieur Infeligo to forgive him his trespass. At this the whole assembly burst out into a loud laughter, to see the man that was even now in his brave terms and vaunting words to come in all submissive manner to entreat for a pardon so ridiculously. He yet not desisting with many a salt tear and hands lifted up towards the Heavens, from whence his pity came, when Faustus came blowing in like a swashbuckler with his Rapier by his side and his hand on his Poynard, swearing all the cross row over.[1] But when he saw the Knight in such a pickle, he sat himself against a wall and laughed so loud and so heartily, that all the whole rout could not choose but laugh with him, and here was laughing, and here and there and everywhere. At length two Ladies rose, to whom perhaps this Knight owed some particular service, and desired Don Infeligo with very mild sermon to be friends with Medesimo again, he told them that they could not demand the thing which he would not readily fulfil, marry he requested this, that as the

---

[1] An incantation over the letters of the alphabet.

disgrace which he had received was too great to be forgotten without some such equal revenge, that he might use some like injury, whereby he might be satisfied and he might again come into his grace : which they granted. Faustus came to Medesimo and reared him up upon his feet, and then got upon his back, and so rid twice about the Chamber, and when he had done he took him by the chin, who had not yet forgotten how to weep, shaking worse then any schoolboy when he fears to climb the horse, and gave him a good box on the ear and went his way. So the Knight was utterly disgraced, and for shame durst not be seen all that day after. They which were there had sport abundance, and Faustus was feared for his brave valour and with his continual delight in knavery got him foes enough too.

CHAPTER XXIV

ANOTHER time he by chance overheard a Gentleman which was talking to a Lady, and said that whatsoever she commanded him to do, he would do it, if she would grant him grace. The Gentlewoman belike willing to hear him speak so not to her, required him to build in that place with one word a Castle of fine silver, at which the Gentleman amazed went away confounded, Faustus followed him fast, and said to him that he had overheard the Lady's unjust demand, wherefore go say (quoth he) thou wilt do it with one word. And so the Gentleman did and it was done, whilst he ran laughing in to many nobles and lusty gallants, telling them he would shew them the strangest thing that ever they saw, and all they came running into the garden together, where they found the Gentleman fast locked in a pair of stocks, and an ugly foul kitchen wench in his arms. O Lord, what wondrous sport did he make them there. And when they had laughed their fill, he loosed the gallant, who went and swore all that he could he would be revenged on him. In such monstrous intolerable knaveries Faustus took especial felicity.

CHAPTER XXV

THESE four honest fellows Faustus, Akercocke, Mephostophiles, and Wagner went out together into the street, and walking there by chance espied four Gentlewomen seeming to be sisters, them they cast to abuse, and they were never content to play any merry pranks for honest sport, but they must be so satirically full of gall, that they commonly proved infamous, sparing neither their good name on whom they committed them nor any kind of villainy, so it might procure mirth : when they had talked sufficiently with them, they did so much that they were contented to ride abroad with them, and so each fetched his horse and came to them masked, and the Gentlewomen were wimpled likewise (for the men as well as women use there to wear masks). Thus they rode to the common furlong where many Italian gentlemen were playing at the Balloon, and there they rode round about, whole armies of shouts accompanying them, they riding still backward and forward, whilst these men-women had sewed their coats to their doublets, and pinned upon their backs things of vile reproach amongst them, then rode they to the Court not yet satisfied, where they were entertained with more merriment and laughter. And when these men-women saw the greatest multitude that was there likely to be, even upon a piece of ground which was higher than all the rest, they leaped down, and by reason of the friendship betwixt their petticoats and their doublets, they haled them all down one after another, the horses ran away, and they lay upon them to their great confusion and reproach, yet they thought all well sith they were personated and masked, but the women stripped off their women's garments and their head attires, and there they were well known to be four brave noble young Gentlemen brethren, and each of them rent off the masks of Mephostophiles and his mates, and detected them to their great shame, who neither durst revenge themselves for fear of further displeasure, nor of revealing what they were, nor could be moaned of any one for their notable abuses aforehand, so that whereas in others it had been but a common jest, on them it was wonderful strange and ridiculous. So they with shame enough went fretting in vain to their lodging.

CHAPTER XXVI

THE Emperor being some five or six days in rest within his walls, caused, as sloth cannot dwell in true noble breasts, the whole Army to set forward, leaving a convenient Garrison within the City of 30,000 men, marched into the fields in sundry embattles with above 130,000 men. And there in the view of the Army Mephostophiles, Akercocke, Wagner, Faustus pricked up to the Turk's camp, armed in complete harness, and there challenged any four to break a staff with them, then came there forth four Janissaries horsemen armed at all assays,[1] and there they ran together to the singular delight of the beholders, so gallantly they demeaned themselves, but in the cope[2] all the four Janissaries were run quite through and through (as they say) and there lay on the cold earth, then made these four fellows in Arms their stop and expected a fresh revenge : which came immediately thundering out of the entry of the Camp, with whom to occur in time they met with the like success as before, to their singular commendations and high praises : then gan the Turk to stamp and fret, and commanded four of the best in his whole camp, and four more with them to run at these villains and to captive them, where they should rue the rashness of their presumption with long eternal torment. These eight came with all their power together and broke their lances very hardly upon their faces, and so did they four on theirs, then they drew their swords committing a brave tourney, till two of the Turks were slain, and the six fled, which were immediately hanged, at which ye Christian laughed heartily, and these four returned thanked highly, and for that the Enemy would not advance himself to the general Fortune of the fight, they marched in again into the City.

[1] Ready for every event.   [2] Encounter.

CHAPTER XXVII

ABOUT two a clock in the night the Turk approached with all his whole army unto the walls of the City, causing particular bands and Pioneers to dig through the countermure, the Sentinels which were on the walls, privily espying by reason the Moon gave some slender light, though she was but three days old, gave warning without any alarm to the chief commanders : so that the whole power of the City almost was gathered into Arms, without any stroke of the Drum. The place wherein the Turk was entering, was right against a street's end of above two yards over and not above thirty yards from the breach, they had digged a deep trench and placed on the scarf nine double cannons thoroughly round and charged with chain and murdering shot, and on each side of the cross street they had erected forts of gravel, etc., like our Barricadoes now, in each of which they placed above fifteen Culverin and Cannon. Now the breach being sufficient, the Turk having entered above 2,000 men, gave ye onset, and sounded the bloody alarm, when suddenly the Flankers discharged and the bulwarks shot freely together, and utterly cut off all them that entered beyond the ditch, and betwixt those three mentioned Forts with their terrible shot, they swept them all out of the place, then began the Turk to thrust his men forward upon the breach (having lost in this assault above 2,100) and ever as they came up to the breach, the Cannon heaved them off, and the small shot from the loops so galled them that they durst not approach. But the Turk cared not, for the murthering of his men might weary the Cannons' insatiate cruelty at length. Then was the alarm given through the City, and everyone fell to their Arms, getting to the walls, and the rest to the assembling places, whilst the Turk freshly filled the breaches with murthered men, he enforcing himself to his power to enter, and they to keep him out. When he saw that how he had stopped the breaches so with dead bodies, which almost made a new red sea with their blood, in a great rage transporting above 30,000 men over the Danuby, furnished them with scaling ladders, whilst he with great store of cannon beat his own slain men off the forenamed breaches, for he was a merciless tyrant, and caused them to assault the wall itself, which they did. Now began the morning to appear, and ye Christian came just upon the backs of the assailants, with the greatest part of the whole power of the city, and put them all to the sword, save those that escaped from them by water, but killed of their own fellows. Then the Christian marched upon the Turk, who seeing his power greatly weakened, having lost at his unlucky assault above 23,000 men, cursing and banning his disastrous fortune, and his Gods the givers of it, retired in a flying pace to his camp, whilst the plenteous spoil made rich the Christian, for upon the dead carcases were found store of jewels and gold in great plenty.

CHAPTER XXVIII

THIS new victory gladded the Christians exceedingly, as much as it grieved the Turk. The breaches now were freshly repaired with all expedition. The Christian princes seeing the inconvenience that followed their keeping within the City, and how great shame it were for them to abstain from the enemy, considering their power to be not much inferior to that of the Turks in number, much more in brave soldiery, wherefore they made a general muster, and determined to offer the battle to them in the plain field, which if they refused, they would give them in their camps, concluding all under one day's valiance, then marched forth the English archers, of whom Wagner desired he might be with his fellows, which when they had taken their stand, they brought store of fletchery[1] to them in carts, which were there disburdened, so every archer being five double furnished, the number of them now was nine thousand, the pike being converted into them, being thereto desirous, and having therefore made great suit, for the Emperor was very loth to forget their first good service : Faustus counselled the Captain to choose a plot of above one hundred acres square, where it was open to each horseman, which they marvelled at greatly, but yet they easily granted to stand anywhere : they were so well placed, that they stood as well to defend the friend, as to offend the foe. Then in due order marched out the whole

[1] Goods made, or sold, by a fletcher (a maker or seller of bows and arrows).

armies of the Christian, and so settled themselves, whilst the Turk brought forward his thick swarms. Now it had been a brave sight, to see the greatest princes of the whole world East and West, attended on by their whole forces set in array, their gorgeous and bright armours and weapons casting up long trammels of golden shine to the heavens, the noise of clarions, trumpets, etc., encouraging the fainting soldier, and increasing the boldness of the resolute. There was at once in this Field all the terror of the world, accompanied with all the beauty. In the City you might have seen the remainders at the churches at prayer, solemn procession round about the town with great devotion, etc. Well, the time was come that the horsemen began to assault the pike, and attempting the ruptures of their array, and the forlorn hopes fiercely skirmishing, whilst with loud outcries the whole use of hearing was taken away : above you nothing but smoke, round about you the thundering cannon, and sharp horrors of sundry weapons, and at your feet death. There might you see the great use of the eughen[1] bow, for the horse no whit fearing the musket, or culiver,[2] as used to it, nor yet respects the piercing of a bullet, by the thick tempest of arrows, hiding their eyes, and hurting their bodies, overthrew the horsemaster to the ground, on that side could not one horseman appear, but straight they fetched him down, so that of thirty thousand horsemen of one assault, there was not one that came within five spears' length of the battle on foot. The great Turk cursing heaven and earth, and all trees that bore such

[1] Yew.   [2] *Caliver*, a light musket or arquebus.

murthering fruit as bows and arrows, caused a troop of five hundred barbed horses, with twenty thousand more to run upon the archers altogether, which they did, but when they came just upon a little ridge, not one horse but suddenly stopped, and the riders which now had rested their staves, lying close upon the saddle pommels, were thrown quite out of the saddle, and either their backs broken, or quite slain. All the whole archery with the camp wondering hereat, as ignorant of the matter, everyone suspending his several judgment, but Faustus laughed heartily, who knew the matter plain, for there had they buried in sand all the way wolves' guts, which by natural magic, as authors affirm, suffers not the horse to come over it in any case, nor any force can carry him over with a rider on him. For the Archers drew just upon, and so universally shot together, that all the troops were put to flight, and above half spoiled and murthered. To be brief, so much the Christian prevailed upon the Turk in three hours and a half fight, that all them were turned and fled, each one advancing forward in his flight, there were slain in this battle and flight above seven score thousand Turks, the great Turk himself fighting manfully on his Elephant, was by the Emperor's own hands slain, all his chief Bassas and men of honour, to the number of three hundred died manfully about him: now the retreat was sounded, and they marched home in most glorious pomp and rejoicing, where the soldiers made rich with the great spoil of the camp, were dismissed, and the princes returned home, and due order taken for the safety of the City. So the Duke of Austria rid of his enemies, gave himself to his forepassed life, and the other princes with great joy caused general feasts and triumphs to be performed in all their kingdoms, provinces, and territories whatsoever.

FINIS

APPENDIX A

LIST OF LOCALITIES

(Where they vary from the modern usage)

ACH : Aachen (Aix-la-Chapelle).
ANHOLT : Anhalt.
AUSPURG : Augsburg.
AUSTRICH : Austria.
BASILE
BASYL } Basle.
BATOBURG : Battenburg.
BETHELEM : Bethlehem.
BEYERLANDT : Bavaria.
BREAME : Bremen (?).
CAMPA DE FIORE : Campo de' Fiori.
CAMPANY : Campania.
CATHAI : China.
COSTUITZ (COSTNITZ) : Constance.
CRACOVIA : Cracow.
CULLIN : Cologne.
DURING : Thuringia.
ELVE : Elbe.
ERFORT : Erfurt.
GEUF (GENF) : Geneva.
GIBLATERRA : Gibraltar.
GINNIE : Guinea.
GOSLARYENS : Citizens of Goslar.
GRACOVIA : Cracow.
KUNDLING : Knittlingen.
LIEFLAND : Livonia.
LIPTZIG : Leipzig.
LITAW : Lithuania.

APPENDIX A

LUSITANY : Lusitania, Portugal.
MAYNE : Main.
MEDERI : Madeira (?).
MENCHEN : Munich.
MENTZ : Mainz.
MILLAIN : Milan.
MISSENE : Meissen.
MOSA : Maas.
NORENBERG : Nuremberg.
NOVA HISPANIOLA : Mexico.
PADOA : Padua.
POLONIAN : Polish.
PRAGE : Prague.
RAVENSPURG : Regensburg.
RHODE : Roda.
SANDETZ : Sandec, in Galicia.
SCLESIA ⎱ Silesia.
SLESIA ⎰
SENA : Siena.
SHAWBLANDT : Schwabenland, Swabia.
SWEITZ : Switzerland.
S. MICHAEL'S ⎱ Two of the Azores.
TERZERA ⎰
TERGESTE : Trieste.
TERRA INCOGNITA : America.
TENORRIFOCIE ⎱ Teneriffe (?).
TRENO RIEFE ⎰
TREIR : Trier (Trèves).
ULME ⎱ Ulm.
ULMA ⎰
WARTZBURG ⎱ Würzburg.
WATZBURG ⎰
WEIM : Vienna.
WEIMER : Weimar.

APPENDIX B

A Ballad of Faustus, about 1670, from the Roxburghe Collection in the British Museum. [Rox II. 235]

THE JUDGMENT OF GOD SHEWED UPON ONE *John Faustus*, DOCTOR IN DIVINITY

Tune of *Fortune my Foe*

All Christian men give ear a while to me,
How I am plung'd in pain but cannot die,
I liv'd a life the like did none before,
Forsaking Christ, and I am damn'd therefore.

At Wittenburge, a town in Germany,
There was I born and bred of good degree,
Of honest Stock which afterwards I shamed,
Accurst therefore for Faustus was I named.

In learning loe my Uncle brought up me,
And made me Doctor in Divinity :
And when he dy'd he left me all his wealth,
Whose cursed gold did hinder my souls health.

Then did I shun the holy Bible book,
Nor on Gods word would ever after look,
But studied accursed Conjuration,
Which was the cause of my utter Damnation.

The Devil in Fryars weeds appeared to me,
And streight to my Request he did agree,
That I might have all things at my desire,
I gave him soul and body for his hire.

323

Twice did I make my tender flesh to bleed,
Twice with my blood I wrote the Devils deed,
Twice wretchedly I soul and body sold,
To live in peace and do what things I would.

For four and twenty Years this bond was made,
And at the length my soul was truly paid,
Time ran away, and yet I never thought
How dear my soul our Saviour Christ had bought.

Would I had first been made a Beast by kind,
Then had not I so vainly set my mind ;
Or would when reason first began to bloom,
Some darksome Den had been my deadly tomb.

Woe to the Day of my Nativity,
Woe to the time that once did foster me,
And woe unto the hand that sealed the Bill,
Woe to myself the cause of all my ill.

The time I past away with much delight,
'Mongst princes, peers, and many a worthy Kt.
I wrought such wonders by my Magick Skill,
That all the world may talk of Faustus still.

The Devil he carried me up into the Sky,
Where I did see how all the world did lie ;
I went about the world in eight Daies space,
And then return'd unto my Native place.

What pleasure I did wish to please my mind,
He did perform as bond and seal did bind,
The secrets of the Stars and Planets told,
Of earth and sea with wonders manifold.

When four and twenty years was almost run,
I thought of all things that was past and done ;
How that the Devil would soon claim his right,
And carry me to Everlasting Night.

Then all too late I curst my wicked Deed,
The Dread whereof doth make my heart to bleed,
All daies and hours I mourned wondrous sore,
Repenting me of all things done before.

I then did wish both Sun and Moon to stay
All times and Seasons, never to decay ;
Then had my time nere come to dated end,
Nor soul and body down to Hell descend.

At last when I had but one hour to come,
I turn'd my glass for my last hour to run,
And call'd to learned men to comfort me,
But faith was gone and none could comfort me.

By twelve a Clock my glass was almost out,
My grieved Conscience then began to doubt ;
I wisht the Students stay in Chamber by,
But as they staid they heard a dreadful cry.

Then presently they came into the Hall,
Whereas my brains was cast against the wall,
Both arms and legs in pieces torn they see,
My bowels gone, this was an end of me.

You Conjurors and damned Witches all,
Example take by my unhappy fall :
Give not your souls and bodies into Hell,
See that the smallest hair you do not sell.

But hope that Christ his Kingdom you may gain,
Where you shall never fear such mortal pain :
Forsake the Devil and all his crafty ways,
Embrace true faith that never more decays.

Printed by and for A. M. and sold by the Booksellers
of London.

APPENDIX C

Bibliography

H. LOGEMAN : *The English Faust Book of* 1592. (*Recueil de Travaux de l'Université de Gand*, 24ᵉ fascicule, Ghent, 1900).

A. E. RICHARDS : *The English Wagner Book of* 1594. (*Literarhistorische Forschungen*, XXXV. Heft, Berlin, 1907.)

W. J. THOMS : *Early English Prose Romances*. (2nd Ed. Vol. III. London, 1858.)

R. PETSCH : *Das Volksbuch vom Doktor Faust*. (Reprint of the first edition of 1587. *Neudrucke*, Nos. 7, 8, 8a, 8b. Halle, 1911.)

G. MILCHSACK : *Historia D. Johannis Fausti des Zauberers*. (Reprint of the Wolfenbüttel MS. Wolfenbüttel, 1892–7.)

W. MEYER : *Nürnberger Faustgeschichten*. (*Abhandlungen der philosoph.-philolog. Klasse der königl. bayrischen Akademie der Wissenschaften*, Bd. XX. Abt. 2. Munich, 1895.)

S. SZAMATÓLSKI : *Das Faustbuch des Christlich Meynenden*. (*Deutsche Literaturdenkmale des* 18. *und* 19. *Jh.*, *No.* 39. Stuttgart, 1891.)

J. SCHEIBLE : *Das Kloster*. (Vols. 2, 3, 5, and 11. Stuttgart, 1846–9.)

A. TILLE : *Die Faustsplitter in der Literatur des* 16. *bis* 18. *Jhdts*. (Berlin, 1898–1904.)

K. ENGEL. *Zusammenstellung der Faust-Schriften vom* 16. *Jh. bis Mitte* 1884. (Oldenburg, 1885.)

326

C. KIESEWETTER : *Faust in der Geschichte und Tradition.* (Leipzig, 1893.)

E. FALIGAN : *Histoire de la légende de Faust.* (Paris, 1888.)

E. SCHMIDT : *Faust und das 16. Jahrhundert. (Charakteristiken*, 1. Reihe, 2. Aufl., Berlin, 1902.)

E. SCHMIDT : *Faust und Luther. (Sitzungsberichte*, 1896.)

E. WOLFF : *Faust und Luther.* (Halle, 1912.)

W. CREIZENACH : *Versuch einer Geschichte des Volksschauspiels vom Doctor Faust.* (Halle, 1878.)

A. W. WARD : *Marlowe's Tragical History of Dr. Faustus.* (4th Ed. Oxford, 1901.)

R. ROHDE : *Das Englische Faustbuch und Marlowes Tragödie.* (Halle, 1910.)

H. LOGEMAN : *Faustus-Notes. (Recueil de Travaux,* 21ᵉ fascicule, Ghent, 1898.)

J. FRITZ : *Ander theil D. Johañ Fausti Historien.* (Reprint of first edition of *German Wagner Book.* Halle, 1910.)

Printed in Great Britain at
The Mayflower Press, Plymouth.
William Brendon & Son, Ltd.